ACRL Publications in Librarianship no. 45

English and American Literature

Sources and Strategies for Collection Development

WILLIAM McPHERON
general editor

with

STEPHEN LEHMANN
CRAIG LIKNESS
MARCIA PANKAKE

American Library Association
Chicago and London 1987

*Association of College and Research Libraries
Publications in Librarianship Committee*

Arthur P. Young, Chair
James Benson
Charles B. Osburn
Robert A. Seal
Julie A. Carroll Virgo
Richard Hume Werking

Library of Congress Cataloging-in-Publication Data

English and American literature.

  (ACRL publications in librarianship; no. 45)
  Includes index.
  1. Libraries—Special collections—English literature.
2. Libraries—Special collections—American literature.
3. English literature—Bibliography—Methodology.
4. American literature—Bibliography—Methodology.
5. Collection development (Libraries) I. McPheron, William. II. Series.
Z674.A75 no. 45 [Z688.E6] 020′.5 s   87-1329
ISBN 0-8389-0476-9   [026′.81]

Copyright © 1987 by the American Library Association.

    All rights reserved except those which may be granted by Sections 107 and 108 of the Copyright Revision Act of 1976.

                      Printed in the United States of America.

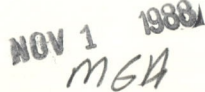

Contents

Preface v

Introduction vii

Collection Development for English and American Literature: An Overview
Eric Carpenter 1

Acquisitions
Craig S. Likness and Kathryn A. Soupiset 20

Current Selection: The Role of Serial Bibliographies and Review Media
Stephen Lehmann 40

Retrospective Collection Development
Richard Heinzkill 56

Serials
Robert Hauptman 82

Contemporary Literature
Charles W. Brownson 102

Textual Studies and the Selection of Editions
Joseph Natoli 127

Literature and Nonprint Media Resources
Peter V. Deekle 144

Building Literary Reference Collections
Scott Stebelman 156

Special Collections
Michael T. Ryan 181

Editors and Contributors 205

Index 207

Preface

The essays in this volume both describe the tasks involved in building collections of English and American literature for academic libraries and discuss the strategies and tools that facilitate their accomplishment. The focus throughout is on practice, with all authors covering the basic bibliographic sources for their chapters' topics as well as incorporating references to other professional writings useful in addressing the problems at hand. The essays are also sensitive to the wide variety of American academic environments and consequently tailor their comments to circumstances ranging from smaller college libraries dedicated to serving classroom activities to multiversities that emphasize faculty research. Though concerns distinctive to public libraries are not considered, much of this volume is certainly appropriate to those which support the serious study of literature. Additionally, care has been taken to make the essays approachable by readers with little knowledge of library procedures as well as to render them interesting to veterans of collection development.

Outside this concern for practical information accessibly presented, no editorial efforts were made to assure philosophical uniformity—a policy which has, in fact, produced some methodological conflicts that greatly enliven the collection as a whole. These disagreements mirror divisions within the discipline of literary scholarship itself and are discussed at some length in the introduction that follows. But what should, perhaps, bear particular emphasis at this point is that while this book offers an abundance of pragmatic advice, it proposes no single, unified philosophy of collection development for English and American literature but rather suggests several competing ideologies.

Though the chapters are bibliographically as well as conceptually self-sufficient and can be read separately, only in conjunction do they reveal the multi-faceted complexity of collection development in the field. The core activities for English-language literature specialists are the subject of the first five chapters. After the introductory overview outlines a planning process for central organizational and policy issues, there are detailed discussions of acquisition methods for literary materials, current selection tools, retrospective collection sources, and serials. The remaining essays concern themselves with narrower topics. The accounts of contemporary literature, textual studies, and nonprint media analyze problems associated with specific classes of resources that are especially important to literary studies. The final two essays deal with the difficulties of constructing separate reference and special collections. Most of the chapters were researched in 1984 and completed in 1985; except for occasional revisions in the final editorial stages, references derive from that earlier time period.

As with most composite projects, the history of this volume is longer and more challenging than originally anticipated. Special obligations have naturally accrued, and it is a pleasure to acknowledge them here. Scott Stebelman, who conceived the idea of this book and assembled the editorial committee, deserves particular mention. The contribution of that editorial committee has been similarly indispensable: less advisors than co-editors, the members have assumed highly active roles, extending to detailed consultation with individual authors. Arthur P. Young, chair of the Editorial Board of ACRL's Publications in Librarianship, has been generous with his time and expertise as this enterprise moved from early planning to completion. And finally, the patience of Joyce McDonald and Julie Sink in processing what at moments must have seemed an intractable manuscript also deserves grateful acknowledgment.

Introduction

This volume originated in 1983 as a project of the English and American Literature Discussion Group, which had been organized the preceding year as a part of the Association of College and Research Libraries within the American Library Association. The conception of both the group and the book may be taken to signal the emerging maturity of the subject specialty of English-language literatures in American academic libraries.

While a few of the premier research libraries in this country traditionally dedicated staff to the systematic building of their general collections of British and American literature, it has only been in the last decade that this need has been more broadly recognized—not only at larger institutions but also in numerous medium-sized university and college libraries. The motives that prompted the widespread creation of such posts are, of course, highly varied and include many factors intrinsic to the evolution of academic librarianship. But also instrumental were profound changes within the worlds of both literature and literary scholarship, and a brief rehearsal of these might usefully introduce this volume's essays.

Perhaps the most striking change in the literary landscape of recent years has been the dramatic rise in the amount of material available. This geometric growth in publishing activity is not, of course, unique to humanistic pursuits; it represents, rather, only one manifestation of the proverbial information explosion that has affected all academic fields since World War II. While symptomatic of a more general trend, the increase in the production of both original literature and literary studies has its own distinguishing features that carry particular consequences for building library collections.

Within the realm of contemporary literature, it is axiomatic to remark how the advent of inexpensive technologies of reproduction has enabled an unprecedented number of small presses and little magazines to print the work of an ever-expanding universe of writers. One simple measurement of the magnitude of this circumstance is the difference between the modest forty-five pages of Len Fulton's first *Small Press Record of Books in Print* issued in 1968 and the massive 1250 pages of its fourteenth edition in 1985. The fact of such quantity has usually been translated by libraries—as by most readers—into a problem of selectivity. Since few institutions either can or wish to collect comprehensively, the sheer abundance of new literature is typically perceived as a challenge of choice.

But the years since World War II have demonstrated how perilous the exercise of such discrimination can be. Many writers marginalized by the aesthetic standards of the 1950s are now the subjects of vigorous critical scrutiny. Yet interestingly, their newly earned attention was not won at the expense of those poets and novelists whose reputations derived from the very different values of three decades ago. The accelerating pace of literary production has tended, in other words, not to perpetuate but to eliminate hierarchies of literary judgment. It has yielded less a prescriptive restructuring than an enormous expansion of the body of seriously regarded contemporary literature. And most crucially, this massive extension of the scope of legitimized writing has fragmented the grounds of judgment, dislocating traditional patterns of cultural authority.

A similarly radical move toward pluralism has also occurred with respect to the literature of earlier periods. Canonicity—once the expression of a comfortably held consensus about our heritage of "the best which has been thought and said"—has been effectively challenged along several fronts. Ethnic and women's studies programs have exposed the prejudicial assumptions about race, class, and gender that historically excluded large bodies of materials from critical consideration. Advocates of popular literature's importance to the construction of social reality have attacked the elitist concept of culture that underlies the very notion of canonicity. And the new historicism—resituating texts in their original socio-political conditions—often privileges works that were formerly treated as non-literary. By rendering problematic old judgments of value and focusing attention on new materials, these and

Introduction ix

other innovative modes of analysis have opened more widely the literary record of the past. And this liberation of the canon has also meant the return of previously neglected texts to commercial availability through a variety of ambitious publishing programs.

Paralleling changes in the production and reception of literature is a remarkable diversification of scholarly interests and methods. The New Critical hegemony of the 1950s has now been displaced by a bewildering range of competing emphases and styles. One convenient index of this complex situation is furnished by the program notes for the Modern Language Association of America's annual conference: all sessions held at the 1960 meeting could be listed in fifteen pages, while more than 100 were required for the Association's centennial conference in 1983. This proliferation of subfields and ideologies has also worked to create new avenues of communication. Though journals and monographs devoted to the academic analysis of literature cannot literally match the number of new primary texts published each year, the proportional growth of secondary sources certainly seems competitive. Items appearing in the English and American literature sections of the *MLA International Bibliography* have, for example, grown by more than 150 percent between 1960 and 1983. And just as in the case of imaginative writing, quantity once again signals a shift in the grounds of quality: for criticism's exponential growth is not ony incremental but also reconstitutive, transfiguring inherited standards of scholarly judgment.

Closely connected to these developments as both causes and effects are major alterations within the teaching profession itself. Most salient are the intensifying pressures on faculty members to publish and the related narrowing of their specializations. Underlying both tendencies are again facts of quantity: the steady growth of professional opportunities from the 1950s through the mid-1960s led not only to a broadened range of research activities but also to the enlargement of graduate programs. The sudden collapse of the job market in the late 1960s and 1970s then left a surplus of unemployed—or, underemployed—scholars whose competition for the dwindling number of positions further increased expectations to publish and encouraged an even greater degree of specialization. And though these difficult economic conditions are now improved, the trends they aggravated remain very strong.

Such centrifugal forces within the teaching profession reflect and reinforce the decentering of cultural authority which since the 1950s has both revolutionized the literary canon and diversified the methods of its analysis. One practical consequence of this process has been the gradual erosion of the faculty's historical role in building the library's

x   *Introduction*

collection of British and American literature. As institutional claims on scholars' energies increased and English studies themselves moved toward greater and more complicated dispersion, the generalist critic who kept alert to developments throughout the discipline became rarer. The task of maintaining a panoptic eye on the field naturally gravitated toward libraries, especially in the last decade as they regularly recruited staff with graduate training in both library science and literature. This process was also repeated in other areas, marking an important phase in that general transfer of responsibility for collection development from the teaching faculty which has occurred throughout the country since the 1960s.

Librarians have taken these newly acquired duties with characteristic seriousness, articulating theories and principles of collection development in a body of professional writing that has grown steadily in sophistication over recent years. Most concern had, however, focused on such larger administrative matters as policy formulation, general criteria for selection, staff organization, budget allocation, and resource sharing until the appearance in 1985 of *Selection of Library Materials in the Humanities, Social Sciences, and Sciences.* Edited by Patricia A. McClung and published by the American Library Association, this volume of essays represents the first sustained attempt to address the practical problems of building library collections in specific academic disciplines. Among its chapters is Susan J. Steinberg and Marcia Pankake's "English and American Literature, with Notes on Some Commonwealth Literatures." Concisely presenting the basic strategies and tools of selection for the field, it serves as both an indispensable primer and a firm foundation for further analysis.

Though the present book was planned independently of their essay, a number of the chapters here act essentially as detailed renditions of the topics and techniques outlined there. While still offering their own distinctive perspectives, this volume's chapters on acquisition methods, current selection, retrospective development, and serials are of this type and should be regarded as refined mappings of a territory already opened by Steinberg and Pankake. But the larger space of this monograph has allowed more than just greater depth of information; it has also enabled the exploration of other issues important to building collections of English-language literary resources. In this category are those chapters that concentrate on the challenges of contemporary literature, textual criticism, and nonprint resources as well as the two essays that address the problems of assembling reference and special collections.

In addition to furnishing a synoptic account of the steps to be taken in establishing a successful collections program, the volume's opening essay also renders explicit a number of assumptions that operate in different, often conflicting manners throughout the other chapters. Since this set of premises sustains whatever conceptual structure these otherwise practice-oriented essays possess, it invites brief examination.

The first of these recurring principles is that effective collection development depends upon a thorough knowledge of the modes of literary research. Carpenter begins his introductory chapter by arguing this point, while Stebelman, Ryan, and Natoli also enforce it at some length. But though the proposition is shared, the meanings assigned it are not. Carpenter and Stebelman form a company—to which Heinzkill also clearly belongs—that largely presupposes traditional styles of scholarship, dominated by literary history, formalist criticism, and conventional bibliography. Ryan and Natoli constitute a very different group—to which Brownson should also be added—that takes its cues from more current schools of thought, most notably the new historicism, deconstruction, and postmodernist nominalism. Had members of either camp written the essays of the other, both the general perspectives and specific judgments would have been different. In other words, once translated into practice, a basic axiom of collection development in English and American literature becomes as unstable as the methodologies of the discipline it serves.

Another common premise is that selectivity is essential to successful collection building. But again understandings of the concept differ sharply. At one pole lies the assumption that aesthetic value is an objective absolute which responsible subject specialists both discern and promote. Such confidence springs from a felt certainty about cultural authority. This attitude informs both Heinzkill's canonical approach to retrospective evaluation and Hauptman's conservative stance toward periodicals. It shapes as well the arguments of other chapters with similarly traditional roots. Operating from a contrary model that regards literary value as highly contingent are Brownson's proposal to displace "good books" with representative collections and Natoli's radically relative notion of textual standards. Such sharp divergences spring directly from the changes in literary production already noted and again suggest that the grounds for collection development in English and American literature are susceptible to sudden shifts.

This disquieting fact is, perhaps, silently acknowledged in a third premise that unites these essays: the insistence that local circumstances should act as the principal determinant of collection policy. Carpenter is most forceful in urging the practical motives for linking library priorities to an institution's individualized teaching and research programs, while Natoli offers an eloquent philosophical defense of the position. And such localism is present with equal prominence in most of the other chapters. Its effect is to establish difference as a governing principle, so that methodological conflict is accommodated by positing diversity itself as the essential condition of collection development in English and American literature. This conclusion is, of course, less the intention of any single author than the product of the volume as a whole, and for that reason it may, indeed, speak all the more emphatically. Certainly the strength that is proverbially said to reside in numbers is needed to enforce any suggestion that the clarity of abstract theory should properly defer to the contradictions of actual practice. That lesson is not easily learned, especially in organizations as devoted to self-rationalization as academic libraries typically are. But it is exactly the message that willy-nilly arises from the contemporary revolutions of literary scholarship and their impact on thoughtful collection development.

More comforting to received wisdom is a final, less problematic premise of these essays: the necessity of understanding with precision the relation between the production of literature and its system of commercial distribution. Likness and Soupiset's densely detailed account of acquisition sources and mechanisms, Lehmann's complementary matrices of current selection tools, Brownson's exhaustive tracing of the bibliographic network of contemporary literature, and Deekle's catalog of entrances into the world of nonprint materials—these chapters embody this central principle of librarianship with particular vigor. Its success in producing information that both enables and improves daily routines is enormous and that alone goes far to justify this book. But the pragmatic value of such bibliographic data should not obscure the difficult issues that occur along the boundaries where literature's anarchic energies disturb the more orderly realms of academic librarianship. Recalling our attention to those ambiguous points of intersection remains a primary service of this volume.

WILLIAM MCPHERON

Collection Development for English and American Literature: An Overview

Eric Carpenter

Building a library's collection in English and American literature is challenging work for any librarian. This introductory chapter provides an overview for beginners, starting with an examination of the research habits of humanists, particularly students and professors of literature. A planning process for developing the collection is articulated, with practical suggestions offered for writing a policy statement, and implementing it through selection, collection management, and resource sharing.

LIBRARY NEEDS OF HUMANISTS

However strong a library's established collection, there are always new, unsatisfied demands for literary materials. How can these needs be met? The first step is to define the research expectations of students and professors of English and American literature in the 1980s.

Some investigation of the library use patterns of humanists has been done. Karl J. Weintraub, noted historian and Dean of Humanities at the University of Chicago, has described "the essential habits of mind and scholarly needs of humanists as these affect issues in acquisition, allocation of funds, book preservation, computerization, problems of access to and use of collections" (p. 22).* While scientists are seldom in-

---

*Here and throughout, full citation for the work quoted or referred to in text is given in Works Cited at the end of the chapter.

terested in the historical development of a topic, for humanists "the whole tradition is often essential and present." Though scientists typically collaborate with colleagues in exploring the objective world, humanists are more often solitary scholars engaged in making "moral, aesthetic, pragmatic, or theological judgments" (pp. 30–31). Weintraub's article and studies by Garfield, Heinzkill, Perrault, Stern, Stone, and a chapter, "New Patterns of Research in the Humanities," in Osburn's monograph, all treat the library needs of humanists and should be read by literature librarians.

The following list of characteristics of humanistic research derives from both this author's experience and Perrault's article:

1. Humanists, particularly literary scholars, are concerned with the text of a given work and its transmission through all the variants in which it has appeared—from original composition to the most recently published edition. Older texts are, therefore, often more important than current publications.
2. This need for older publications makes humanists more concerned than other library users about issues of book and manuscript preservation.
3. Monographs are usually more central to the humanist than journals; the opposite is true for the scientist. The humanists may also need to consult a wide variety of library materials—books, manuscripts, journals, archival materials as well as works of art, or their reproductions.
4. Humanists often require materials in foreign languages, including criticism of English and American literature, works of European literature in their original languages, and important titles in anthropology, linguistics, philosophy, religion, and other disciplines.
5. The ability to browse in the library is crucial to the humanist. Access to published literature in the humanities through both print and electronic reference tools is far less adequate than in the sciences. This fact, plus the humanist's need for retrospective sources, makes him seek proximity to every book which might possibly be related to his topic. The development of on-line library catalogs that provide bibliographic access to materials less accessible physically (in microform collections, or in remote storage, for example) is therefore especially valuable.
6. Ownership and use of a private library are common among humanists. Though contemporary scholars can no longer depend

primarily on personal collections, they still attempt to provide as many of their own materials as possible.

LIBRARY NEEDS OF STUDENTS AND FACULTY IN ENGLISH

These characteristics of library research among humanists apply generally to literary students, but scholars of English also have needs dictated by their specific curricula and research interests. Librarians must be aware of these particularized needs and consequent use patterns to develop literature collections.

The freshman English curriculum consists primarily of composition and introductory literature courses. Composition classes usually require the student to purchase a textbook and an anthology of readings from the college bookstore. Writing short papers based on these texts is often the principal demand, and little use of library materials beyond those placed on reserve (usually in restricted access, multiple-copy collections) is expected. More advanced composition courses, however, often require lengthier papers and library use.

The implications for collection development of the freshman English program are several. Books on composition theory and pedagogy should be acquired for faculty use. Journals such as *College English* and *College Composition and Communication* are similarly appropriate in even small collections, and librarians ought also to read them to identify significant titles for purchase. Basic anthologies of literature like the Norton series also deserve to be added. An efficient reserve book collection must also be developed and maintained to supply multiple copies of books for individual courses. Selectivity should be exercised, however, in adding composition textbooks to the permanent collection. Publication of readers and anthologies for freshman English is one of the most profitable areas of academic publishing. Scores of titles appear each year, and professors may change textbooks frequently. Only those that have enduring value are worthy of acquisition. Pressure on the library by students or faculty to provide multiple copies as a substitute for personal purchase should be resisted. As F. W. Bateson observes, "The undergraduate does not *need* many books; those that he does need are often better bought than borrowed" (p. 5).

At the sophomore and upper division levels the college English curriculum is dominated by literature courses. Students may enroll in author, genre, period, or theme-oriented classes as well as introductions to literary criticism and perhaps even textual study. For all of these, professors usually write course descriptions and syllabi and compile lists of required or recommended readings (often intended for consultation in reserve book collections). Librarians should obtain these lists, preferably well in advance of the beginning of classes, check them against holdings, and order titles lacking. Writing projects in undergraduate literature courses frequently fall into one of two categories. The students may be asked to read and explicate a poem or piece of fiction based primarily on their own aesthetic responses without consulting other sources. Alternatively, the assignment may be to write a paper drawing upon materials found in the library. The English bibliographer ought to know the nature of these assignments and the type of library use involved.

Some general guidelines for developing the literature collection for undergraduates are applicable in most college and university libraries. A core collection of the best modern editions of the standard authors in English and American literature must be acquired. *Books for College Libraries* is a useful tool in identifying these editions, which can typically be purchased in reprint form, if the original is unavailable. Major critical and theoretical works are also needed, as are complete runs of the most important, representative journals publishing both the primary texts themselves and literary criticism. A basic reference collection of literary bibliographies, checklists, concordances, handbooks, and indexes is also necessary. Most undergraduates majoring in English will have their library needs met in a collection built along these lines. Seniors writing honors theses usually require a more comprehensive range of materials, since their research interests may be nearly as specialized as those of graduate students.

Entry level graduate students of English are often required to enroll in courses introducing methods of literary inquiry and the full panoply of research tools in the field. Here they learn the importance of consulting multiple versions of texts, including manuscripts for certain purposes, and the necessity of citing definitive editions. Graduate programs also involve seminars spanning the discipline's chronology as well as covering major authors, critical methodologies, and genres. Depending on the orientation of a particular department, students may be expected to develop both major and minor fields of specialization as well as competence in such extraliterary disciplines as linguistics, philosophy, sociology, or theater.

Library needs of English graduate students are, therefore, many and pressing. Even before beginning to write dissertations, they need texts in various editions, literary criticism (including foreign language works), important titles in other areas of the humanities, and lengthy runs of serials. To identify and locate these materials, graduate students require a strong reference collection consisting of abstracts, bibliographies, chronologies, concordances, dictionaries, handbooks, indexes, literary histories, and other tools of advanced scholarship.

Embarking upon the adventure of writing a doctoral dissertation brings the graduate student into the library with all the needs for resources characteristic of the mature scholar. Bateson, the well-known editor of the *Cambridge Bibliography of English Literature* (*CBEL*), has clearly set forth his basic expectations for a university library supporting doctoral programs in English. The novice bibliographer will find his ambitious program stimulating and provoking:

1. *Manuscripts.* Bateson would require the standard facsimiles, such as the *Beowulf* and other Early English Text Society facsimiles, the *Chaucer Facsimile Series*, H. F. Fletcher's four-volume facsimile edition of Milton's poems, Garland's *James Joyce Archive*, and M. J. Bruccoli's facsimile edition of F. Scott Fitzgerald's *The Great Gatsby*. Students should have as many of these locally available as possible, but librarians must weigh their utility and cost. Not even the largest university library can hope to afford direct access to all the original letters, manuscripts, and other primary materials required by advanced literary scholars. Students and faculty consequently must anticipate travelling to other libraries that possess extensive rare book collections. To facilitate this process, reference works identifying and indexing manuscript and other special literature collections are a crucial part of every library supporting doctoral study.
2. *Original Editions.* Bateson's advice is to acquire at least one first edition for every major author cited in *CBEL*. While such selective representativeness is a good general guideline, purchase of rare first editions is costly and difficult for libraries in the 1980s. He does, however, allow the substitution of facsimile reprints, and, indeed, this will often be necessary.
3. *Standard Editions.* Bateson requires the standard editions of both the major and minor authors covered by *CBEL*. The bibliographer must add to these those writers first cited in the *New Cambridge Bibliography of English Literature* (*NCBEL*). Though definitive modern editions constitute a first priority, each library must reconcile its own needs and budgetary resources in determining the depth and thoroughness with which they are acquired.
4. *Standard Bibliographies, Biographies, Special Studies, Works of Reference.* Though Bateson combines biography, criticism, and reference works, each deserves separate comment. Graduate collections should contain standard biographies of major and

minor authors, and their acquisition ought to be a high priority. But literary criticism, while obviously important, may not have the same urgency as buying editions of primary works. Judicious selection from the torrent of secondary studies appearing each year is a necessity even in larger academic libraries. Perhaps most crucial is the development of a first-class reference collection, one containing all the tools needed to support sophisticated library research.

5. *Periodicals.* Bateson cites the periodicals on which the *MLA International Bibliography* is based as a *sine qua non*, but the passage of time has made this advice less valuable, given the dramatic expansion of titles and the increasing number of nonliterary journals indexed by this bibliography. He also urges purchase of the great literary monthlies and quarterlies now extinct, though it is virtually impossible for any but the largest research libraries to follow this advice because of the price of these serials in the 1980s. Resource sharing among libraries supporting doctoral programs has become essential in providing much of this periodical literature for students and scholars.

6. *Microfilms.* Bateson describes microfilms as "necessary evils" yet advises libraries to subscribe to the major series. Serious students of Renaissance and Restoration literature must consult early editions of works cited in Pollard and Redgrave's *Short-Title Catalogue* of English books to 1640 and the continuation by Donald Wing for 1641–1700. The books entered in both bibliographies are being reproduced on microfilm as *Early English Books: Series I* and *Series II* by University Microfilms International. These and other major microform sets in literature, such as *English Literary Periodicals*, are described in Suzanne Dodson's *Microform Research Collections*. But Bateson's recommendations for the ideal collection can be followed by few, if any, libraries. Those without strong rare book collections certainly must consider acquisition of some of these microform sets, perhaps in cooperation with consortia partners in a resource sharing agreement. Others may also be available for borrowing from the Center for Research Libraries in Chicago by institutions holding membership in CRL.

Meeting the expectations of graduate students for library materials in these six categories is a difficult and challenging task. Additional information on the research habits of advanced literary scholars is found in Chapter Five, "Finding Materials, " and Chapter Six, "Libraries," of Richard D. Altick's engaging book, *The Art of Literary Research*.

PLANNING COLLECTION DEVELOPMENT

Having gathered and examined as much information as possible about the students of literature in general, what should the English librarian do next? The best advice is put simply: define a plan of action.

The remainder of this chapter describes such a plan, whose essential elements may be summarized:

1. Determine the library needs of the *specific* English department served.
2. Evaluate the collection, ascertaining its strengths and weaknesses as related to that department's teaching and research program.
3. Write a policy for building the English collection within the context of local, regional, and national collection strengths and resource sharing arrangements.
4. Implement the policy, making the thousands of daily book selection/deselection decisions necessary.
5. Manage the collection, considering short- and long-range requirements for replacing, preserving, storing, and weeding categories of materials as well as individual titles.
6. Engage in resource sharing and cooperative collection development.

The first essential task is to identify local patterns of needs. The programs of English departments vary considerably, and consequently the demands made upon library collections differ greatly from one institution to another. Most programs are defined by a mixture of emphases on particular authors, periods of literature, methods of inquiry, and critical approaches. But others stress interdisciplinary research, with faculty teaching and doing research more outside than inside literature.

One can begin learning about the orientation of a department by assembling and reading various documents relating to its activities. All colleges and universities have catalogs that contain brief course descriptions and listings of faculty, whose specializations can be ascertained from the classes they teach. Departmental brochures, syllabi, lists of reserve books, faculty publications, and dissertations completed and in-progress should also be gathered. The latter two provide especially valuable information about both overall patterns of research and specific titles consulted or sought in the library. Analyzing these citations serves as a useful method of collection evaluation. It is also useful to read some of the books, articles, and dissertations written locally, since this keeps the librarian in touch with research interests and also provides a foundation for informed contact with faculty.

In addition to studying the English department and its publications, the librarian should meet its members. Establishing and maintaining close, collegial relationships with them is a first priority for the bibliographer. It is simply impossible to identify the needs of patrons or build collections for them if these ties are not strong. Every possible avenue of approach, both formal and informal, must be explored. Arrange to speak at department meetings. Sometimes, orientations for new graduate students are held annually, and an introduction then is a good beginning. More relaxed contacts over meals can also be arranged.

Perhaps most importantly, a new English librarian should make an appointment with each faculty member to discuss the professor's research activities and library expectations and those of his students. A standard repertoire of questions may serve as the focus for the interview: What are your research interests? How do you and your students use the library? What do you perceive as its collection strengths and weaknesses, and what should be done about them? Are there any particular titles the library lacks? Are there bibliographies you recommend be checked against library holdings?

Another approach is to organize these questions into a written survey of the faculty, results of which can be entered in computer-based profiles such as used at Arizona State University by Borovansky and Machovec. A record for each professor registers his research area, publications, and current projects. The records must be actively maintained, since changes of interest and personnel are constant, and shifting patterns of demands on the collection can remain undetected if not monitored closely.

Still another method of discovering the resource needs of the English department is by participating in library instruction, which helps a bibliographer establish and maintain liaison with both students and faculty. Instruction can take a variety of formats. Some bibliographers teach courses (either credit or noncredit) in research methods, sponsored by the English department, the library, or under the auspices of both. Librarians also give library-oriented lectures in particular English courses in cooperation with professors. Term paper clinics conducted for undergraduates and conferences for graduate students centered on their dissertation topics are other viable avenues of instruction. Informal consultations with professors on their research projects also offer occasions for librarians to learn about new directions in scholarship.

Also of occasional value is work at the reference desk. Many libraries now combine public service and collection development on the assumption that extensive public contact improves book selection decisions. While this point is debatable, it is true that the reference desk can teach something about library use. But extensive public service assignments can also drain a bibliographer's energies and leave insufficient time for effective collection development.

COLLECTION EVALUATION

Once the English department's use patterns and needs are understood, the bibliographer should next evaluate the existing collection. Needs assessment and evaluation may proceed together to a certain extent, provided the librarian has achieved at least a basic understanding of the clientele's requirements. José Ortega y Gasset has been quoted by Eli Oboler on the role of the librarian: "I imagine the librarian of the future as a filter interposed between men and the torrent of books" (p. 71). This is apt. The collection builder's role is to mediate between the reader and the universe of information, and to do this he must measure the collection's strengths and weaknesses in the light of the users' needs.

A valuable tool in this second stage of the librarian's plan for collection development is the American Library Association's (ALA) *Guidelines for Collection Development*, which contains the section, "Guidelines for the Evaluation of Library Collections." This document argues that the purpose of evaluation is to "determine whether the collection is meeting its objectives, how well it is serving its users, in which ways or areas it is deficient, and what remains to be done to develop the collection" (p. 9).

A good way to begin is by engaging in what Hendrik Edelman calls "library archaeology," or the search for information on "who bought what when?" This task involves excavation in old files to locate documents left by previous bibliographers, including letters, memos, and reports detailing the genesis and growth of the collection. A history of the library, or book exhibit catalogs describing the provenance of parts of the collection, may exist. How did the library originate? Who were its early benefactors? What collections were acquired and added *in toto*? Dealers' catalogs previously marked for purchase and accession books now gathering dust are other sources of useful information.

But often little written evidence of the library's history remains. This is especially true in newer university libraries, where patterns of rapid growth and movement of both collections and staff have destroyed much documentation. In these libraries a bibliographer can interview older faculty and staff colleagues. Sometimes one or more of them serve as living memories of the library and enjoy reminiscing for a novice bibliographer. The collection itself can also yield information from bookplates inserted by owners of volumes later donated or sold to the library.

With available evidence in hand, the librarian can then choose his methods of evaluation, an inventory of which is provided in the ALA *Guidelines* and is abbreviated here for the sake of discussion:

1. Check the collection against standard lists, catalogs, and bibliographies.
2. Examine the collection directly.
3. Conduct document delivery tests.
4. Compile statistics.
5. Check citations from papers of library users (pp. 12-19).

Measuring the collection against standard bibliographies is one of the most important techniques of evaluation for English librarians. Achieving several objectives simultaneously, it deepens knowledge of the collection, identifies gaps in holdings, and leads to compilation of desiderata lists for retrospective collection development. Selection of the proper bibliographies is vital and must be made with great care. Some work may have already been done in a particular library, and copies of previously annotated lists should be studied for information about the shape and strength of the collection at the time the evaluation occurred. Duplication of effort ought to be avoided, since this work is tedious and time-consuming.

Standard tools like *CBEL* and *NCBEL* should be used with collections supporting doctoral research. Depending on the level and number of degrees, the range and sophistication of patrons' needs, and special subject emphases in the English department, other bibliographies can be employed. While many smaller libraries look to the language and literature volume of *Books for College Libraries*, larger institutions may need to compare holdings with specialized author, genre, or period compilations to guide their programs of retrospective acquisition. In all cases, it is incumbent on the bibliographer to analyze the results carefully. Copies of books annotated and records of work accomplished must be kept to prevent future duplication. Desiderata lists should also be prepared and sent to antiquarian dealers or advertised in the out-of-print trade journals, as funding permits.

Inspecting the collection directly and testing the quality of document delivery are also important. The *Guidelines* offer the excellent advice that the bibliographer "physically look over the materials on the shelf. The examination may reveal size, scope, depth, and significance of the collection; currency of material, and physical condition. Furthermore, preservation, conservation, restoration, or replacement of materials may be taken into consideration in the process" (p. 14). There is no substitute for these regular walks through the bookstacks.

In addition to examining the cataloged collection, the bibliographer should locate *hidden*, partially or totally uncataloged collections. Large libraries usually have these pockets of materials, perhaps a backlog of gift books, or even unprocessed special collections. Find out where these are and what access tools exist for them. Lobby to have records for them included in the public card or on-line catalog. Review microform collections carefully as well. They are often less than fully accessible through the main public catalog. This situation is especially vexing in newer research libraries, where the only copies of many early editions of fifteenth to nineteenth-century works are contained in large microform sets.

Tests of shelf availability should also be conducted. These can be done quite simply. Select a particular title, a classification number, an author section, or a systematic sample. Are the books on the shelf? In circulation? If titles cannot be accounted for, there may be a more widespread problem of poor shelf availability that can seriously frustrate patrons and that deserves further investigation. Is there demand for more copies of heavily used titles? Is theft a common occurrence? Are books reshelved promptly and properly? A bibliographer can attempt to solve these problems by ordering replacement copies and encouraging the circulation staff to improve shelving practices.

The *Guidelines* also recommend compilation of statistics as an evaluation technique. Figures on the size of the English department faculty, numbers of undergraduate majors, graduate students, and dissertations in progress should be assembled. These can be analyzed to discern actual and potential patterns of collection use. Many libraries have also conducted shelflist measurements, according to the Library of Congress (LC) National Shelflist Count breakdown provided in the *Guidelines* (pp. 42–54). These statistics indicate the size and growth patterns of holdings in the P and other LC classes relevant to literary scholars.

Use studies, including citation analysis, are another collection evaluation tool. What areas of the literature collection are most heavily used? What other parts of the collection are being consulted by English department members? Data from automated circulation systems can be retrieved and manipulated to answer such questions. A major study of this kind is Paul Metz's *The Landscape of Literatures: Use of Subject Collections in a University Library*. Interlibrary loan represents another source of user information. Borrowing records indicate what books and serials requested by patrons are not available locally, highlighting materials that should be acquired. Conversely, some segments of the collection may be used more to support interlibrary lending than to meet local needs. If so, is this the result of consortia resource sharing agreements? The answers to these questions contain collecting implications that the bibliographer must ponder and act upon.

Evaluating collections through citation analysis is another ALA-endorsed method of evaluation. Heinzkill and Stern employ this technique to define the general characteristics of materials cited by literary scholars. These studies do not, however, provide bibliographers with *specific* information on the citation habits of researchers working in their home institutions. References in books, articles, and dissertations written locally must be examined to discover the use patterns in individual libraries. Charles J. Popovich describes a technique for localized analysis of citations in business management dissertations that could be applied in English.

A variety of evaluation approaches ought to be employed by English bibliographers to learn about their collections. Having gained this knowledge, librarians must next place their own collections in the context of others on the campus, in the city, and in the region. This broader measurement permits the librarian to work intelligently in the resource sharing environment where important collection development and management decisions will increasingly occur.

The bibliographer should begin on the campus. Are there special literary or humanities collections in other libraries—a rare books collection, for example, within the university library system, or perhaps an independent grant-funded research institute library? What are their strengths and lending policies? Libraries off-campus can also be visited. College and university bibliographers located near large public libraries should acquaint themselves with colleagues and collections there. These contacts not only increase familiarity with local resources but may also become the first step in the process of reaching cooperative collection building agreements.

Most academic libraries now belong to one or more consortia. Knowledge of the strengths of participating institutions and working relations with professional counterparts are important. Many large academic libraries also now hold full or associate membership in CRL, which librarians can visit, perhaps while attending an ALA conference in Chicago. Publications of the Center describe its considerable holdings in literature.

All of this investigation of other collections helps an English librarian understand the context within which the local collection must be evaluated and developed. It also prepares the bibliographer for meaningful participation in resource sharing.

WRITING A COLLECTION DEVELOPMENT POLICY

But before considering resource sharing, the English bibliographer must complete the third stage of the overall plan for collection development—writing a policy for the literature collection. Having identified the library needs of English department patrons, evaluated the existing collection, and explored literature holdings of local libraries and consortia partners, a librarian is well prepared to write the policy.

Presuming the library does not already have a comprehensive written policy, the ALA *Guidelines* provide a rationale, framework, and procedure for writing one. Sources of sample policies, cited in the bibliography, include the Association of Research Libraries (ARL) SPEC (Systems and Procedures Exchange Center) Kits containing working documents, and copies of policies from selected ARL libraries. Also especially useful are the policies of Stanford University and the University of Texas at Austin, available from those libraries.

A good initial step in the preparation of a policy is writing a report summarizing the previous assessment of existing program needs and collection strengths. A basic issue the report will confront is whether the existing collection is adequate for the teaching and research needs of the department it serves. If not, where and how is it weak, and what course of action is possible to remedy the situation? At this stage of the collection development plan, the librarian must be prepared to answer those questions, answers that, once reformulated, will constitute the collection development policy statement.

Broadly based discussion is crucial in the formulation of a policy. Often the bibliographer writes a policy for English as part of a library-wide effort to produce a comprehensive document. But whatever the situation, the librarian must consult with the English department's library committee, if one exists, or its chairperson, or perhaps even the individual members of the department as a whole. Before initiating these contacts, it is wise, however, to have at least a list of recommendations, and ideally a draft policy in hand. Especially in a gloomy fiscal climate, considerable negotiation may be necessary to establish priorities. This can be difficult, and the librarian must remain sensitive to the faculty's advice, even while taking into account the library's budgetary limits.

The specific content of the policy itself will depend on local needs, of course, but a description of its overall structure is possible. The ALA *Guidelines* suggest arrangement by academic program, linked to appropriate areas of the LC classification schedule, with an index by LC class to "facilitate cooperative resources planning with other libraries" (p. 16). In English and American literature this translates into an arrangement by periods, for each of which the bibliographer must define the desired degree of collecting intensity. The *Guidelines* explain these (3–5), ranging from minimal to comprehensive levels, adaptable to libraries of any size. For example, one institution may specify that modern English literature (PR 6000–6076) be acquired at the research level to support doctoral dissertations, but that Anglo-Saxon (PR 1490–1799) be built to a lesser extent because no advanced degrees are awarded in Old English. For each literary period or area of the collection, the language of publication, the format, and geographic coverage must also be indicated. In addition, priorities should be set for current versus retrospective collecting, acquisition of primary versus secondary texts, and foreign versus English language publications. Resource sharing agreements, as these affect each collecting area, are noted as well.

But at this point, a cautionary note deserves sounding. The ALA *Guidelines* are being rewritten, with completely different designations for collecting intensities. Prompted by the Research Libraries Group's (RLG) Conspectus (see Gwinn and Mosher) and the North American Collection Inventory Project (see Farrell), this radical revision is occurring under the auspices of the Collection Management and Development Committee of ALA's Resources and Technical Services Division. New policy statements should take into account these changes.

IMPLEMENTING THE POLICY IN DAILY SELECTION

The next stage of the collection development process translates theory into practice. The library's particular needs are met by appropriate selection from the total universe of books, journals, and other forms of relevant materials.

The administrative organization of this process is a key factor. Staffing patterns will vary considerably, with some libraries dividing selection responsibility by discipline or department, others by broad division (humanities, social sciences, natural sciences), and yet others by geographic areas (Western Europe, Latin America, East Asia, etc.). Chief collection development officers usually coordinate this activity, especially in large libraries, but they are often so involved with budgetary and personnel matters that little time is available for individual title decisions. It is, therefore, finally the English bibliographer's responsibility to insure that the clientele's expectations are satisfied, both within the field and in related areas. If the psychology department, for example, has no interest in psychoanalysis but English does, books in psychoanalysis should be purchased from the English funds.

Coordination of the use of selection tools is also important. For some libraries *Choice* cards alone might suffice. In larger institutions, a broad range of selection tools is employed, typically including one or more approval plans. In the absence of, or in conjunction with, these plans, selection may proceed through a combination of national bibliographies, Alert Service cards from the Library of Congress' Cataloging Distribution Service, and book reviews.

Acquisition of noncurrent titles can proceed simultaneously. The methods and degree of developing the retrospective collection must depend upon policy, staffing, and funds. Some out-of-print purchasing may be done by circulating disiderata lists and buying from dealers catalogs. Books from University Microfilms' Books on Demand program may also be acquired. Other microform facsimiles and large reprint sets represent alternative avenues for adding older materials.

COLLECTION MANAGEMENT

The penultimate task in the bibliographer's overall plan is collection management. Like selection, this too is a daily activity. Added copies of heavily used titles must be reordered and missing books replaced or records withdrawn. This work requires close collaboration with colleagues in the acquisitions, circulation, and cataloging departments.

Planning collection growth involves similar cooperation. Many libraries face severe space problems, and obtaining funds for new construction is often difficult or impossible. Both compact storage and weeding may be necessary, requiring decisions about the disposition of particular titles as well as categories of materials. Academic libraries find these situations especially trying. If patrons are to acquiesce in the storage or weeding of parts of the literature collection, the project must be well planned, including systematic consultation. Acting on the sound advice of Stanley J. Slote's *Weeding Library Collections* can help the bibliographer grapple with the challenges of this problem.

Preservation is an aspect of collection management that increasingly concerns the profession. Many larger libraries have appointed preservation officers or added preservation responsibilities to the duties of present staff members. These librarians not only coordinate the work of daily repair and physical maintenance but also plan longer-range preservation projects. English specialists typically participate in this work, usually by selecting titles for restoration and preservation, sometimes specifying the method of treatment. Should the old but still definitive edition be replaced? Is reprint or microform copy available? Should the volume be preserved in a special container? Can it be discarded? These questions must be answered for thousands of deteriorating titles in both large and small English collections. Preservation is also now being done cooperatively in some consortia.

COOPERATIVE COLLECTION DEVELOPMENT

Resource sharing is the context in which all other collecting functions must be conducted. Needs assessment, evaluation, policy writing, daily selection, and collection management are activities in which libraries are increasingly cooperating. Resource sharing has become an article of faith, and the novice bibliographer can expect to spend part of each day in this work.

For the English specialist, cooperation must begin at home with the special collections department in his own library. It is essential that selection for the circulating and special collections be closely coordinated. As Perrault observes: "Most humanities scholarship makes use of materials housed in library special collections. Because of uniqueness, scarcity, value, and format, rare printed books, original manuscripts, early photographs and films, rare maps, personal memorabilia, and ephemera of all varieties are located in special collections. All these materials are the subjects of research in the humanities disciplines" (p. 13). The English bibliographer and the special collections librarian must work together to overcome such potentially divisive issues as restricted access and the need for duplicate purchasing. Techniques for sharing information on authors collected and specific titles added should be worked out. Similar agreements ought to be reached with other literature librarians and collections on campus.

Establishing cooperative arrangements with local academic and public libraries off-campus is also important. These can develop naturally through personal contact. Among many possibilities might be an arrangement about current fiction. The public library, for example, may agree to collect best-selling novels and popular genre fiction (detective, mystery, and Western novels), while the academic library acquires science fiction, experimental prose, and small press publications in all genres. Lists of authors treated by each might be exchanged.

Similar understandings may be reached by libraries working together regionally. These consortia can undertake cooperative serials review projects, which try to insure that members consult each other before cancelling the last subscription to a particular title held in the area. Commitments may also be made to collect at ALA-defined levels in specifically assigned literary periods or genres.

More broadly, the Association of Research Libraries' NCIP is using the RLG Conspectus to specify levels of existing collections and intensities of current collecting. These standardized descriptions, along with resource sharing through membership in CRL or other consortia, are but two ways in which English bibliographers can hope to strengthen collections nationally. Much work lies ahead. Many university libraries are forced to support doctoral programs in a very large number of disciplines with tight budgets for acquisitions. In an era of shrinking support for humanities study and collections, perhaps the greatest challenge to English bibliographers is to develop their own collections on stringent budgets, while making additional resources in other libraries easily available to local scholars.

So the task of building the literature collection for both the present and the future beckons the English bibliographer. Student and faculty needs must be evaluated in light of collection strengths and budgetary constraints. Policies must be written, books chosen, and library resources shared daily. For all its difficulties, the quest is still a noble one. James Holly Hanford eloquently states that the challenge "can be met successfully only by those who have subscribed to the contract of their great community, as Edmund Burke so nobly defined it: a partnership not only between those who are living, but between those who are living, those who are dead, and those who are to be born, a partnership in all science, a partnership in all art, a partnership in every virtue, and in all perfection" (p. 36).

WORKS CITED

Altick, Richard D. *The Art of Literary Research*. 3rd ed. New York: Norton, 1981.

American Library Association. *Guidelines for Collection Development*. Ed. David L. Perkins. Chicago: American Library Association, 1979.

Association of Research Libraries. Office of Management Studies. Systems and Procedures Exchange Center. *Collection Development Policies*, Kit 38, November 1977.

———. *Cooperative Collection Development*, Kit 111, February 1985.

Bateson, F. W. "The Function of the Library in Graduate Study in English." *Journal of General Education* 13 (April 1961): 5-17.

Beowulf: Reproduced in Facsimile from the Unique Manuscript, British Museum MS. Cotton Vitellius A.xv. 2nd ed. London: Oxford Univ. Press for the Early English Text Society, 1959.

Books for College Libraries. 2nd ed. Chicago: American Library Association, 1975. (A new edition is in preparation.)

Borovansky, Vladimir T., and George S. Machovec. "Microcomputer-Based Faculty Profile." *Information Technology and Libraries* 4 (December 1985): 300-5.

Cambridge Bibliography of English Literature. Ed. F. W. Bateson. 5 vols. Cambridge: Cambridge Univ. Press, 1940-57.

Center for Research Libraries. *Handbook, 1981* and *1984 Supplement*. Chicago: The Center, 1981, 1984.

Chaucer Facsimile Series. Norman, Okla.: Pilgrim Books, 1978-83.

Choice. Middletown, Conn.: Association of College and Research Libraries, 1964- . 11/yr.
College Composition and Communication. Urbana: National Council of Teachers of English, 1950- . 4/yr.
College English. Urbana: National Council of Teachers of English. 1939- 8/yr.
Dodson, Suzanne Cates. *Microform Research Collections: A Guide*. 2nd ed. Westport, Conn.: Meckler, 1984.
Edelman, Hendrik. Address. Annual Conference of the Academic Library Association of Ohio. Athens, 7 October 1983.
Farrell, David. "The NCIP Option for Coordinated Collection Development." *Library Resources & Technical Services* 30 (January-March 1986): 47-56.
Fitzgerald, F. Scott. *The Great Gatsby: A Facsimile of the Manuscript*. Ed. Matthew J. Bruccoli. Washington: Microcard Editions Books, 1973.
Garfield, Eugene. "Is Information Retrieval in the Arts and Humanities Inherently Different from That in Science? The Effect That ISI's Citation Index for the Arts and Humanities Is Expected to Have on Future Scholarship." *Library Quarterly* 50 (January 1980): 40-57.
Gwinn, Nancy E., and Paul H. Mosher. "Coordinating Collection Development: The RLG Conspectus." *College & Research Libraries* 44 (March 1983): 128-40.
Hanford, James Holly. "The American Scholar and His Books." *PMLA* 74 (May 1959): 30-36.
Heinzkill, Richard. "Characteristics of References in Selected Scholarly English Literary Journals." *Library Quarterly* 50 (July 1980): 352-65.
James Joyce Archive. Ed. Michael Groden. 63 vols. New York: Garland, 1977-80.
Metz, Paul. *The Landscape of Literatures: Use of Subject Collections in a University Library*. Chicago: American Library Association, 1983.
Milton, John. *Complete Poetical Works Reproduced in Photographic Facsimile*. 4 vols. Ed. Harris Francis Fletcher. Urbana: Univ. of Illinois Press, 1943-48.
MLA International Bibliography of Books and Articles on the Modern Languages and Literatures. New York: Modern Language Association of America, 1921-
New Cambridge Bibliography of English Literature. Ed. George Watson. 5 vols. Cambridge: Cambridge Univ. Press, 1969-77.
Oboler, Eli M. "A Brief Rejoinder to Bateson." *Journal of General Education* 14 (April 1962): 69-71.
Osburn, Charles B. *Academic Research and Library Resources: Changing Patterns in America*. Westport, Conn.: Greenwood, 1979.
Perrault, Anna H. "Humanities Collection Management—An Impressionistic/Realistic/Optimistic Appraisal of the State of the Art." *Collection Management* 5 (Fall/Winter 1983): 1-23.

Pollard, A. W., and G. R. Redgrave. *Short-Title Catalogue of Books Printed in England, Scotland, and Ireland and of English Books Printed Abroad, 1475-1640.* London: Bibliographical Society, 1946. (2nd ed. in progress since 1976.)

Popovich, Charles J. "The Characteristics of a Collection for Research in Business Management." *College & Research Libraries* 39 (March 1978): 110-17.

Slote, Stanley J. *Weeding Library Collections—II.* 2nd rev. ed. Littleton, Colo.: Libraries Unlimited, 1982.

Stern, Madeleine. "Characteristics of the Literature of Literary Scholarship." *College & Research Libraries* 44 (July 1983): 199-209.

Stone, Sue. "Humanities Scholars: Information Needs and Uses." *Journal of Documentation* 38 (December 1982): 292-313.

Weintraub, Karl J. "The Humanistic Scholar and the Library." *Library Quarterly* 50 (January 1980): 22-39.

Wing, Donald. *Short-Title Catalogue of Books Printed in England, Scotland, Ireland, Wales, and British America, and of English Books Printed in Other Countries, 1641-1700.* 3 vols. New York: Index Society, 1945-56. (2nd ed. in progress since 1972.)

Acquisitions

Craig S. Likness and Kathryn A. Soupiset

Acquisitions, Edelman argues, implements selection decisions generated by collection development (pp. 33-34). While this principle may seem obvious, many librarians think of acquisitions only as an organizational unit rather than as part of a process which demands the constant participation of selectors. English and American literature specialists should be involved in establishing and monitoring the acquisitions mechanisms that bring materials into libraries. Every selector needs to understand acquisitions methods and local procedures as well as supply subject and bibliographic expertise. Even when they perform a wide variety of collection development and public services assignments, selectors must not overlook acquisitions involvement.[1]

PROCEDURES AND TECHNIQUES FOR IN-PRINT MATERIALS

Selectors have traditionally depended on a wide variety of sources to identify and select new materials. English and American literature specialists use publishers' catalogs and other promotional literature, special advance publications created by book jobbers, advance notification slips, book trade publications, book reviews and books received lists in journals, specialized small press tools, and recommendations of library users. The *ALA Glossary* defines verification as "the process of determining that a requested bibliographic item has actually been published and that the supplied bibliographic data are current and adequate for use in order information" (p. 238). While most sources identifying current publications available for purchase supply enough information to verify a title, standard national bibliographies remain important English and American literature verification tools, notably the *National Union Catalog (U.S.A.)*, *Canadiana*, *British National Bibliography*, the *Australian National Bibliography*, and *New Zealand National Bibliography*. In addition, each country is served by at least one trade bibliography of books in print:

United States

Books in Print. New York: Bowker. Issued annually with supplements, this set has author, title and subject volumes. Bowker also publishes a variety of related titles, including *Forthcoming Books* and *Books in Series*. Publishers' directory included.

Cumulative Book Index. New York: Wilson. Published monthly with annual cumulations, *CBI* is strong on Canadian publishing and includes selected titles from other English-speaking countries. Publishers directory included.

American Book Publishing Record. New York: Bowker. This classified list of American book production and of titles distributed in the United States by agents of foreign publishers cumulates monthly and annually into *ABPR*. Other multiyear retrospective cumulations available. No publishers list included.

Small Press Record of Books in Print. Paradise, Calif.: Dustbooks. Annual.

Canada

Canadian Books in Print. Toronto: University of Toronto Press. This annual, with author and title selections, includes a publishers directory.

Great Britain

British Books in Print. London: Whitaker. An annual in single alphabetical author-title sequence, with a publishers directory.

Whitaker's Cumulative Book List. London: Whitaker. An annual classified list.

Australia

Australian Books in Print. Melbourne: D. W. Thorpe. Author, title and subject approaches.

New Zealand

New Zealand Books in Print. Wellington: New Zealand Book Publishers Association.

Africa

African Books in Print. London: Mansell. Irregular, supplemented by *African Book Publishing Record*, a quarterly also published by Mansell.

In recent years, bibliographic utilities, notably OCLC and Research Libraries Information Network, have also been successfully used for verification. Many bibliographers and acquisitions personnel now think of these resources first because of database size, up-to-date information, and searching strategy alternatives not available in the printed sources. Increasingly, as acquisitions procedures become automated, the utilities will deliver the service formerly supplied by national and trade bibliographies.

Closely related to verification is the activity called "acquisitions pre-order, or precatalog searching" which determines whether or not a bibliographic unit is already available locally or on order (*ALA Glossary* pp. 173-74; see also Reid). After a book title is verified and searched, it will be ordered directly from a publisher or from a book wholesaler, typically called a vendor or a jobber. Acquisitions departments need to maintain policies which help identify the appropriate vendor for a book. On most occasions, individual, or "firm," orders are directed to vendors because of substantial discounts and the services they render on the library's behalf. Vendor services may include payment of postage, return options, and invoicing flexibility. The latter can be especially valuable if a particular library has idiosyncratic invoicing and payment procedures. In addition, vendors can even help verify inadequately described titles if such assistance is requested. Thus, libraries typically find it more efficient and cost-effective to work with selected vendors who in turn handle a large number of publishers for the client library.

Acquisitions departments may sometimes find it advantageous to order directly from publishers, especially when speedy delivery is crucial, or prepayment is required. Some publishers show little interest in working with book jobbers but will do business directly with libraries. Publishers, unlike vendors, rarely offer discounts on firm orders. Vendors can supply, however, most prepayment-required, obscure, and difficult-to-obtain titles. They should also be able to provide a list of publishers with whom they do not deal as well as the publishers who refuse to offer their books through jobbers.[2]

Every medium- to large-sized library, whether academic or public, needs a strong up-to-date collection of publisher directories to meet general patron demands. These same tools serve as useful acquisitions aids. The following list is representative rather than comprehensive. Remember that most of the trade bibliographies previously cited include publisher directories as well:

African Book World and Press: A Directory. 2nd ed. Detroit. Gale Research Co., 1980.
Book Publishers Directory: A Guide to New and Established, Private and Special Interest, Avante Garde and Alternative, Organization and Association, Government and Institution Presses. 4th ed. Detroit: Gale Research Co., 1984.
Cassell's and the Publishers Association Directory of Publishing in Great Britain, the Commonwealth, Ireland, South Africa, and Pakistan. 10th ed. London: Cassell, 1983. Triennial.
Fulton, Len, and Ellen Ferber, eds. *International Directory of Little Magazines and Small Presses.* Paradise, Calif.: Dustbooks. Annual.
International ISBN Publishers Directory. 4th ed. New York: Bowker. 1983.
International Literary Market Place. New York: Bowker. Annual.
Kurian, George Thomas. *A Directory of American Book Publishing: From the Founding Fathers to Today's Conglomerates.* New York: Simon and Schuster, 1975.
Literary Market Place. The Directory of American Book Publishing. New York: Bowker. Annual.
Publishers, Distributors, & Wholesalers of the United States: A Directory. 6th ed. New York: R. R. Bowker, 1985.
Publisher's International Directory. 10th ed. Detroit: Gale Research Co., 1983.
Singh, Amritjit, Rajiwa Verma, and Irene M. Joshi. "Select List of Indian Publishers." *Indian Literature in English, 1827-1979: A Guide to Information Sources,* pp. 497-99. Detroit: Gale, 1981.
Taubert, Sigfred, ed. *The Book Trade of the World.* New York: Bowker, 1972-84.
Whitaker's Publishers in the United Kingdom and Their Addresses. London: Whitaker, 1984.
Who Distributes What and Where: An International Directory of Publishers, Imprints, Agents, and Distributors. New York: Bowker, 1981.
Zell, Hans M., Carol Bundy, and Virginia Coulon. *A New Reader's Guide to African Literature.* 2nd ed. London: Heinemann, 1983.

While the firm order process is well established, approval plans are relatively new acquisitions mechanisms which libraries use to gather books; they prove effective in their delivery of English and American literature and literary scholarship as well as of books in other related subject areas. (See approval plan section of this chapter's bibliography for references.) While firm orders acquire specific titles selected by a library, approval plans identify and deliver titles determined by subject and nonsubject parameters chosen by the individual library. With book in hand, librarians decide whether or not to purchase the title. Because of staffing limitations, many acquisitions departments cannot keep up with both current and retrospective book ordering in a title-by-title mode. Selectors themselves often have a difficult time staying abreast of current bibliography in their subjects, if other collection development and public services tasks are assigned. Approval plans should get appropriate new books into the library quickly. While they require staff involvement, such plans simplify the identification of titles and production of order requests, thus allowing personnel to invest time in other assignments.

All major book vendors offer approval plans. While details vary from company to company, the plans operate basically in the same manner. First, a company representative profiles the library collection development interests, usually during an on-site visit, according to subject and nonsubject guidelines. This initial step defines the subjects to be treated. For instance, a library may want criticism on eighteenth-century English literature to come on approval. At the same time, the library can, for example, request that coverage be limited to university press titles costing less than $75.00 per volume. Such a directive excludes titles from trade publishers, like Doubleday and Random House. Other nonsubject categories, in addition to type of publisher and cost, include: language of book, level of book, country of origin, amount of illustrated material, reference genres, and nonbook formats. Thus, a matrix of subject and nonsubject mandates encoded by vendor and client in the profiling process determines which books are identified and supplied to a library.

Second, most approval plans have a form or slip notification option for those titles excluded from automatic shipment by a nonsubject parameter or for titles in subject areas of lesser interest. These slips usually contain complete bibliographic information as well as subject and nonsubject assignments. They may be reviewed by selectors and/or faculty and then used to generate orders. Some vendors extend return options on titles selected by form; others do not. Many libraries subscribe to "slips-only" plans for certain subject areas. English and American literature could certainly be acquired with this approach in many libraries.

Third, any book shipped automatically on approval may be returned if deemed unsuitable by the selector. Vendors automatically send titles when the subject and nonsubject descriptors assigned to both book and library match. If a library produces a high return rate, a service representative may want to discuss how the profile can be improved. Obviously a vendor feels the plan is not working efficiently if too many books are returned. Be sure to discuss return rates with vendors when establishing approval plans. Expectations may vary. While approval plans are designed to supply a library with appropriate materials quickly, efficiently, and at a reasonable discount, they are not blanket orders or comprehensive gathering plans. Vendors treat only a certain universe of publishing for approval (certain publishers are excluded, specific titles will be judged inappropriate) and individual libraries are profiled for only a percentage of that universe. Selectors need to be aware of likely problem areas where titles are not treated for approval review. Vendors can inform you if a title will arrive at your library as a book or a slip notification. They can also tell when a title will not be treated on your behalf.

Fourth, vendors offer various discount options. These options are often quite diverse and can frequently be modified to meet a library's unique needs. At the same time, customer service from the vendor is a crucial matter.Library staff and vendor service representatives must develop a strong, professional working relationship if approval plans are to be understood for their possibilities and limitations and to be made to work effectively for the library. Quality of service may outweigh a higher discount offer.

While some librarians oppose approval plans with the argument that identification is a library task, the preselection done by vendors is in itself a valuable collection development service and should be understood as such. The identification or preselection done by approval plan vendors is not without error of oversight or faulty inclusion; however, other selections methods are vulnerable to these same problems. Remember that approval plans offer the option of return. While a book may be an important work of scholarship, it may not be suitable for a specific collection. Examining a book can be very informative, perhaps as useful as reading reviews. In addition, approval plans should be assessed systematically with regard to coverage and timely performance. Profile modifications may improve approval plan performance in significant ways. Most plans accommodate change with minimal disruption.

A variety of approval plan options are available for English and American literature collection development. Both literature and literary scholarship can be acquired via approval. Several vendors, notably Blackwell North America and Baker & Taylor, have author-based plans for contemporary literature as well as literary criticism about these authors. This means that a library can specify that works in a particular genre by a listed living author be sent automatically on approval. A library could decide to select plays and poetry by a particular author as well as criticism about these works, but exclude the novels of the same author. Again, this does not mean that all appropriate titles by the author will be selected for approval treatment; approval plan vendors may exclude certain publishers.

Many reference books, in addition, can be acquired via approval mechanisms as can popular literature, including mysteries, westerns, science fiction, and fantasy. Several vendors include first novels as well. Since special British plans are available from United Kingdom vendors, a library may wish to exclude books of British origin from a North American plan. English and American literary scholarship published in Europe and Australia can be acquired through special foreign approval plans, although many foreign publishers are represented in the larger North American plans if their titles are distributed in the United States.

Approval plans offer the following advantages over exclusive firm ordering for current titles:

1. Prompt delivery of new books
2. Freeing selectors for collection development matters beyond monitoring new book publishing as well as for other library assignments
3. Quality vendor selections based on knowledge of both the book trade and libraries
4. Return option after examination.

If collection development goals are clearly defined, approval plans can be used by most libraries, regardless of size, to acquire English and American literature. Acquisitions staff and selectors should actively explore the potential of approval plans and keep abreast of vendor developments in the field.

Another acquisitions mechanism, the book club, operates like an approval plan on a personal scale. Clubs are typically subject-focused and deliver a pre-selected title on a regular basis. The book can be returned if inappropriate. While most libraries do not need to include book clubs in their acquiring efforts, smaller libraries have used the Fireside Theater Book Club, the Poetry Book Society, and others sucessfully.

In contrast to the selectivity of approval plans, the standing order is the acquisitions mechanism which acquires all titles in both numbered and unnumbered monographic series, all titles produced by a specific publisher, or all titles handled by a book vendor in a specific genre or subject area. The standing order can also acquire all new volumes in a multivolume set or edition of collected works as they are published. The standing order is appropriate only when comprehensiveness is the objective. Since a commitment to a vendor (or publisher, or bookstore) is required for a standing order, careful evaluation of vendor service record and discounts is essential. Discounts vary significantly. Typically, there are no return options with standing orders; this is the major disadvantage. At the same time, a standing order should acquire all designated works, and this can be an especially effective way to gather series from academic departments, associations, and other obscure publishers, as well as materials in elusive subject areas.

If a library is absolutely certain it wants every title in a series or knows that titles in a particular series or from a particular publisher are not systematically identified and reviewed, the standing order may be the appropriate acquisitions device. For instance, many libraries acquire all volumes in such series as the Early English Text Society publications, because approval plans and firm ordering of titles offer less precision and demand more staff involvement in identifying, selecting, and ordering. The same argument can be advanced for acquiring volumes in a set or the collected edition of an author's work. This type of title, often called a continuation, as well as the monographic series can be deleted from approval plan coverage.

Firm orders can create duplication problems if acquisitions personnel fail to identify which series and continuations are maintained on standing order. Selectors must be very careful in this regard as well. Libraries need to develop mechanisms which help avoid duplication. Many libraries have in recent years cancelled standing orders for series and continuations to reduce "committed" money allocations. Librarians are doing this because standing order commitments have sometimes grown larger in inflationary years and because approval plans offer nearly comprehensive coverage, with the additional option of return on many series and continuation titles. Carefully evaluate any standing order before cancelling it. Cancellation may lead to more bibliographic and acquisitions work, as well as weaker collections, if the alternative acquisitions approach implemented is not reliable or timely.

While the standing order is an acquisitions mechanism, a serial is a kind of publication.[3] Standing orders or subscriptions procure most serials for libraries. At the same time, individual volumes or issues of a serial can be acquired via firm order. Serials acquisition is typically handled in the acquisitions department or in a serials department where receiving and perhaps cataloging and some public services functions also take place. Libraries maintain standing orders and subscriptions for serials with one or more vendors who specialize in the serials format. They are often called subscription agents. Despite the confusing array of terms used, selectors need to understand, first of all, which titles are serial and which are not. They also need to know the local standing orders list which may include some non-serial titles that behave like, but do not meet the exact definition of, a serial. Reference books dominate this category.

Only with significant knowledge of serials can selectors avoid unnecessary confusion over these bibliographically complex titles. Serials volumes can be sent on approval plans. Most vendors will send only a first volume for review and then require a standing order for the future volumes or future notification slips. Vendors are also able to take a library's standing orders list, which may include all types of monographic series and nonserial titles, and delete from approval plan coverage those materials obtained via standing order.

Serials bibliography is served by the following resources:

Current British Journals. London: The British Library, published in association with the UK Serials Group, 1982.

EBSCO Subscriptions Services. *Librarian's Handbook.* Birmingham, Ala.: EBSCO-Industries. Annual.

Faxon. *Faxon Librarian's Guide.* Westwood, Mass.: Faxon. Annual.

Fulton, Len, and Ellen Ferber, eds. *International Directory of Little Magazines and Small Presses.* Paradise, Calif.: Dustbooks. Annual.

The Serials Directory: An International Reference Book. Birmingham, Ala.: Ebsco 1986.

Irregular Serials and Annuals. New York: Bowker. Annual.

Magazine Industry Marketplace: The Directory of American Periodical Publishing. New York: Bowker. Annual.

Sources of Serials: International Serials Publishers and Their Titles, with Copyright and Availability Information. 2nd ed. New York: Bowker, 1981.

Perryman, Wayne, and Lenore Wilkas. *International Subscription Agents.* 5th ed. Chicago: American Library Association, 1985.

Standard Periodical Directory. New York: Oxbridge Publishing Co. Biennial.

Ulrich's International Periodical Directory. New York: Bowker. Annual.

In addition to these important trade bibliographies and directories, two union list projects remain basic resources: the *Union List of Serials in Libraries of the United States and Canada*, succeeded by *New Serials Titles*, and the *British Union Catalogue of Periodicals* followed in 1981 by *Serials in the British Library*. As is the case with monographs, the bibliographic utilities are becoming increasingly important serials acquisitions aids.

PROCEDURES AND TECHNIQUES FOR OUT-OF-PRINT MATERIALS

The antiquarian book world consists of remarkable people, unique businesses, and extremely diverse materials. It defies description. Either librarians enjoy dealing with this aspect of acquisitions, or they willingly leave it to other librarians who do. English and American literature selectors are served well by dealers throughout North America and Great Britain; acquisition of out-of-print literary materials is a common specialty for dealers who buy and sell used books. English and American literature specialists need to establish productive dealer contacts in the antiquarian book world if any retrospective collection development is underway. Moreover, these dealers can be important sources of collection development and bibliographic expertise. While advertisements and listings in journals, such as *AB Bookman's Weekly* and *American Book Collector,* identify specialist dealers, the telephone typically produces the best results. A subject selector should rely on the leads and recommendations offered by experienced library colleagues. Referrals are a key component of most out-of-print success stories. Often reputable dealers inform their colleagues in the antiquarian business about library special interests. Faculty may have used particular dealers to build personal research libraries; their suggestions can prove invaluable. In addition, the following antiquarian book dealer directories usually prove useful; many are regularly revised.

AB Bookman's Yearbook: The Specialist Book World Annual. Newark, N.J.: AB Bookman's Weekly. Annual.

American Book Collector. *Directory of Specialized American Booksellers 1984–1985.* New York: Moretus Press, 1984.

American Book Trade Directory. New York: Bowker. Annual.

Antiquarian Booksellers Association of America, Inc. (ABAA). *Membership Directory.* New York. Annual.

Book Dealers in North America: A Directory of Dealers in Secondhand and Antiquarian Books in Canada and the United States of America. 9th ed. London: Sheppard Press, 1977.

Book Dealers in India, Pakistan, Sri Lanka, &c.: A Directory of Dealers in Secondhand and Antiquarian Books in the Sub-Continent of South Western Asia. London: Sheppard Press, 1977.

Burgess, William E. *The Collector's Guide to Antiquarian Bookstores.* New York: Macmillan, 1984.

Dealers in Books: A Directory of Dealers in Secondhand and Antiquarian Books in the British Isles. 11th ed. London: Sheppard Press, 1984.

Directory of American Book Specialists. 4th ed. New York: Continental Publishing Co., 1981.

European Bookdealers: A Directory of Secondhand and Antiquarian Books on the Continent of Europe. 5th ed. London: Sheppard Press, 1982.

Fox, John. *Literary Bookstores: A List in Progress.* 3rd ed. New York: Poets & Writers, 1983.

International League of Antiquarian Booksellers. *International Directory of Antiquarian Booksellers.* (Frequency varies.) Note: Grant Uden, "The Antiquarian Booksellers' Association (International): List of Members in England, Scotland, and Wales, 1981" in *Understanding Book Collections,* 221–40. London: Antique Collectors' Club, 1982.

Marcan, Peter. *Directory of Specialist Bookdealers in the United Kingdom Handling Mainly New Books.* 2nd ed. High Wycombe: Peter Marcan, 1982.

Because out-of-print acquisitions can consume a great deal of time for both selectors and acquisitions staff, it is important to develop a strategy which gets orders out and books in as efficiently as possible. Selecting the best vendor for the titles in question is the key to a successful out-of-print acquisitions program. Selectors should inform the acquisitions staff of likely dealers or advise with regard to approach. It may be helpful for the selector to establish initial contact with a dealer to exchange information concerning library collection needs and priorities as well as dealer capabilities. Reichman describes well the common mechanisms used in ordering out-of-print English and American literature and literary scholarship, including:

1. Placing the orders with a major vendor who offers an out-of-print search service or with a specialist dealer who has appropriate interests and inventory
2. Placing the order with a book scout who has access to major used book inventories or will employ other finding methods on the library's behalf
3. Maintaining a desiderata file and searching dealers' catalogs as they are received
4. Advertising in *AB Bookman's Weekly*
5. Taking a book buying trip to search book dealer inventories or book fair stock, or attending book auctions.

Placing an order or want list with an out-of-print vendor requires the least deliberation, but it does not necessarily produce a book faster. It gets the order out, however, and presumably the vendor begins searching actively. The process of locating an out-of-print book can take a very long time; it may never prove successful. A book scout or book finder should be approached when it is crucial that an out-of-print book be obtained as quickly as possible. It is important to identify eager book scouts who have access to major book inventories or who travel widely in their searching efforts. Urban areas such as New York, Boston, and San Francisco are obviously good locations for scouts. Selectors of English and American literature should stay informed of the many specialist bookdealers within the field of literature who can be recommended to acquisitions staff. For instance, the current antiquarian book scene boasts dealers in twentieth-century poetry, women's literature, drama, science fiction, gay literature, travel narratives, and all U.S. regional literatures, to name only a few specialties. Similarly, a number of other dealers focus on used scholarly books in various subjects appropriate for academic libraries. This type of dealer is often a good choice for literary biography and criticism as well as quality literature.

Searching dealers' catalogs against desiderata files is time consuming and inefficient. But if a selector regularly reads the catalogs, it can be a productive way of identifying and acquiring needed books. Of course, catalogs can be simple lists or major tools of learning, containing extensive bibliographical and subject information. All English and American literature specialists can benefit from reading quality catalogs that advance one's subject knowledge; they are much more than acquisitions tools. Ordering from dealers' catalogs involves certain constraints, notably time. The possibility of the book already being sold necessitates prompt action. Usually acquisitions departments establish special procedures to handle these orders efficiently. Most dealers permit libraries to reserve titles with a telephone call. If a library decides to cancel the hold after a search of the public catalog or the on-order file reveals local availability, dealers appreciate a quick response. Dealers often make available proof copy for future catalogs. A head start can prove a very useful service to the busy selector. This service, however, is typically a privilege only accorded special clients. Often dealers will prepare inventories or lists of stock for special clients if they are requested to do so in specific subject areas. Many dealers have stock they never plan to list in catalogs.

Advertising is another out-of-print acquisitions alternative, although many libraries prefer to let dealers employ this mechanism. While use of a book scout means paying top dollar, advertising may bring in a wide range of quotes on a title, even for identical condition.

Whatever techniques are used, bookdealer-librarian relations are an important part of any successful involvement in the antiquarian book trade. It is worth taking the time to inform dealers about special subject interests and collection development priorities for English and American literature. Good dealers know not only the technicalities of bibliography but also their subject specialties and are often able to recommend important titles if they understand a client's interests and constraints. Think of bookdealers as collection development and selection specialists in their own right. Obviously, librarians must never forget that these "friends" are also in business to make a profit. Most antiquarian bookdealers are, indeed, small businesses with cashflow concerns and other problems. Take care that the library's business office practices, which may delay payment, do not interfere with your good working relationships.

Among antiquarian dealers in English and American literature, a distinction needs to be made between the specialist in fine condition modern first editions and the dealer who sells good used books. Collectors typically want the former, while libraries are usually satisfied with the latter, unless buying for special collections. Frequently dealers carry both inventories. A library not requiring mint copies and thus top price may have difficulty conveying this message. Be persistent. Also be very careful when reading catalogs to note what prices dealers are asking for particular titles. A library does not need to pay mint condition prices for out-of-print materials.

Reading the antiquarian book trade journals is important for all English and American literature selectors actively involved in retrospective collection development and acquisitions. *AB Bookman's Weekly* (U.S.A.) and *Antiquarian Book Monthly Review* (Great Britain) are the principal titles. *American Book Collector* has useful advertisements and a list of new catalogs received as well as important bibliographical articles in each issue. Other titles include *Australian Bookseller and Publisher* and *New Zealand Book World*.

ACQUIRING SPECIAL MATERIALS

Many English and American literature publications remain elusive even when comprehensive approval plans and standing orders are used. Acquiring publications of associations, societies, and academic departments can be especially problematic. Even the publications of the Modern Language Association of America are sometimes difficult to identify. Newsletters and announcements in society and association journals are filled with leads to important creative, scholarly, and professional titles which might be otherwise overlooked. The wide range of titles published by small presses is discussed elsewhere in this book. As Kniffel explains, they can be quite fugitive and frequently need special acquisitions attention (p. 35).

Reprints have in recent years developed into a major component of the publishing industry. Arno, Garland, AMS Press, Greenwood, Virago, and many other companies have built noteworthy lists of literary titles. Reprint companies usually produce limited runs and supplies can often be quickly exhausted. If illustrations are significant in a book, a reprint edition may prove unsatisfactory to users because of poor print quality. Many approval plans include new reprint titles of scholarly merit in their notification plans. Rarely will approval plans supply a reprint automatically—the assumption being that the library may already have it in the original edition. Many publishers of reprints encourage direct orders with significant discounts, all future volumes at a fixed price in a large continuation or series, prepublication savings, and other ways of garnering institutional commitment to a title. Publishers thereby are better able to determine print runs needed. Because actual publication details for reprints are frequently difficult to uncover with regard to what is actually available, many libraries prefer ordering reprints from vendors despite potential loss of discounts. An interesting publishing trend worth noting is that major publishers identified with quality reprints, such as those noted above, are including many more original titles in their lists. Reprints now seem to be a less attractive publishing option—an ironic turn as preservation and collection maintenance become increasingly significant collection management issues for libraries of all sizes.

While the standard bibliographical tools already listed include reprints, a special tool is *Guide to Reprints*. This annual cumulative list cites books, journals, and other materials from over 400 worldwide publishing firms. It includes a directory of publishers as well.

Like reprints, microform collections can dramatically enhance a library's holdings, especially the library's research potential. The major microform bibliographic and acquisitions tools are the following:

Dodson, Suzanne, ed. *Microform Research Collections: A Guide*. 2nd ed. Westport, Conn.: Meckler, 1984.
Guide to Microforms in Print. Westport, Conn.: Meckler. Annual.
Microform Market Place. Westport, Conn.: Meckler. Biennial.
Microform Review. Westport, Conn.: Meckler. Quarterly.
National Register of Microform Masters. Washington, D.C.: Library of Congress. Annual.
Newspapers in Microform. Washington, D.C.: Library of Congress. Annual.
Niles, Ann, ed. *An Index to Microform Collections*. Westport, Conn.: Meckler, 1984.

Libraries usually acquire microforms directly from publishers, although some vendors or distribution companies act as suppliers. Distributors typically handle titles and collections produced outside the United States. Often the available literature represents the distributor as publisher. Because microforms typically demand significant expenditures, research on prospective acquisitions is crucial. As with reprints, good acquisitions advice is, "Be Careful." The large microform publishers, such as University Microfilms International and Readex, employ sales representatives who can provide acquisitions and collection development information.

Many libraries have occasion to need microform copies of titles which are uniquely held by institutions and not available from publishers or vendors. For instance, a university may have microfilmed a manuscript in its special collections department. If permission is granted, microfilms can be easily and cheaply reproduced. Some libraries produce a microform copy if another library wishes to purchase it. Others will make arrangements to lend the microform and permit the borrower to make a microform or paper copy.

Microform collections have equipment and storage needs often not recognized by university administrators when equipment budgets are approved. Fortunately, many microform companies now offer equipment and cabinet bonuses in lieu of discounts for large purchases. This important trend will hopefully be advanced by other publishers in the future as many libraries can pursue microform purchases when liberated from equipment and storage concerns.

Paperbacks, because they often quickly replace hardcover editions which a library may not have acquired, can be problematic to English and American literature selectors. Does the selector postpone purchase until the hardcover is located by an out-of-print search? Does the selector rely on the paperback only until the appropriate hardcover edition is secured? In some settings, another English-language hardcover edition, such as the British or Canadian edition, may suffice. And in other settings, paperbacks may be entirely appropriate for purchase of popular genre fiction acquired for browsing or light reading collections. Many literary works now appear only as trade paperback originals, and many specialized scholarly titles appear only in paperback as well. Binding is, of course, an option for any trade paperback purchased which is likely to receive heavy use, but selectors must let acquisitions personnel know when paperback editions are not suitable substitutes.

Specialist companies publish dissertations and theses, the largest being University Microfilms International. Collection development policies should provide bibliographers and acquisitions staff with guidance in how to deal with requests for these materials: how many, if any, should be acquired; in what areas; in what format—hardcopy or microform? Some publishers are now producing monographs which are, in fact, dissertations. Be aware of this publishing trend. Foreign dissertations pose special problems. Often verification can be as difficult as locating a copy. Several companies now publish or make these publications available. Directly contacting the university may, however, prove the most productive procurement method.

Regional literature plays a role in collecting for almost every English and American selector. It also poses special acquisitions problems because many of these publications usually escape approval plans and identification in standard bibliographical tools. Most regions of the United States are served, however, by literary newsletters and book review journals as well as little magazines which identify important authors and titles. Catalogs from specialist bookdealers also prove useful in this regard. Usually the regional literature book dealers will include both current and out-of-print titles for consideration.

GIFTS AND EXCHANGES

Selectors should actively solicit gifts which help achieve collection development objectives. Gifts can enhance literature collections because many readers purchase quality books and thereby build significant personal libraries. While such libraries are built to meet the leisure reading, research, and collecting interests of individuals, they are often highly appropriate additions for institutional libraries.

A gifts operation, however, demands the full cooperation and support of library administration. A vital gifts policy should offer guidelines which can be uniformly applied. Selectors need to have the authority to refuse gifts as well as accept them; this, of course, means saying "yes" or "no" to donors, not only materials. Finally, a gifts operation has processing, staffing, and storage requirements which must be recognized for their costs. Gifts are not free.

Donors are not always motivated by altruism. Frequently their principal concern is a tax deduction, and they often press a library to appraise the materials. But gift appraisal is a controversial issue and is likely to remain so as long as tax laws periodically change. ACRL has strongly encouraged libraries not to appraise collections, but rather to direct donors to qualified book people. Advise the donor to choose an appraiser and deduct the appraisal cost, as well as the appraised value of the gift, from his or her taxes. The Antiquarian Booksellers Association of America (ABAA) is a good source for appraisal referrals. In spite of firm library policy, it may be necessary for the English and American literature specialist to research on occasion the value of particular titles. The tools which aid in this task include:

American Book-Prices Current: A Record of Literary Properties Sold at Auction in England, the United States, and in Canada. New York: American Book-Prices Current. Annual with cumulations. British counterpart is *Book-Auction Records.*

Bookman's Price Index. Detroit: Gale Research Co. Annual. British counterpart is *Book-Prices Current.*

Bradley, Van Allen. *The Book Collector's Handbook of Values.* 4th ed. New York: Putnam, 1982.

Heard, Joseph N. *Bookman's Guide to Americana.* 8th ed. Metuchen, N.J.: Scarecrow, 1981.

Acquisitions department staff usually manage exchange units. Typically only large universities establish formal exchange relationships with other institutions. Exchanges are acquisitions mechanisms which are designed to deliver materials hard to identify and obtain in subject areas important to a library. In return, a university's own publications may be exchanged as may duplicates and other unwanted materials. In some cases, specially purchased books may be included in exchange agreements. Exchanges are primarily gathering mechanisms; they only secondarily act as means for dispersal of a library's unwanted materials.

While exchange operations of any magnitude may be unnecessary and impractical for most academic libraries, especially with regard to English and American literature, all libraries need to establish ways of disposing of unwanted materials. Some libraries produce and distribute exchange lists. Often area bookdealers appreciate first choice of unwanted book stock and will offer cash or credit for what they remove. Other area libraries might be willing to do some purchasing or exchanging. Membership organizations such as USBE, the Universal Serials and Book Exchange, are an option. Book sales and donations to local institutions are good ways to make friends for the library, but they can consume considerable staff time. Selectors are often called upon by acquisitions staff to suggest creative alternatives which assist in dispersing unwanted materials.

CONCLUSION

All English and American literature selectors, including bibliographers in large research institutions as well as those selecting in smaller settings, need to understand the processes involved in acquiring library materials. The collection development policies followed by selectors, whether highly detailed documents or well-established traditions or somewhere in between, should influence acquisitions procedures. Selectors in all subject areas must share their priorities and subject expertise with acquisitions personnel if quality collections are to be developed. Selectors also need to define clearly the actual acquisitions tasks they—as selectors—will undertake and be aware of what the acquisitions staff can and cannot, should and should not, do for them. All personnel involved must remember that organizational structure influences interaction, policy formation, and procedures.

It is important for selectors to communicate processing priorities and time expectations if an acquisitions department handles large numbers of orders submitted by different subject specialists. It is important to understand how mechanisms such as approval plans, standing orders, and gifts processing work and to monitor their effectiveness. It is important to ask questions when procedures become problematic or service seems unsatisfactory. It is particularly important for selectors to be clear and accurate. If one agrees with Charles Osburn that selecting and acquiring materials to build library collections is the foremost public service (pp. 12-13), then every selector should view working creatively and effectively with library acquisitions staff as a very high priority indeed.

NOTES

1. The issue of reference positions expanding to include collection development, as well as other assignments, is reported in William Miller, "What's Wrong with Reference: Coping with Success and Failure at the Reference Desk," *American Libraries* 15 (1984): 128-33, and Charles A. Bunge, "Potential and Reality at the Reference Desk: Reflections on a 'Return to the Field,'" *Journal of Academic Librarianship* 10 (1984), 128-33.

2. The American Library Association's *Guidelines for Handling Library Orders for In-Print Monographic Publications* notes that "librarians and bookdealers conduct their business on a contractual basis, whether formal or informal. The object is to provide the best possible service to the library at a reasonable cost" (p. 2).

3. *ALA Glossary* defines a serial as: "A publication in any medium issued in successive parts bearing numerical or chronological designations and intended to be continued indefinitely" (p. 203). Many libraries add or delete elements if the local situation warrants modification. The *Anglo-American Cataloguing Rules*, 2nd ed. (Chicago: American Library Association, 1978) continues the above definition with the following sentence: "Serials include periodicals; newspapers; annuals (reports, yearbooks, etc.); the journals, memoirs, proceedings, transactions, etc. of societies; and numbered monographic series" (p. 570).

WORKS CITED AND RELATED MATERIALS

General Works and Bibliographies

ALA Glossary of Library and Information Science. Ed. Heartsill Young. Chicago: American Library Association, 1983.

Edelman, Hendrik. "Selection Methodology in Academic Libraries." *Library Resources & Technical Services* 23 (Winter 1979): 33-38.

Godden, Irene P., Karen W. Fachan, and Patricia A. Smith. *Collection Development and Acquisitions, 1970-80: An Annotated Critical Bibliography*. Metuchen, N.J.: Scarecrow, 1982.

Osburn, Charles. "Marketing the Collection Development Aspects of Serials Control." In *Serials Collection Development: Choices and Strategies*. Ed. Sul H. Lee. Ann Arbor: Pierian Press, 1981.

Welsch, Erwin K. "Resources: The Year's Work in 1982." *Library Resources & Technical Services* 27 (1983): 323-329.

Wynar, Bohdan S. *Library Acquisitions: A Classified Bibliographic Guide to the Literature and Reference Tools*. 2nd ed. Littleton, Colo.: Libraries Unlimited, 1971.

Acquisitions: In-Print and Out-of-Print

American Library Association. Bookdealer-Library Relations Committee. *Guidelines for Handling Orders for In-Print Monographic Publications.* 2nd ed. Chicago: American Library Association, 1984.

Bonk, Wallace J., and Rose Mary Magrill. *Building Library Collections.* 5th ed. Metuchen, N.J.: Scarecrow, 1979.

Ford, Stephen. *The Acquisitions of Library Materials.* Rev. ed. Chicago: American Library Association, 1978.

Grieder, Ted. *Acquisitions: Where, What, and How: A Guide to Orientation and Procedure for Students in Librarianship, Librarians, and Academic Faculty.* Westport, Conn.: Greenwood, 1978.

Kim, U. C. *Policies of Publishers: A Handbook for Order Librarians.* 2nd ed. Metuchen, N.J.: Scarecrow, 1982.

Magrill, Rose Mary, and Doralyn J. Hickey. *Acquisitions Management and Collection Development in Libraries.* Chicago: American Library Association, 1984.

―――, and Mona East. "Acquisitions Trends in the 1960's" and "Acquisitions Environment in the 1970's." *Advances in Librarianship* 8 (1978): 3–20.

Melcher, Daniel, and Margaret Saul. *Melcher on Acquisitions.* Chicago: American Library Association, 1971.

Perez, Ernest R. "Acquisitions of Out-of-Print Material." *Library Resources & Technical Services* 17 (1973): 42–59.

Reichmann, Felix. "Purchase of Out-of-Print Material in American University Libraries." *Library Trends* 18 (1970): 328–53.

Reid, Marion. "Searching and Verification: How Much is Enough?" *RTSD Newsletter* 10 (1985): 52–54.

Wulfekoetter, Gertrude. *Acquisitions Work: Processes Involved in Building Library Collections.* Seattle: Univ. of Washington Press, 1961.

Approval Plans

Association for Research Libraries. *Approval Plans in ARL Libraries* (SPEC Kit, 83). Washington, D.C.: Systems and Procedures Exchange Center, 1982.

Cargill, Jennifer, and Brian Alley. *Practical Approval Plan Management.* Phoenix: Oryx Press, 1979.

Kevil, L. Hunter. "The Approval Plan of Smaller Scope." *Library Acquisitions: Practice and Theory* 9 (1985): 13–20.

McCullough, Kathleen. "Approval Plans: Vendor Responsibility and Library Research: A Literature Survey and Discussion." *College & Research Libraries* 33 (1972): 368–81.

―――, Edwin D. Posey, and Doyle C. Pickett. *Approval Plans and Academic Libraries: An Interpretative Survey.* Phoenix: Oryx Press, 1977.

Serials Acquisitions

Katz, Bill, and Peter Gellatly. *Guide to Magazine and Serials Agents.* New York: Bowker, 1975.

Lee, Sul H., ed. *Serials Collection Development: Choices and Strategies.* Ann Arbor: Pierian Press, 1981.
Melin, Nancy Jean, ed. *Serials Collection: Organization and Administration.* Ann Arbor: Pierian Press, 1982.
Osborn, Andrew. *Serial Publications: Their Place and Treatment in Libraries.* 3rd ed. Chicago: American Library Association, 1980.
Taylor, David. *Managing the Serials Explosion. The Issues for Publishers and Librarians.* White Plains, N.Y.: Knowledge Industry Publications, 1982.
Tuttle, Marcia. *Introduction to Serials Management.* Greenwich, Conn.: JAI Press, 1983.

Alternative Materials and Formats Acquisitions

Buzzell, Bonnie G., and Rosemary L. Cullen. "Special Collections, Small Presses, and Gathering Plans." In *Shaping Library Collections for the 1980's.* pp. 110-14. Ed. Peter Spyers-Duran and Thomas Mann, Jr. Phoenix: Oryx Press, 1980.
Kniffel, Leonard. "What about the Library?" *Small Press* 1 (March/April 1984): 34-40.
Meckler, Alan. *Micropublishing: A History of Scholarly Micropublishing in America, 1938-1980.* Westport, Conn.: Greenwood, 1982.
Meredith, Joseph C. "Scholarly Reprint Publishing in the United States: A New Look." *College & Research Libraries* 46 (March 1985): 133-39.
Nemeyer, Carol A. *Scholarly Reprint Publishing in the United States.* New York: Bowker, 1972.
Sullivan, Robert C. "The Acquisition of Library Microforms: Parts I and II." *Microform Review* 6 (1977): 136-44, 205-11.

Gifts

Association of College and Research Libraries. "Statement on Appraisal of Gifts." *College & Research Libraries News* 34.3 (March 1973): 49.
Lanier, Don, and Glenn Anderson. "Gift Books and Appraisals." *College & Research Libraries* 40 (1979): 440-43.
Leonhardt, Thomas W. "Gift Appraisals: A Practical Approach." *Library Acquisitions: Practice and Theory* 3 (1979): 77-79.
Payne, John R. "A Closer Eye on Appraisals." *College & Research Libraries News* 46 (1985): 52-56.
Schenck, William Z. "Evaluating and Valuing Gift Materials." *Library Acquisitions: Practice and Theory* 6 (1982): 33-40.
Schreyer, Alice D., ed. *Rare Books 1983-84: Trends, Collections, Sources.* New York: Bowker, 1984. Lists of auctioneers and appraisers as well as dealers included.

Current Selection: The Role of Serial Bibliographies and Review Media

Stephen Lehmann

The primary collection responsibility for most bibliographers is currently published material. This is made bibliographically accessible through (1) *serial bibliographies* that appear on a continuing basis and at regular intervals, (2) *review media*, especially journals devoted partially or exclusively to evaluating recently published scholarship, (3) *promotional and sales materials*, including publishers' catalogs and advertisements, and (4) *vendors' notification slips*. This chapter explores the role of the first two of these categories in the selection process.

A librarian assessing the suitability of a given bibliography—or, since the choice of one bibliography may effect a chain of such decisions, a set of bibliographies—will need to consider factors existing in both the collecting environment and in the selection tools themselves. Book selection, as Ross Atkinson's very useful model shows, is a highly contingent undertaking, whose course and outcome will be affected by the complex interaction of each element in the selection process, including the selector, the collection, the users, the universe of publishing, and the bibliographic tools which chart that universe. Atkinson's point regarding book selection—"There can be no final, impartial, objective determination as to precisely what belongs in a collection and what does not"

The author gratefully acknowledges the assistance of Phyllis Bischoff, Michael Durkan, Margaret Felts, Jeffery Larson, Warren Osmond, Eva Sartori and Jim Spohrer.

(p. 118)—can be extrapolated to serially published selection tools. Certainly it would be very difficult to recommend with confidence a set of these tools for any single type of library, let alone for all libraries: the contingencies are too many, too individual, too fluid. It would be like recommending a recipe without knowing the cook, or the guests, or the availability of possible ingredients. What is an egregiously inefficient mode of selection for one library is necessary and standard procedure for another, and one library will have no reason to have heard of another's most indispensable selection source. By the same token, there are few better ways to understand the character of a collection than by knowing the tools through which it is built. This substantial range of possible differences requires the selector to understand the major variables which govern specific alternatives. Precisely because the choices are determined locally and individually, the selector's ability to make an informed decision regarding current selection tools is of enormous consequence to the library's collection.

In the selecting environment the primary variable is the scale and scope of the library's collecting activity, from which derive the major secondary factors: (1) the existence and extent of approval plans, and (2) the amount of staff time and subject expertise available for selection. A third, largely technical but still important factor involves the mechanics of selection. These include the extent of the selector's reliance on publisher's announcements, bibliographic notification slips supplied by some vendors, and other sales and promotional media as well as the degree to which selection activity is centralized in a bibliographer, or dispersed among library staff and teaching faculty, as is sometimes the case in smaller institutions.

Many research libraries receive the bulk of their material in Anglo-American literary scholarship through approval plans and standing orders. They also have subject-trained staff responsible for catching material not netted by the plans. In these libraries it is likely that bibliographers will use only the most comprehensive or highly specialized tools since general and selective bibliographic and review media list exactly those titles received "automatically," and are therefore of little use for selection purposes. Given the collection goals of research libraries, the subject matter of a book is often more important than its perceived quality, rendering reviews superfluous as primary selection tools.

In smaller academic libraries, on the other hand, selection is generally done on a title-by-title basis. There are fewer librarian selectors, therefore less aggregate subject expertise, and selection is only one of their many disparate responsibilities. Since, in addition, the relative cost of each book increases in inverse ratio to the size of the collection, and the collections of smaller libraries are targeted closely to the local curriculum, the matter of quality, the need for expertise in evaluating citations and reviews, and the relative significance of a given title become correspondingly more important. For all these reasons, then, the teaching faculty is often deeply involved in the selection process, and the librarian's responsibility, beyond planning, coordinating, and some selecting, is to insure that faculty are provided with the tools that will enable them to do their part of the job well. This brings in a new set of factors, seemingly trivial but nonetheless important, involving the mechanics of making the sources available to a dispersed constituency. *Times Literary Supplement*, for example, might be an ideal review medium for a small library, but surely it cannot be removed from the premises for weeks while being routed through departmental offices. Such considerations can give *Choice* cards, a very practical, even decisive advantage.

Because existing studies of actual selection practices in academic libraries are dated, or provide only aggregate statistics that are not broken down by type of library, they are of limited use for the purposes of this chapter. Still, some of the tabulations are worth citing. Perhaps the most interesting is Géza Kósa's, showing that while each selector in six disciplines ordered from half to three-quarters of the selected titles from only six sources, each used from twenty to forty tools in all (averaging twenty-nine). Kósa's study was done at Indiana University, Bloomington, and reflects the typical situation in a research library, where considerable effort is spent on the relatively small proportion of the titles listed outside the major sources. It is safe to predict that in a smaller library the percentage of orders emanating from key sources is even larger, and that the total number of tools used is much smaller. While Kósa found that "book reviews in professional or book review journals did not appear to be the most productive selection sources for the subject specialists in the sample" (p. 18), according to Elizabeth Futas' recent survey, 97 percent of 204 American academic libraries—many of them presumably not research libraries—used review media for selection (56 percent as first choice), with 83 percent using *Library Journal*, 79 percent *Choice* and 48 percent the *New York Times Book Review* (p. xxi).

While choosing selection sources is partly a question of institutional priorities and constraints, the differences among the tools themselves also obviously have to be considered. One will need to look at (1) comprehensiveness of the scope of coverage; (2) currency of information, which can range from prepublication to delays of as much as four years in some scholarly reviews; (3) type and quality of indexing and classification of bibliographic data—selectors usually prefer a classified organization over the scattered specificity of subject indexing; (4) quality and quantity of evaluative commentary.

Edelman very usefully identifies three stages in the selection process. The first, "a rough cut," uses current bibliographic tools and book review journals as well as ads, fliers, vendors' slips, and approval plans. The second "serves as a quality check on the first stage," and draws on reviews in scholarly journals. The process is rounded out by the retrospective evaluation of both the collection and the process itself, which Edelman designates as the third stage (pp. 37-38). It is an appealing and effective model, not the least because it imposes conceptual neatness on a supremely messy activity.

In the pages that follow only the principal types of selection tools (generally corresponding to Edelman's initial two stages) are analyzed. Not included are (1) sources for contemporary *belles lettres*, alternative press materials, and interdisciplinary studies; (2) listings lacking subject access (e.g., *Weekly Record*) when classified or indexed alternatives are available (*American Book Publishing Record*); and (3) tools more suitable for bibliographic verification or retrospective collection building. Rather, the focus is on those serial publications that treat the basics of Anglo-American literary scholarship: literary texts, criticism, theory, history, and biography produced by university presses, "serious" trade presses, and scholarly, academic, and literary societies. Since the Anglo-American literary industry has become decidedly multinational, major European sources have also been cited: French and German tools for titles in those languages as well as for the considerable amount of English-language publication taking place in German-speaking Europe. With the exception of the section on continental Europe, the area or country arrangement is generally made according to the *coverage* of a tool rather than by its place of publication. Although selection using such online bibliographic data as the MARC records is even now an option, it is not discussed here, since it is still very much on the fringes of current practice; in another five years the situation will no doubt have changed. (See also Kenneth Quinn's "Using DIALOG as a Book Selection Tool.") Finally, if a source is clearly of marginal utility in the selection of Anglo-American literary scholarship (e.g., *Cumulative Book Index, Publishers Weekly*), it has been omitted, whatever its status in the bibliographic canon.

In short, this is meant to be a practical guide. Within each geographic division, the two major bibliographic genres, national and trade bibliographies, precede the remaining types of selection sources in approximate order of their currency (review journals, critical surveys, subject bibliographies, reviews in scholarly journals). Following this area arrangement is a section devoted to indexes of composite collections.

1. *National bibliographies* attempt to be fully comprehensive records of the publishing output of a given country and are usually issued by the national library. In theory and usually in fact, they are the authoritative bibliographies. Some are now current within a year or two. Increasingly, they also include Cataloging in Publication (CIP) entries, which renders them as up-to-date as the trade bibliographies. For some major national bibliographies (e.g., the *British National Bibliography*), subject access is excellent, with both subject classification and a subject index provided. In the listings below, national bibliography has been construed to include titles which have attained that status *de facto*, if not officially.

2. *Trade bibliographies* are the most current source for books published by a country's commercial book industry. Their greatest liability for many libraries is limited coverage: in addition to small, private, and alternative presses, many scholarly, research, and professional institutions, as well as other noncommercial publishers of academic interest are generally not represented in trade listings. Also, since they are usually compiled from information provided by the publishers, often in advance of publication, the listings are not always accurate, and books have been known to make their first and last appearance in the pages of a trade bibliography.

3. *Book review journals* are intended either for the book trade, the buying public, or the library market, and are therefore considerably more timely than reviews in scholarly journals. (Scholarly review journals are published in some disciplines, history, for example, but nothing along these lines is being done in literary scholarship.) *Choice*, which reviews from the published text rather than from proof copy and is sometimes faulted for being slow, generally prints its reviews within six months of the book's appearance, compared to a two to three year lag for many scholarly journals. The limitation of book review journals is their extreme and inevitably arbitrary selectivity. Even *Choice*, the most comprehensive of the reviewing journals, covers only a quarter of the approximately 25,000 books it receives annually from publishers.

4. *Critical surveys* are less current than book review journals, but generally more current than reviews in scholarly journals. Typically they pull together into one source the publishing activity of a discipline for the previous year, and while they are neither comprehensive nor current, they are convenient. The fact that coverage is limited to major studies will be an advantage where collecting activity is limited. Some libraries will also find the brief evaluations helpful: indeed, the brevity, itself, may be the basis for their appeal.

5. *Subject bibliographies*, like critical surveys and scholarly book reviews, appear at least two years after the fact and are therefore too late to be useful to many libraries as a major selection source. On the other hand, they are comprehensive (more so than critical surveys) and thus potentially useful to even the largest libraries, at least as a check. There are literally scores of serial subject bibliographies in Anglo-American literature, and selectors needing very specialized lists may find them useful. In the section below only the more comprehensive are listed, in addition to those covering particular geographic areas. Serial bibliographies specific to literary periods, genres, and authors will be found in Wortman's *A Guide to Serial Bibliographies for Modern Literatures*, Patterson's *Literature Research Guide, and her Author Newsletters and Journals*.

A related type of selection aid exists in the form of "Books Received" columns printed in many scholarly journals. Because they are not the result of systematic effort on the part of the journals, they are generally current within a year. While obviously making no claim to comprehensiveness, they offer selectors reasonably deep and current coverage in areas of special interest where for one reason or another the standard selection tools are deficient (e.g., because of the interdisciplinary nature of the subject, or the international scope of the literature in that field). Examples of good and potentially useful listings of this kind may be found in *Comparative Literature Studies* (fall and spring issues), *Drama Review*, Feminist Studies, and Speculum.

6. *Scholarly book reviews* are so slow to appear and by and large so scattered thoughout dozens of journals that they constitute a most inefficient form of selection tool, even as a "quality check," except in a few special areas like African literary studies, where a journal with an excellent, comprehensive review section compensates for the field's highly imperfect bibliographic apparatus. Still, there are situations in which inefficiency is a price worth paying. Further, scholarly reviews can help beginning selectors learn the lay of the land in terms of issues, scholars, publishers, etc. and thus may have heuristic value beyond their usefulness as selection tools. A sampling of major journals with significant book review sections is listed below; further titles will be found in Patterson's *Literary Research Guide* (pp. 447-58) and in a series of articles by Virginia Seiser in *Serials Review*. (For an overview, see also Young's "Scholarly Book Reviewing in America.")

7. *Indexes to collections* provide subject and author access to essays, poetry, plays, short stories, and other contributions published in anthologies. Although not designed as selection tools, they should be checked to insure that the titles are held by the library to the extent desired. These are generally current within a year.

UNITED STATES

National Bibliography

National Union Catalog: Books. LC Subject Index. Washington, D.C.: Library of Congress, 1983- . A monthly updating and cumulation of the subject index to the *National Union Catalog (NUC)*, published since 1983 on microfiche. The subject index includes only those titles cataloged by the Library of Congress (regardless of country of publication) and does not index those items in the *NUC* processed by the approximately 1100 contributing libraries. For full bibliographic information, the register must be consulted (via the register number given in the subject index), since the subject index provides only author, title, and publication date. Prices are not included. The advantage of the *NUC* is the unique scope of its coverage, but the specificity of its subject approach makes it an awkward general selection tool.

CDS Alert Service. Washington D.C.: Library of Congress, Cataloging Distribution Service. Successor to the Library of Congress' proof-slip program, the Alert Service allows libraries to receive current MARC and non-MARC cataloging (for English and/or non-English materials) as well as prepublication CIP records in the form of 3"x5" laser-printed cards selected according to a subject profile submitted by the library. This may be as broad as "Language & Literature," i.e., the Library of Congress "P" class, but usually no narrower than, say, "English Literature—Literary History & Criticism" (PR 1-56), although there is a separate category "English Literature—Women Authors" (PR 11-116). While many of the citations are likely to duplicate those found in other sources, this service can function as a kind of acquisitions list of the Library of Congress, useful especially for foreign and nontrade titles. The CIP records, compiled sometimes from scanty and tentative data provided by the publisher, are distributed up to eighteen months prior to publication. For information call (202) 287-6171 or (202) 287-6100 or write: CDS Alert Service Desk, Customer Services Section, Cataloging Distribution Service, Library of Congress, Washington, D.C. 20541.

Trade Bibliographies

American Book Publishing Record (ABPR). New York: Bowker, 1960- . A monthly cumulation of the *Weekly Record*, this is the single most comprehensive list of current U.S. publications, generally providing complete order information. The citations include MARC records, CIP data, and Bowker cataloging, and are organized by Dewey classification with a rudimentary subject index. Cumulates annually.

Subject Guide to Forthcoming Books. New York: Bowker, 1967- . According to its preface, this bimonthly tool "aims to list all books expected to be published or exclusively distributed in the U.S.A. during the next five months." Although this can be useful for keeping on top of publishing in very specific subject areas, unless the advance notification provided by *Forthcom-*

ing Books is vital, selectors are likely to find the classified organization of *APBR* more convenient and reliable.

Book Review Journals

Choice. Middletown, Conn.: Association of College and Research Libraries, 1964– . Published eleven times a year in magazine and card format. Including approximately 600 brief reviews per issue, this is the major review medium for many college libraries. It covers critical editions of standard works as well as literary scholarship received from U.S. publishers and distributors. According to one set of figures (Macleod, p. 24), 32 percent of *Choice*'s reviews are of university press books, which means, as data supplied by the American Association of University Presses indicates, that approximately 61 percent of these titles are reviewed by *Choice*. Although there is good reason for G. Edward Evans to write, "The best thing you can do in the United States is to use *Choice*" (p. 163), one must do so in full awareness of its limitations and supplement it with other tools to the extent required by the library's collection needs. *Choice* reviews are particularly useful because editorial policy encourages contributors to make comparisons to relevant titles. Further, the card format can be of great convenience, especially where faculty is involved in selection. On the whole, *Choice* meets its stated goal of publishing reviews within four to six months of the book's publication (Sabosik, p. 935). (For details regarding *Choice*'s coverage, see the Selection Policy Draft in the September 1983 issue.)

Library Journal. New York: Bowker, 1876– . Although not specifically aimed at academic libraries, *LJ*'s book review section is consistently cited as a popular source by college and even university librarians (Futas, p. xxi; Kósa, 17). Since reviewers work from proof copy, *LJ* is the most current general review medium after the *New York Times Book Review*. Each biweekly issue reviews about six books in Anglo-American literary scholarship. (For comparisons of reviewing journals, see also the articles by Ream and Macleod.)

The University Publishing New Books Supplement. Oakland: Wilstead & Taylor, 1984– . Attempting to furnish thumbnail reviews of all English-language university press titles, this quarterly, until recently issued by the University of California Press, has just suspended publication. Resuscitation is still possible and should be welcomed by libraries which select heavily from university press materials and want a larger cut from which to select than *Choice* offers.

New York Review of Books. New York: 1963– . Although too limited in coverage to be a useful selection tool, this is the source if you need to know which books the faculty will want on the shelves yesterday. The panoptic nature of the review essays, which often pull together and summarize recent scholarship on topics and methods, can give valuable insight into current developments in the field of literary studies as well as related disciplines.

New York Times Book Review. New York: New York Times, 1896– . The most current general review medium.

Critical Surveys

American Literary Scholarship. Durham, N.C.: Duke Univ. Press, 1965- . Providing chapter-length reviews of current scholarship on major authors, literary periods, and genres, this annual also includes separate sections on black literature and foreign scholarship. *Year's Work in English Studies.* See under United Kingdom, below. The last two chapters are devoted to American literature.

Subject Bibliographies

MLA International Bibliography of Books and Articles on the Modern Languages and Literatures (MLAIB). New York: Modern Language Association of America, 1922- . Annual. The most comprehensive and inclusive bibliography of literary scholarship. "American (U.S.A.) Literature," v. 1, section 5. "General Literature and Related Topics" (e.g., criticism, literary theory, genres, etc.), v. 4.

Annual Bibliography of English Language and Literature. See under United Kingdom, below. Includes American authors.

Scholarly Book Reviews

American Literature. Durham: Duke University Press, 1929- . Published quarterly, this journal contains up to thirty reviews an issue, which are generally current within a year or two, remarkably timely for publications of this type. See also the listing under United Kingdom, below, especially *Journal of Modern Literature.*

UNITED KINGDOM AND IRELAND

National Bibliography

British National Bibliography (BNB). London: British Library, Bibliographic Services Division, 1950- . The *Weekly List* and its monthly indexes cumulate three times a year. Arranged according to the Dewey Decimal Classification with a very useful subject index, the *BNB* is the most comprehensive bibliography available for British imprints, though small press and other fugitive items are typically not included. It is generally current within a year, more so for CIP entries, and prices are often listed. While most selectors avoid using a British source to order a University of Nebraska Press title from its London office, they will not always be alerted to the fact of copublication, as when a book published by the University of Chicago is issued in Britain by Secker & Warburg—under a different title. Annotated bibliographic citations will help, but when copublication or overseas distribution goes unremarked, the potential for initiating a duplicate order is unavoidable.

Trade Bibliographies

Whitaker's Books of the Month & Books to Come. London: Whitaker, 1970- . Weekly listings cumulate monthly in *The Bookseller*, the journal of the British book trade. Quarterly and annual cumulations appear in *Whitaker's Cumulative Book List*. Subject access is generally inadequate for selection.

Book Review Journals

British Book News. London: British Council, 1940- . Featuring informed, informative reviews of manageable length (about 600 words), each issue of this monthly contains ten to fifteen reviews in English literary scholarship. The special section, "Next Month's Books," includes a substantial listing of literary criticism under the rubric "Literature."

Times Literary Supplement. London: Times Newspaper, Ltd., 1902- . This weekly offers authoritative reviews of significant publications in all fields and languages.

London Review of Books. London: 1979- . British clone of the *New York Review of Books*.

Irish Literary Supplement: A Review of Irish Books. Selden, N.Y.: Irish Studies, 1982- . Appearing in April and October, this relatively new journal covers books on Irish studies, with a heavy emphasis on literature. Also included are news items and articles pertaining to Irish publishing and of interest to selectors in Irish studies.

Critical Surveys

Year's Work in English Studies (YWES). London: John Murray for the English Association, 1921- . Annual. Arranged by literary period, *YWES* is "a selective, comprehensive, and evaluative narrative bibliography of scholarly writing in the fields of English and American literature" (from the preface to the 1981 edition). It is useful not only for focusing attention on those works it mentions and recommends, but also for highlighting trends and controversies in the discipline. As of the 1981 volume, a separate chapter on literary theory is included, and beginning with the 1982 volume (published in 1985), a chapter on Commonwealth literary scholarship has been added.

Studies in English Literature. Houston: Rice University Press, 1961- . Each quarterly issue brings a review article on a given period in British literary history: Winter, "Recent Studies in the English Renaissance"; Spring, "Recent Studies in Elizabethan and Jacobean Drama"; Summer, "Recent Studies in the Restoration and Eighteenth Century"; Autumn, "Recent Studies in the Nineteenth Century." Coverage is highly selective.

Subject Bibliographies

Annual Bibliography of English Language and Literature. London: Modern Humanities Research Association, 1921- . Superior coverage of scholarship published outside England and America, most notably Eastern European material, and the inclusion of references to book reviews warrant what may seem a redundant effort if one uses the "Literature of the British Isles" section of *MLAIB*.

Annual Bibliography of Scottish Literature. Edinburgh: Scottish Group of the University, College and Research Section of the Library Association, 1970- . Issued as an annual supplement to *The Bibliotheck*, this is a comprehensive bibliography of scholarship in the field of Scottish literature from the previous year.

Etudes irlandaises. Villeneuve d'Ascq, France: Université de Lille, 1979- . Previously "Livres et revues," "The Year's Work in Anglo-Irish Literature" furnishes an annual list of scholarship.

Irish University Review. Shannon: Irish University Press, 1970- . Compiled by members of The International Association for the Study of Anglo-Irish Literature, "IASAIL Bibliography Bulletin" appears in each autumn issue.

Scholarly Book Reviews

The Review of English Studies. Oxford: Oxford University Press, 1925- . Quarterly. Each number reviews up to sixty books.

Selectors seeking depth in particular literary periods may wish to consult the journals entered below. While most are interdisciplinary and go beyond national and subject boundaries, all will regularly identify highly specialized materials not treated elsewhere.

Speculum: A Journal of Medieval Studies. Cambridge, Mass.: Medieval Academy of America, 1926- . Quarterly.

Renaissance Quarterly. New York: Renaissance Society of America, 1948- . Quarterly.

Eighteenth-Century Studies. Northfield, Minn.: American Society for Eighteenth-Century Studies, St. Olaf College, 1967- . Quarterly.

Studies in Romanticism. Boston: Boston University, 1961- . Quarterly.

Victorian Studies. Bloomington, Ind.: Program for Victorian Studies, 1957- . Quarterly.

Journal of Modern Literature. Philadelphia: Temple University, 1970- . The Annual Review issue (November) provides short reviews of English-language scholarship. While the emphasis is on the period 1885 to 1950, the 1984 issue, for example, includes reviews of books about Graham Greene, Seamus Heaney, Doris Lessing, and other contemporary writers.

CANADA

National Bibliography

Canadiana. Ottawa: National Library of Canada, 1951- . Appears monthly with annual cumulations, this tool comprehensively covers Canadian titles as well as books published elsewhere on Canadian subjects. Part 1 consists of Canadian publications, part 2 of titles published elsewhere; both are organized by the Dewey Decimal Classification and are indexed by subject (Index B). Generally current within a year, it is also issued in microfiche.

Current Selection 51

Trade Bibliography

Quill and Quire. Toronto: 1935- . This magazine lists forthcoming titles in each monthly issue as well as semianually (spring and fall) for the entire spring and fall publishing seasons. Broad subject classifications are employed.

Book Review Journals

Canadian Book Review Annual. Toronto: Simon & Pierre, 1976- . Provides brief reviews of major works of Canadian interest, including Canadian literary scholarship.

Critical Surveys

Year's Work in English Studies. See under United Kingdom and Ireland, above.

Subject Bibliographies

MLA International Bibliography. See under United States, above. Includes "British Commonwealth Literature: Canadian Literature," v. 1, section 2.

Journal of Commonwealth Literature. Munich, New York: Hans Zell, 1965- . The annual bibliographic listing in the December issue includes an introductory essay reviewing the year's work in Canadian literature, and is followed by a record of bibliographies, research aids, and criticism, as well as *belles lettres.* This is a major source.

"Canadian Literature: An Annotated Bibliography" in *Journal of Canadian Fiction,* 1973- . Though it has not appeared since 1979, the compiler, Bruce Nesbitt of Simon Fraser University, intends to resume publication, but when and in which journal is not yet certain.

Scholarly Book Reviews

For a comprehensive, annotated list see Jarvi, MacKenzie and McLean (pp. 17-23).

Canadian Literature. Vancouver: University of British Columbia, 1959- . Quarterly.

University of Toronto Quarterly. Toronto: University of Toronto Press, 1935- . "Humanities" section in each July issue ("Letters in Canada") is notable.

AFRICA

National Bibliographies

The state of African national bibliographies has been recently and vividly described by G. E. Gorman: "Of the nineteen ... compilations which are properly constituted, ongoing national bibliographies very few can be regarded as adequate: incomplete and inaccurate coverage, greatly delayed production, poor quality and inadequate overseas distribution continually plague all but a handful of these services" (p. 98).

One must rely, then, on other tools to keep more or less on top of current publishing in Africa: accessions lists, trade bibliographies, review media, etc. The LC Alert Service is also considered a necessary and useful source for U.S. Africanists.

SANB: South African National Bibliography. Pretoria: State Library, 1960- . Published quarterly (the fourth quarter included in the annual cumulation). Because of its reliability, this is the African national bibliography American librarians are likely to find most useful. Includes virtually everything received through the national depository system. The State Library also offers the same bibliographic information through a weekly card service. Items are arranged by Dewey classification.

Library of Congress. Library of Congress Office, Nairobi. *Accessions List, Eastern Africa.* Nairobi: The Office, 1968- . Although obviously not a national bibliography, this list does attempt to provide broad coverage for Eastern Africa. It is published bimonthly, organized by country (no subject indexing), and is generally current within two years.

Joint Acquisitions List of Africana (JALA). Evanston: Northwestern University, 1962- . Bimonthly. An important selection source in African studies, although the citations are only in main entry order. Lists recent acquisitions of twenty-one contributing libraries, with imprints going back five years.

Trade Bibliography

African Book Publishing Record (ABPR) Oxford: Hans Zell, 1975- . Quarterly. Besides being a wonderfully informative source of news on African publishing, *ABPR* includes a bibliographical section in each issue, intended to supplement the relatively infrequently published *African Books in Print* (London: Mansell, 1975, 1978, 1984). It records new and forthcoming books by subject and country of publication. Listings are generally current within two to three years and include the price.

Critical Surveys

Year's Work in English Studies. See under United Kingdom and Ireland, above.

Subject Bibliographies

MLA International Bibliography. See under United States, above. "African Literature," v. 2, section 6.

Journal of Commonwealth Literature. See under Canada, above. Separate sections for East and Central Africa, Southern Africa, Western Africa and South Africa.

Scholarly Book Reviews

Research in African Literatures. Austin: University of Texas Press, 1970- . Published quarterly. Offers approximately ten to twenty reviews per issue.

AUSTRALIA AND NEW ZEALAND

National Bibliographies

Australian National Bibliography. Canberra: National Library of Australia, 1961– . Classified according to Dewey, with author, title and subject indexes, this tool is published bimonthly, with monthly and annual cumulations available in microfiche.

New Zealand National Bibliography. Wellington, N.Z.: National Library of New Zealand, 1968– . This listing is now published in the microfiche, index-register format used by the Library of Congress. It is updated monthly.

Trade Bibliographies

Australian Bookseller & Publisher. Melbourne: D. W. Thorpe, 1921– . Published eleven times a year. This magazine features "Australian Books Published" (by main entry) and "Next Month's New Books" (by publisher, annotated) which cumulate monthly in the microfiche update of *Australian Books in Print*.

New Zealand Bookseller & Publisher. Publication announced for 1984, now (temporarily?) suspended.

Book Review Journals

Australian Book Review. Carlton, Vic.: National Book Council, 1961– . Published ten times a year. An excellent source for current reviews.

Critical Surveys

Year's Work in English Studies. See under United Kingdom and Ireland, above.

Subject Bibliographies

MLA International Bibliography. See under United States, above. Includes "British Commonwealth Literature: Australian Literature," v. 1, section 2; "New Zealand Literature," v. 1, section 4.

Australian Literary Studies. St. Lucia: English Dept., University of Queensland. The "Annual Bibliography of Studies in Australian Literature" has appeared in the May issue since 1964. This is a comprehensive listing of scholarship published within the previous two years.

Journal of Commonwealth Literature. See under Canada, above. Separate sections on Australia and New Zealand.

Scholarly Book Reviews

Australian Literary Studies. See under Subject bibliographies, above.

CONTINENTAL EUROPE

National Bibliographies

Bibliographie de la France: Bibliographie Officielle, Livres. Paris: Editions du Cercle de la Librairie, 1857– . Twice monthly. Works of literary scholarship are found in Section 8, "Histoire et critique littéraires." Monographic series are included in the monthly supplement *Publications en serie*.

Deutsche Bibliographie. Wöchentliches Verzeichnis. Frankfurt am Main: Buchhändler-Vereinigung GMBH, 1947– . Weekly. Reihe A covers trade books, Reihe B lists titles emanating from scholarly and academic societies and other nontrade publishers. Listings from German-speaking Switzerland, Austria, and the German Democratic Republic are also included. Anglo-American literary scholarship is found in Section 52, "Englische Sprach- und Literaturwissenschaft." Even more timely than the very prompt *Deutsche Bibliographie*, although less comprehensive, is the Buchhändler Vereinigung's weekly *Neuerscheinungen-Sofortdienst* (1975–) which lists CIP titles from two to three months prior to publication.

Trade Bibliographies

Les Livres de la semaine. Published in *Livres-Hebdo*, Paris: Editions Professionnelles du Livre, 1979– . Cumulates as a monthly supplement, *Livres du mois*, which is also published as a section of the monthly *Livres de France*. Literary criticism will be found in Section 80, "Histoire littéraire, Théorie, Critique..."

English Language Titles from German Publishers. Frankfurt am Main: Buchhändler-Vereinigung, 1972– . Annual. The 1983/84 edition lists in section 800, "Philology, Literature," over twenty titles in literary theory and Anglo-American literary criticism.

Harrassowitz Book Digest: Languages, Literature. Wiesbaden: Harrassowitz, 1984– . (Previously *German Book Digest*.) Each quarterly issue includes a section, "Anglo-American Languages and Literature," and lists German and English titles published in German-speaking Europe as well as English-language titles published elsewhere on the Continent.

Book Review Journals

Amsterdam Review of Books. Amsterdam, October 1984– . Includes reviews of new and forthcoming books published in the Netherlands in English as well as Dutch.

Critical Surveys

American Literary Scholarship. See under United States, above. Includes a chapter on foreign scholarship.

Subject Bibliographies

English and American Studies in German: Summaries of Theses and Monographs. Tübingen: Max Niemeyer Verlag, 1969– . Published as a supplement to *Anglia*. This tool furnishes very useful summaries, sometimes with evaluative comments, of German, Swiss and Austrian scholarship in British, American and Commonwealth literatures, linguistics and pedagogy. There are almost 100 abstracts per issue.

Indexes to Collections

Arts & Humanities Citation Index. Philadelphia: Institute for Scientific Information, 1978– . Includes approximately twenty-five collections in Anglo-American literary scholarship in the "Guide & Journal Lists" section of the annual "Permuterm Subject Index" volume.

Essay & General Literature Index. New York: Wilson, 1934– . Over three hundred collections of essays, many of them in or related to literary studies, are listed in this annual index.

Play Index. New York: Wilson, 1953– . Appears every five years. Treats numerous anthologies as well as singly published plays.

Poetry Index Annual. Great Neck, N.Y.: Granger Book Co., 1982– . Indexes about fifty collections.

Short Story Index. New York: Wilson, 1953– . Lists approximately 200 anthologies. Published annually.

WORKS CITED

Atkinson, Ross. "The Citation as Intertext: Toward a Theory of the Selection Process." *Library Resources & Technical Services* 28 (1984): 109–18.

Edelman, Hendrik. "Selection Methodology in Academic Libraries." *Library Resources & Technical Services* 23 (1979): 33–38.

Evans. G. Edward. *Developing Library Collections*. Littleton, Colo.: Libraries Unlimited, 1979.

Futas, Elizabeth. *Library Acquisition Policies and Procedures*. 2nd ed. Phoenix: Oryx Press, 1984.

Gorman, G. E. "Current African National Bibliographies." *African Book Publishing Record* 9 (1983): 97–101.

Jarvi, Edith, Catherine MacKenzie, and Isabel McLean, comps. *Canadian Selection*. Toronto: University of Toronto Press, 1978.

Kósa, Géza. "Book Selection Tools for Subject Specialists in a Large Research Library: An Analysis." *Library Resources & Technical Services* 19 (1975):13-18.

Macleod, Beth. "*Library Journal* and *Choice*: A Review of Reviews." *Journal of Academic Librarianship* 7 (1981): 23–28.

Patterson, Margaret C. *Author Newsletters and Journals*. Detroit: Gale Research Co., 1979.

──────. *Literary Research Guide*. 2nd ed. New York: Modern Language Association of America, 1983.

Quinn, Kenneth. "Using DIALOG as a Book Selection Tool." *Library Acquisitions: Practice & Theory* 9 (1985): 79–82.

Ream, Daniel. "An Evaluation of Four Book Review Journals." *RQ* 19 (1979): 149–153.

Sabosik, Patricia E. "Currency of *Choice* Reviews." *Choice* 22 (1985): 935.

Seiser, Virginia. "Review Sources." *Serials Review* 5 (1979): 69–73; 6 (1980): 67–73.

Wortman, William A. *A Guide to Serial Bibliographies for Modern Literatures*. New York: Modern Language Association of America, 1982.

Young, Arthur P. "Scholarly Book Reviewing in America." *Libri* 25 (1975): 174–82.

Retrospective Collection Development

Richard Heinzkill

Retrospective collection development involves those activities by which titles not recently published are identified and added to the collection. It contrasts with current selection, which focuses on materials that have been newly published or reviewed.

While there are many types of tools that assist the English librarian in building the collection retrospectively (e.g., biographical dictionaries, literary handbooks and histories, critical studies), the most valuable sources are bibliographies. This chapter discusses retrospective bibliographies, emphasizing selective ones and excluding those issued serially. These retrospective compilations may be published separately, appended to scholarly studies, or appear within more inclusive serial publications, like the bibliographical essays in *Choice*. Of course, serial bibliographies themselves, such as *American Literary Scholarship*, can also be employed retrospectively with a run of several years used to generate a list of works on a topic.

The opportunity to strengthen a collection retrospectively may be occasioned by a number of circumstances: new developments in the curriculum, shifts in research interests, requests from library users, and the acquisition of gift materials. Depending on funds, staff time, and the number of titles under consideration, different procedures will be followed when selecting noncurrent items. It is not possible to set up a simple flow chart for judging a title's value to a specific library. Primary works may be checked in the major reference sources, and secondary studies can be assessed by the credentials of the scholar or the reputation of the publisher. In some cases, interest in the subject is so strong, or the collection so weak in a field, that almost anything is acceptable. But of particular interest to this chapter are those selective bibliographies which define a core, or basic list of works, either for the whole of English and American literature, or for specific periods.

Selective bibliographies are also useful in evaluating the collection, an important component of the decision-making process in retrospective development. Whether a faculty member observes that there are not enough books on a given period, or a student complains that a certain title seems to be missing from the collection, or a broad quantitative measure such as a shelflist count reveals an inadequacy, the bibliographer can refine these general impressions by employing selective bibliographies, which act as precise yardsticks of the collection. Evaluation, whether pursued systematically or *ad hoc*, may be undertaken for a variety of reasons:

1. To determine if a collection meets standards
2. To upgrade the support of an established academic program
3. To support a new academic program
4. To restore balance to the existing collection
5. To gather data for management decisions about budgeting, preservation, or storage
6. To establish the strength of the collection when writing and reviewing collection development statements.

But to state that retrospective bibliographies are the principal tools of evaluation is not to say that all of them are equally useful. One needs to keep the following characteristics in mind.

1. *Comprehensiveness.* Although an exhaustive bibliography is useful for verification, it offers little help in deciding to add a title, especially to a smaller collection, since it says nothing about the book's relative importance.
2. *Selectivity.* A selection can be voluminous (e.g., the *New Cambridge Bibliography of English Literature*), much smaller, like the Goldentree bibliographies, or balanced, aiming to present a core collection for the study of a particular author, period, or genre.
3. *Layout.* Some tools integrate bibliographic information into the text in such a way that it cannot be extracted without great difficulty.
4. *Timeliness.* Many bibliographies are seldom if ever updated. Serial bibliographies, reviews of research, and similar tools must be used to supplement most retrospective bibliographies.

Determining which bibliography will function as the library's standard for evaluative purposes is obviously an important decision. The crucial concern is a proper fit between the bibliography's scope and the library's desired level of collecting. If there is no published list that can serve effectively, it is possible to compile one from literary histories, handbooks, and scholarly works on the subject or period. How the selected writers will be represented is the next decision, whether by primary, secondary, and/or supporting background works. Relevant titles can then be obtained from reference sources supplemented by such standard tools as the *National Union Catalog, Books in Print, Cumulative Book Index*, and bibliographical utilities like OCLC and RLIN. Once the bibliography has been checked against local holdings and a desiderata file established, in-print and reprint catalogs ought to be consulted for current availability, with the remaining titles referred to out-of-print dealers.

Requests for funding retrospective collection building should be presented as positively as possible, not strictly in terms of rectifying past mistakes. If there is not a separate budgetary line for retrospective purchasing, there ought to be an agreement on the approximate ratio of current to retrospective outlays. Something is seriously wrong with a materials allocation that is spent entirely on recently published titles.

Grants can be a useful source for funding retrospective purchasing. They are, perhaps, more easily obtained for specific subject areas, such as ethnic and women's studies. The National Endowment for the Humanities as well as foundations dedicated to improving the quality of higher education sometimes support retrospective collection development. Other sources, closer to home, are campus-wide capital improvement drives, memorial funds in honor of distinguished faculty, and special projects undertaken by friends of the library groups.

Whatever the arguments against involving faculty in current book selection, there is a strong case for their engagement in retrospective activities, at least in a limited fashion. The identification of problem areas in the collection, the decision to undertake a formal evaluation, and the choice of standard bibliographies and checklists all benefit from the participation of knowledgeable faculty members. Furthermore, retrospective collection building can be costly, and faculty involvement encourages their support in obtaining funds.

The reporting of retrospective collection projects demonstrates that the library is both interested in building a quality collection and concerned to communicate its activities. One may send out a news release, invite a reporter from the campus newspaper or alumni paper, or put an article in the library's own newsletter. More often such publicity will take the form of memos to interested faculty and heads of appropriate departments as well as to library administrators. It is especially important to contact persons whose advice and support have been asked in selecting titles. Unlike publicity couched in statistical terminology, stories about retrospective buying show progress in a tangible way.

There are several developments that should be watched because of their potential impact on retrospective collection development. The first is the microcomputer, which promises much help, though little yet has been done with it. Second, the growth of large shared cataloging databases will increasingly require careful justification for acquiring older titles, especially when they are already held in the region. Persuasive arguments on this point remain possible for English bibliographers because older material is more frequently used in literature than in other scholarly fields. Primary works are a basic library resource to which researchers require immediate, not deferred access. Furthermore, these materials are needed for browsing, which is so important for the humanistic scholar (Stone, p. 295).

The remainder of this chapter is based upon the assumption that there is a scholarly consensus, sometimes shaky but nevertheless present, about which authors constitute the canon of English and American literature. The bibliographer should, however, be aware that this consensus is under attack (Fiedler, Hubbell, Nordloh). The canon is being expanded to include previously neglected women writers, ethnic minorities, popular literature, genre fiction (Westerns, science fiction, detective fiction, romance) and the products of popular culture generally.

It is, finally, necessary to emphasize that collection development cannot be done simply "by the book." Despite comments in the following pages about bibliographies that are useful for evaluating and building collections, local interests remain a major influence on selection decisions. But the bibliographer must also strike a balance between ideal and immediate concerns. Because trends in scholarship shift, because academic programs change focus, or new ones emerge, and because faculty members come and go, English literature specialists ought to realize that the collection is being gathered not only for the present, but also for the future. The broader it is, the better the base upon which to build when changes come. Use of bibliographic tools and exact methods will vary, but the goal remains the same—to assemble a body of literature that meets the needs of the majority of present and prospective library users.

The bibliographies discussed in the following pages are together intended to define a core research-level collection. To reiterate, comprehensive bibliographies of both primary and secondary materials have been excluded, because they exercise no judgment about the relative importance of titles but are concerned only with whether works fit the scope of time or format of the compilation. They certainly are important scholarly tools in their own right and belong in the collection, but inasmuch as few, if any, libraries will attempt to acquire all of the items in a comprehensive bibliography, they have been omitted here, where the aim has been to identify bibliographies that give direction and advice. Further references to comprehensive bibliographies can be found in Margaret C. Patterson's *Literary Research Guide*, and Robert C. Schweik and Dieter Riesner's *Reference Sources in English and American Literature*.

ENGLISH LITERATURE
General Bibliographies

Among retrospective bibliographical sources in English literature, the Cambridge bibliographies have no equal for authority and prestige. Individual parts have competitors, but as sets they are unrivaled. The original *Cambridge Bibliography of English Literature (CBEL)* was issued in 1941; a supplement providing coverage through 1955 was published in 1957. Then starting in 1969 with the appearance of volume three, a thorough revision began as the *New Cambridge Bibliography of English Literature (NCBEL)*. Cut-off dates for the inclusion of material in the individual volumes varies; to be safe, subtract three years from the imprint date of each. Much background material relevant to literary studies was not treated in *NCBEL*, and therefore *CBEL* remains helpful as a guide to earlier scholarship in many areas.

The beginner using these tools should keep several points in mind. First, the listing of editions of an author is not an endorsement of worth but merely a statement of fact. Only rarely is there some indication of which edition is to be preferred. For guidance on the relative authority of editions, other bibliographies will have to be consulted. Second, as large as the sections of secondary material are under some authors, they still are meant to be selective. (Of course, for minor writers who have received little critical attention, a short list of references may be virtually comprehensive.) For purposes of collection development, at least for a basic collection, a less generous list of secondary sources is more desirable. Third, even allowing for changes of interest in the scholarly world, the division by NCBEL of major and minor authors can be trusted. If anything, history will elevate some minor authors to higher status, but it is unlikely that any of those enthroned by NCBEL will be toppled.

Bibliographies accompanying literary histories furnish other avenues to the full range of English literature. Notable are the appendices of Boris Ford's *New Pelican Guide to English Literature*; because those in his original *Pelican Guide to English Literature* were compiled by different persons, they also remain useful. The bibliographical supplements to Alfred C. Baugh's *A Literary History of England* and the *Oxford History of English Literature* are worth noting as well because they represent the judgments of respected scholars on the outstanding works in their fields. The typography and format of both, however, render them somewhat difficult to use.

A shorter, highly recommended general tool is *A Guide to English and American Literature* by F. W. Bateson and Harrison T. Meserole. This revised version of Bateson's classic *A Guide to English Literature* benefits from his experience and discernment as general editor of *CBEL*.

Period Bibliographies for Old English

There are several sound bibliographies of Old English. Fred C. Robinson's *Old English Literature: A Select Bibliography* concentrates on more recent works and is extremely selective. Drawing on his vast erudition, Robinson offers a good basic Old English collection as of 1968. William Matthews' *Old and Middle English Literature* has a broader scope because it extends to older commentary. Unlike Robinson, Matthews does not, however, discuss individual titles. A third selective bibliography, found in David M. Zesmer's *Guide to English Literature from Beowulf through Chaucer and Medieval Drama*, was compiled by another Old English scholar, Stanley B. Greenfield, and remains worth consulting. He makes interesting observations on the outstanding editions and scholarly works. Old English studies do not move at such a furious pace that these titles cannot still serve as a first step toward building the collection.

Period Bibliographies for Middle English

The Middle English portion of the collection can be formed by following the advice of Matthews' *Old and Middle English Literature* and Bateson and Meserole's *Guide*. Their recommendations concerning the basic texts of the period are very similar. However, following Matthews will produce a fuller collection of the critical works. For example, he records eleven book titles and twenty-one journal articles about Thomas Malory, but Bateson confines his suggested readings to six books. While Matthews' bibliography is an unadorned listing, Bateson's incisive and succinct comments make for lively reading. But unlike Matthews, Bateson has not remarked extensively on the drama for the period, instead deferring to Stanley Wells' *English Drama (Excluding Shakespeare)*.

Period Bibliographies for the Renaissance

Because literature flourished during the Renaissance, there are easily several hundred writers who could be called the major authors of the period. A minimal group is the seventy-five covered by Bateson and Meserole. Further guidance in determining the outstanding figures can be found in the Goldentree bibliographies for the period: John L. Lievsay's *The Sixteenth Century: Skelton through Hooker* and Arthur E. Barker's *The Seventeeth Century: Bacon through Marvell*. They give the most important editions of the collected works and a careful selection of secondary material, but neither identifies the principal genres in which the authors wrote.

S. K. Heninger, Jr.'s *English Prose, Prose Fiction, and Criticism to 1660* divides Renaissance prose into different categories: religious, historical, travel, scientific and technical, ephemeral and polemical, essays, narrative fiction, literary criticism, education, and translations. Within each section, the most important authors are listed chronologically, and for each title the best modern editions are cited.

Frieda Elaine Penninger identifies thirty-four significant playwrights in her *English Drama to 1660 (Excluding Shakespeare)*. She comments on available collected editions but does not list each dramatist's works individually. A more select list of twenty-two major figures with coverage of collected editions as well as important editions of individual plays is in Irving Ribner and Clifford Chalmers Huffman's Goldentree bibliography, *Tudor and Stuart Drama*. These two tools can also be relied upon to indicate important secondary literature on Renaissance drama. Of the two, Penninger's emphasizes more recent scholarship.

Collecting Shakespeareana is an important yet sometimes overwhelming task for the English selector. The editing of Shakespeare's works is a complicated story, and the commentaries on the plays are beyond enumeration. The handiest summary of the textual history from the "good quartos" to the present is provided by Norman Sanders in Stanley Wells' *Shakespeare: Select Bibliographical Guides*. This work is also a source for recommended editions of the plays as well as one of the best places to learn about the highlights of Shakespearean scholarship that should be included in most libraries. Good advice on the most recent collected editions is also in *Shakespeare: A Study and Research Guide* by David Bergeron.

NCBEL furnishes information on the thirty-seven more prominent Tudor, Jacobean and Caroline poets, and also lists many others of lesser rank. Libraries generally will be content to represent many of these poets only by anthologies, both Renaissance gatherings as well as recent compilations. Modern editions of older anthologies, such as Hyder E. Rollins' exemplary versions of *Tottel's Miscellany, The Paradise of Dainty Devices, England's Helicon,* and other contemporary miscellanies, constitute a good foundation. The best of recent anthologies are cited by Bateson and Meserole, and by C. S. Lewis in *English Literature in the Sixteenth Century, Excluding Drama,* a volume of the *Oxford History of English Literature.*

Period Bibliographies for the Restoration and Eighteenth Century

Literary histories of this period are so full of names, it is sometimes difficult to determine who are the most important writers. Help can be obtained from Bateson and Meserole's *Guide*, which lists eighty-six principal figures in chronological order between the Renaissance and 1800. The best edition of primary texts is cited, accompanied by a short selection of secondary works.

Donald F. Bond has compiled two Goldentree bibliographies to cover this period, *The Age of Dryden* and *The Eighteenth Century.* Entries indicate preferred scholarly editions and a minimal selection of critical works, but fiction writers are excluded. Twenty-nine of these whose reputations endure today are treated in Jerry C. Beaseley's *English Fiction, 1660–1800*, which covers both primary and secondary works. All three of these titles include generous selections of background materials in such areas as science, religion, and the fine arts, which are essential for an understanding of the literature of the times.

Period Bibliographies for the Romantic Movement

Although the principal Romantic writers can be easily ascertained, there is a plethora of minor authors. For instance, *NCBEL* lists only five major novelists of the early nineteenth century (Maria Edgeworth, Walter Scott, Jane Austen, Thomas Love Peacock, and Frederick Marryat) but seventy-three others are recorded as minor. Furthermore, most of the Romantics were prolific, and many had dual or multiple reputations, variously as novelists, poets, essayists, and critics. About the only genre the period fails to be noted for is successful stage drama.

The major poets and essayists are dealt with in two excellent volumes of bibliographical essays sponsored by the Modern Language Association (MLA). *The English Romantic Poets: A Review of Research and Criticism*, edited by Frank Jordan, is limited to five poets, while *The English Romantic Poets and Essayists: A Review of Research and Criticism*, edited by Carolyn Washburn Houtchens and Lawrence Huston Houtchens, covers an additional eleven authors. In both there are detailed evaluations of editions, biographies, and critical works concerned with each author.

The only work in Gale's Information Guide Library devoted solely to this period is Donald H. Reiman's *English Romantic Poetry, 1800–1835*, which treats Wordsworth, Coleridge, Byron, Keats, and Shelley. Besides coverage of primary texts, Reiman's volume is also rich in background sources. Like many other titles in the Goldentree series, the very selective *Romantic Poets and Prose Writers* compiled by Richard H. Fogle is becoming dated. Nevertheless, it furnishes bibliographical information on fourteen authors, with editions and other works of special importance marked with an asterisk.

Period Bibliographies for the Victorian Era

It is estimated that over 40,000 novels were written during the Victorian period. *NCBEL* considers only twenty novelists of the era as major ones, while another 126 are regarded as minor. The MLA guides discussed immediately below treat only seventeen novelists, twelve of which are common to *NCBEL*.

Lionel Stevenson edited the first MLA volume, *Victorian Fiction: A Guide to Research*, which covers scholarship to 1962. Its successor, *Victorian Fiction: A Second Guide to Research*, edited by George H. Ford, analyzes scholarship published between 1963 and 1974, and also furnishes complete coverage for Robert Louis Stevenson and Samuel Butler. These tools record judgments on matters bibliographical and critical by some of the best scholars in Victorian studies.

A more selective guide to fiction is Ian Watt's *The British Novel: Scott through Hardy* in the Goldentree series. Watt mentions collected works, occasionally commenting on editions of the major authors. Minor authors are represented only by their main novels, while the importance of another 105 novelists is registered by simply listing their names in alphabetical order in an appendix.

Nonfiction prose also plays a central role in Victorian literature. Excellent coverage of these writers is found in David J. DeLaura's *Victorian Prose: A Guide to Research*. The annotations of editions and secondary works are most helpful. Prose writers, along with valuable auxiliary reading on the cultural background of the time, are treated in a much shorter Goldentree volume, *Victorian Poets and Prose Writers* by Jerome H. Buckley. Still another selective guide to Victorian prose is Harris W. Wilson and Diane L. Hoeveler's *English Prose and Criticism in the Nineteenth Century*. The principal works of thirty-four writers are listed here, although not in their latest editions.

Frederick E. Faverty's *The Victorian Poets: A Guide to Research* is an excellent introduction to the work of eleven major poets and has good advice on primary and secondary works up to the time of its publication. However, there has been considerable research on the Victorian period in recent years, so a new edition of this work is badly needed. Buckley's bibliography is also useful for Victorian poets.

In *English Drama and Theatre, 1800-1900*, L. W. Conolly and J. P. Wearing list the collected works and editions of the principal plays for 110 dramatists, excluding George Bernard Shaw and J. M. Barrie. *NCBEL* is more conservative in its selection: only seven dramatists are regarded as major, including Shaw and Barrie, although an additional forty playwrights are ranked as secondary.

Period Bibliographies for the Modern Period

Determining which twentieth century authors to collect can be a problem. The aim is to identify those writers who already are, or will soon become, the outstanding figures of the century. Inclusion in biographical dictionaries suggests that an author may be noteworthy. There are also several broad but selective bibliographical works pertinent to the job. *Twentieth Century British Literature: A Reference Guide and Bibliography*, by Ruth Z. Temple, includes 400 authors, many of whom are still living. Only creative works are listed, and the genre of each title is indicated, a feature often useful in selection. International in its coverage of English-language novelists, James Vinson's *20th Century Fiction* provides a full bibliography of the works of just over 300 authors. Although each writer's country of origin is given in the entry, there is no separate index to identify specifically British writers. E. C. Bufkin's *The Twentieth Century Novel in English: A Checklist* is confined strictly to novels separately published in book form. The results are interesting: Max Beerbohm has one entry and much of D. H. Lawrence's literary work fails to qualify for inclusion, but Bufkin's book is excellent for the novels of about 700 authors. A biocritical dictionary of living authors, Vinson's *Contemporary Novelists* features writers from throughout the English-speaking world, providing for each a checklist of works in all genres.

These more comprehensive tools offer little guidance to selectors in smaller libraries which seek to focus on authors whom an emerging consensus identifies as the century's best writers. A start in this direction is Thomas Jackson Rice's two-volume *English Fiction, 1900-1950*, which confines itself to the thirty-five authors Rice identifies as both major and the "'second echelon' of major-minor novelists" (vol. 1, p. xix). Paul L. Wiley undertook the same assignment in his *British Novel: Conrad to the Present*. This Goldentree bibliography focuses on the major authors and those "somewhat less celebrated but nevertheless distinctive enough" to merit attention. Despite a 1973 copyright date, selection ends about 1950. The volume cites complete works where they exist and enumerates titles, if there is not a collected edition. Interestingly, twenty-five authors are common to Rice and Wiley.

For a selection of novelists prominent after 1950, two guides can be recommended. *Contemporary Fiction in America and England, 1950-1970* by Alfred F. Rosa and Paul A. Eschholz highlights fifty-six recently published British novelists who are worthy of serious consideration. Rosa and Eschholz had to contend with the arbitrary cut-off date of 1950 to avoid duplicating writers already treated in other volumes of Gale's Information Guide Library. *The Contemporary English Novel: An Annotated Bibliography of Secondary Sources*, compiled by Horst W. Drescher and Bernd Kahrmann, concentrates on seventy-nine novelists who emerged after 1954, a date the authors see as a turning point in the history of the British novel. This tool serves well in directing the bibliographer to the best writers of recent British fiction.

Identifying the most significant poets of the first half of this century is a perilous challenge for any critic, yet several have boldly undertaken the task. Emily Ann Anderson narrowed the field to twenty-one in her *English Poetry, 1900-1950*, which records the principal titles of each poet and annotates important secondary literature. John Press offers another selection in his *A Map of Modern English Verse*, which furnishes limited bibliographies of the primary works of thirty-nine poets. A similar tool, *English Poetry, 1900-1950: An Assessment* by the poet C. H. Sisson is valuable less for its bibliographical advice than its choice of thirty-five poets who show "the best English verse" of the period (p. [11]). Press and Sisson agree on sixteen names, but only seven of these commonly cited writers are included by Anderson.

Martin E. Gingerich's *Contemporary Poetry in America and England, 1950-1975* is part of Gale's Information Guide Library and therefore included no writers that are mentioned elsewhere in the series. Gingerich has chosen a generous number of poets, most of whom are still alive. He registers titles of separately published volumes of poetry as well as critical studies. To update Gingerich's list of primary texts, one must use *Contemporary Poets*, edited by James Vinson and D. L. Kirkpatrick. This large gathering of practicing poets from all nations of the English-speaking world lists not only poetry but also other types of creative work by each writer.

Modern British drama is not usually thought to have begun with T. W. Robertson's plays of the 1860s, but that is where Charles A. Carpenter starts his Goldentree bibliography, *Modern British Drama*. Limited to only fifty-four dramatists, this short list of primary and secondary works inevitably omits names that should have been included, but nonetheless still acts usefully as a starting place. Another view of the drama of the period, E. H. Mikhail's *English Drama, 1900–1950*, selects seventy-nine dramatists, weighted in favor of his specialty, the Irish stage. His cut-off date prevents incorporating the burst of theatrical activity often called the "New Drama," which began in 1956 with the production of John Osborne's *Look Back in Anger*.

Too inclusive to guide the development of basic collections but certainly useful for its coverage of living playwrights from the entire English-speaking world is *Contemporary Dramatists*, edited by James Vinson. Like other volumes in St. Martin's Contemporary Writers of the English Language series, there is no separate index by country of origin, and bibliographies record all literary works, not just an author's dramatic writing.

SCOTTISH LITERATURE

Though much of Scottish literature is so closely intertwined with the English scene that many writers are equally prominent in both Edinburgh and London, there yet remain works that are distinctively Scottish. Several sources are valuable in building a rounded collection representative of this literature thought by Scots to be central to their tradition.

A sizeable basic collection is laid out by David Daiches in "Further Reading" in *A Companion to Scottish Culture*. Arrangement is by literary period, with about fifty titles of both primary and secondary works mentioned for each era. Another chronological approach is available in the bibliographical appendix to *A History of Scottish Literature* by Maurice Lindsay. Sixty-one authors from the fifteenth century to the present are treated. One drawback is Lindsay's greater interest in works of criticism about the authors than in editions of their work, so that other sources have to be used to identify primary materials.

W. R. Aitken offers a more generous selection of writings "of interest to those who wish to comprehend what Scottish literature is—or is not" in his *Scottish Literature in English and Scots* (p. xviii), which treats thirty-two medieval and Renaissance authors, twenty-five writers who flourished in the period 1660–1800, fifty from the nineteenth century, and 102 representing the twentieth century. Both primary and secondary sources are entered for each author, and there is also a listing of background studies for Scottish literature.

IRISH LITERATURE

The Irish contribution to the mainstream of English literature ranges from a seventeenth-century poet laureate, Nahum Tate, to such major modernist masters as George Bernard Shaw and James Joyce. Before the later part of the eighteenth century, Irish writers usually made their literary reputations in London and were largely assimilated into English culture. For this reason many books about Anglo-Irish literature start with Maria Edgeworth (1767–1849), whose career was based in her native country. She begins Richard J. Finneran's *Anglo-Irish Literature: A Review of Research*, which continues through the Irish Renaissance. Finneran's supplement, *Recent Research on Anglo-Irish Writers*, updates the original volume, also discussing newer drama, fiction and poetry. Although these volumes are principally designed to comment on the secondary literature, outstanding editions of primary works are discussed. The writers considered in these essays are those around which a collection of Irish literature should be built.

Another approach to the canon of Irish literature can be derived from Maurice Harmon's *Modern Irish Literature, 1800–1967: A Reader's Guide*. There are short sections for various aspects of Irish culture as well as for important critical studies of poetry, drama, and fiction, but not for creative works. The list of authors should, however, be used with caution, since writers have been included only if they are the subject of a bibliography—not always the best criterion of significance.

Not as selective are two other tools. Brian McKenna's *Irish Literature, 1800–1875* covers the principal works of 114 authors. Richard Fallis' *The Irish Renaissance* treats secondary works for about forty-seven authors from the late nineteenth century through 1940. The writers chosen are representative of this period of Irish literary history, which has strongly influenced English Literature.

AMERICAN LITERATURE

General Bibliographies

The Literary History of the United States, edited by a group of scholars headed by Robert E. Spiller, is usually regarded as the most important bibliography of American literature. The bibliographical section of the first edition (1948) covered 207 authors. The supplements to subsequent editions added thirty-two contemporary writers. Nevertheless, the twentieth century is not as well represented in Spiller as it should be in a library's collection. By contrast, the background material on American civilization occupies a substantial portion of the tool's bibliography and provides a thorough outline, with supporting titles on the social, cultural, and intellectual influences on American literature. But as important as Spiller's work continues to be, from the collection developer's point of view it is not ideal. The use of supplements instead of a fully integrated new edition requires three separate searches for most writers. Furthermore, the titles are embedded in paragraphs, rather than listed in columns, making them time-consuming to check.

A second important bibliography, Jacob Blanck's projected eight-volume *Bibliography of American Literature,* is often regarded as definitive, but neither is it nor was it intended to be. A committee of the Bibliographical Society of America determined its scope, employing the principal criteria that writers had to be in the field of *belles lettres* and "in their own time at least, were known and read" (vol. 1, p. xi). Hence its inclusion of many writers more newsworthy than literarily noteworthy. Futhermore, no one living in 1930 could be included, which eliminated most twentieth-century literature. The resulting list of 281 authors features many who are not at present, nor are likely to be, of scholarly interest, among which Joyce Kilmer and Emma Lazarus might be mentioned. Indeed, only eighty-seven of Blanck's authors are also in Spiller. In fact, the motive of this enormous undertaking was to help book collectors as much as the academic community. Entries, while providing a wealth of bibliographic detail, are designed less to furnish an easily consulted list of primary works than to aid in identifying specific issues and states of editions.

First Printings of American Authors, edited by Matthew J. Bruccoli, could be used to supplement the *Bibliography of American Literature*. Although not done with Blanck's loving attention to detail, it does provide information about first printings for over 354 authors. There are no stated criteria for inclusion. Many writers outside *belles lettres* are represented, and the selection is weighted in favor of the twentieth century.

Another general bibliography is James Vinson's set, *American Writers to 1900* and *American Writers since 1900*. The first volume treats 131 authors, the second, 251. Taken together they cover a substantial portion of American literature. Especially useful are references to more recent writers not mentioned in other general bibliographies. But despite Vinson's wide scope, 34 percent of the authors in Spiller are omitted, with early American literature particularly slighted, including numerous colonial and Revolutionary figures. Titles are listed in columns according to genre, an arrangement that facilitates use at the catalog. There is also a selection of secondary works. Though bearing a 1983 date of publication, few imprints later than 1977 are entered.

Selective Bibliographies

Judging by these general bibliographies, there are between 400 and

500 American authors that should interest a research library. Several compilers have undertaken the challenge of reducing this corpus. Lewis Leary offers the most concentrated selection in *American Literature: A Study and Research Guide*. He asked ninety-five of his academic colleagues to list the twenty writers every undergraduate student of American literature should be acquainted with. The voting was so close that he felt duty-bound to enlarge his final tabulation to twenty-eight authors. Leary comments on the collected and selected editions for each writer and also recommends critical works—a combination that makes this volume a good tool for retrospective evaluation.

Valmai Fenster's *Guide to American Literature* limits itself to 100 authors who in her estimation are most frequently studied in courses by undergraduate majors and graduate students in English. For each writer, separate publications are listed as well as any collected works or edited texts. Citations to critical studies are kept to a minimum. Most academic libraries would not want to limit collections to so little secondary material, but at least this volume identifies the most essential titles.

Andrew Wright, who has labored long in the field of American literature, selected ninety-six authors ranging from William Bradford to Flannery O'Connor for his *Reader's Guide to English and American Literature*. Citations are too few and too dated to form a sound working collection, but the volume does define well a central core of American authors.

Another reflection of the scholarly consensus on the canon of American literature can be found in three highly recommended volumes featuring bibliographical essays on thirty-nine writers. Although not conceived as a set, the books have developed into one. The original volume, *Eight American Authors: A Review of Research and Criticism*, was first edited by Floyd Stovall and subsequently revised under James Woodress. It deals with the most important figures in American literature. Later, scholars were asked to name the outstanding authors prominent prior to 1900 not listed in Stovall-Woodress. Bibliographical essays about these were then published as *Fifteen American Authors before 1900*, under the editorship of Earl N. Harbert and Robert A. Rees. The modern period was treated in similar fashion. Authorities were polled to determine the most crucial writers excluded from *Eight American Authors*, and bibliographic essays were commissioned and edited by Jackson R. Bryer in *Fifteen Modern American Authors*, later revised as *Sixteen Modern American Authors*. Evaluations in these volumes are of the highest quality, covering both primary and secondary sources thoroughly. Although comments on editions are useful, it must be remembered that some of the essays were written before the Center for Scholarly Editions began its work and prior to the Library of America.

Bibliographies for the American Novel

C. Hugh Holman and Janis Richardi's Goldentree bibliography, *The American Novel through Henry James*, focuses on thirty-eight novelists, listing texts and criticism for each. The section on general studies of the American novel is also important. A companion Goldentree volume is Blake Nevius' *The American Novel: Sinclair Lewis to the Present*. Although forty-eight novelists are covered, many important names were excluded because serious commentary on them was lacking at the time of the guide's compilation.

In its Information Guide Library, Gale has issued three useful volumes. David K. Kirby's *American Fiction to 1900* treats the principal works and most reliable collected editions for forty-one authors. James Woodress' *American Fiction, 1900-1950* provides especially valuable comments on editions and reprints of the primary works for forty-four writers. *Contemporary Fiction in America and England, 1950-1970* by Rosa and Eschholz furnishes unannotated lists of texts by eighty American novelists.

Also useful for contemporary American novels is Bufkin's *Twentieth-Century Novel in English: A Checklist*, which covers numerous less prominent figures who are nonetheless of a caliber that is appropriate to graduate level collections. Not as discriminating is Vinson's *Contemporary Novelists*, which lists works in all genres by 500 living English-language writers. No attempt has been made here to isolate the essential authors.

Bibliographies for American Poetry

Most valuable for defining the historical canon are the bibliographies appended to two anthologies, Gay Wilson Allen's *American Poetry*, which covers fifty-four major figures from the seventeenth century forward, and Hyatt H. Waggoner's *American Poets from the Puritans to the Present*, which provides checklists for the creative works of seventy-one writers along with a selection of secondary works about the American poetical tradition. More recent American poets of note appear in Gingerich's *Contemporary Poetry in America and England, 1950-1975*, which similarly records published volumes of poetry as well as critical studies. Too inclusive to be called carefully discriminating, Vinson and Kirkpatrick's *Contemporary Poets* is nonetheless an important source for biobibliographical information about living poets. Unfortunately, there is no index to identify the Americans as a group.

Bibliographies for American Drama

Except for some verse plays and closet dramas, dramatic works are written to be acted. Since their usual dissemination is through performance, obtaining texts is not always easy. Indeed, many early American theatrical pieces were meant to be no more than occasional entertainments and were not published for the reading public. Because they are now consulted more for their historical interest than literary merit, most libraries rely on anthologies and collections to represent this earliest period of American theater. These are listed in Walter J. Meserve's *American Drama to 1900*, which also includes both primary and secondary bibliographies for major nineteenth century dramatists.

Though Gale intends to cover fully twentieth-century American drama, only Richard H. Harris's *Modern Drama in America and England, 1950-1970* has appeared. Here are listed the published plays of 255 playwrights, accompanied by references to critical works about them. While the selection of dramatists is very good, their nationality is not indicated, an annoyance if the focus is on American drama.

Perhaps the most balanced coverage of American theater is in E. Hudson Long's *American Drama from Its Beginning to the Present*. This Goldentree guide divides its fifty-two playwrights into categories of greater and lesser importance. Regrettably, concentration is on criticism, with primary texts inadequately reported. Therefore, other sources will have to be consulted to ascertain the published plays of this group.

To date there is no succinct bibliography for the drama of the past fifteen years. Under the general editorship of Daniel Hoffman, the *Harvard Guide to Contemporary American Writing* includes a chapter that usefully identifies fifty playwrights prominent since World War II. Vinson's *Contemporary Dramatists*, furnishing biobibliographical accounts of over 300 living practitioners of the genre, can be employed to gather titles by these and other writers emerging on the contemporary scene. This tool has the great advantage of being regularly revised.

CANADIAN LITERATURE

Although books were written in Canada from the earliest settlement, a distinctive Canadian literature was not evident until the middle of the nineteenth century. The bibliographies presented in this section cover the historical development of Canadian literature, while also offering differing visions of its canon.

A minimum list of Canadian writers is represented by Reginald E. Watters' bibliography accompanying his and Carl F. Klinck's *Canadian Anthology*. It registers works by and about forty-six authors. The ongoing

Annotated Bibliography of Canada's Major Authors, edited by Robert Lecker and Jack David, is an ambitious work that eventually will comprise ten volumes, covering in detail primary and secondary materials on forty-nine writers. Because the majority are living, plans are to update the entries by issuing supplements. With only three authors from the nineteenth century and two more whose careers straddle both the nineteenth and twentieth centuries, this tool clearly has a contemporary bias. But otherwise, it is well done.

Although not intended to be a reference work, David Stouck's *Major Canadian Authors: A Critical Introduction* can serve as a selection guide. Chapters on seventeen authors are supplemented by an appendix, "Guide to Other Canadian Writers," that lists seventy-one further names of note. Bibliographies identify the more important titles, though the appendix is necessarily more restrictive. In *A Concise Bibliography of English-Canadian Literature* Michael Gnarowski records primary works and a short selection of critical studies for each of 117 writers.

Another overview of Canadian literature is furnished by two complementary handbooks. Clara Thomas in *Our Nature, Our Voices: A Guidebook to English-Canadian Literature* briefly treats fifty figures from the beginning to the present. Frank Davey's *From There to Here: A Guide to English-Canadian Literature since 1960* profiles about sixty authors, only four of whom are cited by Thomas. Each volume provides a selection of the author's major works as well as secondary literature. Taken together, these volumes would suggest that the best of Canadian writers number 106, with the emphasis about equally divided between the living and the dead.

AUSTRALIAN LITERATURE

There are now about one hundred authors that most authorities would agree belong in the pantheon of Australian literature. Among various representative lists, the most concise is Joseph and Johanna Jones' *Authors and Areas of Australia*, which contains sketches of thirty-four writers and selectively records their works.

Fred Lock and Alan Lawson identify forty-eight authors in *Australian Literature—A Reference Guide*, including some who have been relatively neglected by scholars. While not listing primary works, their guide indicates available bibliographies of them. A few critical works are also listed. L. T. Hergenhan offers another version of the canon in the bibliographical appendix to *The Literature of Australia*, edited by noted Australian writer Geoffrey Dutton. Sixty-five writers are entered, with selected coverage of materials both by and about each.

The most recent effort to define the Australian corpus is *The Oxford*

History of Australian Literature, edited by Leonie Kramer. The volume's bibliography, compiled by Joy Hooton, covers seventy-eight individual authors, listing principal primary works and major secondary studies as well as sometimes commenting on the better editions.

NEW ZEALAND LITERATURE

The most interesting account of New Zealand's best creative writing is Peter Alcock's article, "New Zealand Literature: A Select List with Some Background Titles." Derived from his effort to measure a library's collection of the field, Alcock's list features sixty titles, many first published after World War II. John Thomson's *New Zealand Literature to 1977* accords lengthy bibliographical treatment to thirty-one authors. A supplementary chapter covers seventy-three minor figures in an extremely brief fashion. Another version of the New Zealand canon is the twenty-six authors in William H. New's *Critical Writings on Commonwealth Literatures*. Although New concentrates exclusively on secondary works, the scholarly interest in these writers suggests their importance.

AFRICAN LITERATURE

The rise of English literature in Africa occurred on two fronts. Paralleling the development of a white colonial culture was the emergence of English as a means of self-expression for the indigenous black population. Many bibliographies of African literature reflect this duality. However, there are two that encompass both traditions. Anne Tibble appends a select reading list of 110 authors to her *African-English Literature: A Short Survey and Anthology of Prose and Poetry Up to 1965*. Martin Tucker includes both white and black writers in the bibliography for his *Africa in Modern Literature*, which covers the primary works of ninety-four authors who flourished after World War II. Both of these books are now nearly twenty years old and regrettably no other select bibliography taking an overall view has appeared.

A surge of interest in black literature in the 1950s produced some fine bibliographies devoted solely to native authors. One of the most recent is *A New Reader's Guide to African Literature*, edited by Hans M. Zell and others. Though multilingual in scope, for each country there is a section exclusively for English literature, with the added attraction that many entries are evaluative. Supplementing the volume's bibliographic section is a biographical dictionary of ninety-five prominent contemporary African writers, many of whom write in English. An older tool more generally interested in early writers is Janheinz Jahn and Claus Peter Dressler's *A Bibliography of Creative African Writing*. This work is awkward to use because to identify the 736 titles in English by 368 authors, all entries must be scanned, inasmuch as the arrangement is only by country. More manageable is O. R. Dathorne's *The Black Mind: A History of African Literature*. Though restricted to the most accessible works, the book nonetheless offers a good representative collection of 102 authors, including a few from the eighteenth and nineteenth centuries for historical perspective. Dathorne's section on general critical works is also very useful.

For South African literature alone, the *Pilot Bibliography of South African English Literature (from the Beginnings to 1971)* seeks to provide a representative listing of the most significant South African writings in English. Compiled by the Reference Department of the University of South Africa Library, the book emphasizes 159 writers of more than popular or ephemeral interest. For "indisputably major writers" a full record of works is given; for others, selectivity has been exercised. Banned books as well as black writings are included. Another perspective is offered by a library exhibition catalog, *Our English Heritage: South African English Literature* which focuses on fifty novelists, thirty-eight poets, and nine dramatists. A more concise list, limited to the twentieth century, is the twenty-three authors in the index to Harry Blamires' *A Guide to Twentieth-Century Literature in English*.

The rise of the South African novel is traced by Jacobus Petrus Lodewicus Snyman in *The South African Novel in English (1880–1930): A Critical Study*. Aviva Astrinksy's *Bibliography of South African English Novels, 1930–1960* continues Snyman's work. Also of interest is *CBEL*'s coverage of English–South African literature to 1914, which features twenty novelists. And for the other tradition of fiction in English, there is Ursula A. Barnett's *A Vision of Order: Black South African Literature, (1914–1980)*, which has a separate chapter on the novel with a bibliography for a different set of twenty novelists.

The best and most balanced historical survey of South African poetry in English is the anthology, *A New Book of South African Verse in English*, edited by Guy Butler and Chris Mann. It begins with Thomas Pringle and concludes with some younger poets writing today. The short biographical sketches of the ninety-nine featured poets include a selective bibliography of their works. Fifteen poets prominent before 1914 are in *CBEL*. The more comprehensive *Critical Survey of South African Poetry in English* discusses numerous poets, but G. M. Miller and Howard Sergeant regard fifteen as distinguished enough to merit individual treatment in their bibliography, only two of whom are black.

If concentrating on West Africa is the goal, Eliane Saint-Andre-Utudjian's *A Bibliography of West African Life and Literature* usefully supplements coverage of the region provided by the more general African bibliographies. For the newly emergent literature in English of East Africa, two bibliographies published in *The Journal of Commonwealth Literature* are noteworthy: Elizabeth Knight and two colleagues treat the poetry and fiction of forty-two writers along with related critical studies, while Margaret MacPherson covers dramatists and play collections.

WORKS CITED

Aitken, W. R. *Scottish Literature in English and Scots: A Guide to Information Sources*. Detroit: Gale Research Co., 1982.

Alcock, Peter C. M. "New Zealand Literature: A Select List with Some Background Titles." *World Literature Written in English* 13 (1974): 231–34.

Allen, Gay Wilson, Walter B. Rideout, and James K. Robinson, eds. *American Poetry*. New York: Harper & Row, 1965.

Anderson, Emily Ann. *English Poetry, 1900–1950: A Guide to Information Sources*. Detroit: Gale Research Co., 1982.

Astrinsksy, Aviva. *A Bibliography of South African English Novels, 1930–1960*. Cape Town: Univ. of Cape Town, School of Librarianship, 1965.

Barker, Arthur E. *The Seventeenth Century: Bacon through Marvell*. Arlington Heights, Ill.: AHM Pub., 1979.

Barnett, Ursula A. *A Vision of Order: A Study of Black South African Literature in English (1914–1980)*. Amherst: Univ. of Massachusetts Press, 1983.

Bateson, F. W., and Harrison T. Meserole. *A Guide to English and American Literature*. 3rd ed. New York: Gordian Press, 1976.

Baugh, Albert C. *A Literary History of England*. 1948; 2nd ed. New York: Appleton-Century-Crofts, 1967.

Beaseley, Jerry C. *English Fiction, 1660–1800: A Guide to Information Sources*. Detroit: Gale Research Co., 1978.

Bergeron, David M. *Shakespeare: A Study and Research Guide*. New York: St. Martin's Press, 1975.

Blamires, Harry, ed. *A Guide to Twentieth-Century Literature in English*. London: Methuen, 1983.

Blanck, Jacob. *Bibliography of American Literature*. New Haven: Yale Univ. Press, 1955– . (In progress.)

Bond, Donald F. *The Age of Dryden*. New York: Appleton-Century-Crofts, 1970.

———. *The Eighteenth Century*. Northbrook, Ill.: AHM Pub., 1975.

Bruccoli, Matthew J., ed. *First Printings of American Authors: Contributions Toward Descriptive Checklists*. 4 vols. Detroit: Gale Research Co., 1977–79.

Bryer, Jackson R., ed. *Fifteen Modern American Authors: A Survey of Research and Criticism*. Durham, N.C.: Duke Univ. Press, 1969. Rev. ed. as *Sixteen Modern American Authors: A Survey of Research and Criticism*. Durham, N.C.: Duke Univ. Press, 1974.

Buckley, Jerome H. *Victorian Poets and Prose Writers*. 2nd ed. Arlington Heights, Ill.: AHM Pub., 1977.

Bufkin, E. C. *The Twentieth-Century Novel in English: A Checklist*. 2nd. ed. Athens: Univ. of Georgia Press, 1984.
Butler, Guy, and Chris Mann, eds. *A New Book of South African Verse in English*. Capetown: Oxford Univ. Press, 1979.
Cambridge Bibliography of English Literature. Ed. F. W. Bateson. 5 vols. Cambridge: Cambridge Univ. Press, 1940–57.
Carpenter, Charles A. *Modern British Drama*. Arlington Heights, Ill.: AHM Pub., 1979.
Conolly, L. W., and J. P. Wearing. *English Drama and Theatre, 1800–1900: A Guide to Information Sources*. Detroit: Gale Research Co., 1978.
Daiches, David, ed. *A Companion to Scottish Culture*. London: Edward Arnold, 1981; New York: Holmes & Meier, 1982.
Dathorne, O. R. *The Black Mind: A History of African Literature*. Minneapolis: Univ. of Minnesota Press, 1974.
Davey, Frank. *From There to Here: A Guide to English-Canadian Literature Since 1960*. Erin, Ont.: Press Porcepic, 1974.
DeLaura, David J., ed. *Victorian Prose: A Guide to Research*. New York: Modern Language Association of America, 1973.
Drescher, Horst W., and Bernd Kahrmann. *The Contemporary English Novel: An Annotated Bibliography of Secondary Sources*. Frankfurt am Main: Athenaeum Verlag, 1973.
Dutton, Geoffrey, ed. *The Literature of Australia*. 1964; rev. ed. Ringwood, Vic.: Penguin Books Australia, 1976.
Fallis, Richard. *The Irish Renaissance*. Syracuse, N. Y.: Syracuse Univ. Press, 1977.
Faverty, Frederick E. *The Victorian Poets: A Guide to Research*. 2nd ed. Cambridge, Mass.: Harvard Univ. Press, 1968.
Fenster, Valmai Kirkham. *Guide to American Literature*. Littleton, Colo.: Libraries Unlimited, 1983.
Fiedler, Leslie. *What Was Literature: Class, Culture, and Mass Society*. New York: Simon & Schuster, 1982.
Finneran, Richard J., ed. *Anglo-Irish Literature: A Review of Research*. New York: Modern Language Association of America, 1976.
———, ed. *Recent Research on Anglo-Irish Writers*. New York: Modern Language Association of America, 1983.
Fogle, Richard Harter. *Romantic Poets and Prose Writers*. New York: Appleton-Century-Crofts, 1967.
Ford, Boris, ed. *The New Pelican Guide to English Literature*. 8 vols. Harmondsworth, Eng.: Penguin, 1982–83.
———, ed. *The Pelican Guide to English Literature*. Rev. ed. 7 vols. London: Cassell, 1961–64.
Ford, George H., ed. *Victorian Fiction: A Second Guide to Research*. New York: Modern Language Association of America, 1978.
Gingerich, Martin E. *Contemporary Poetry in America and England, 1950–1975: A Guide to Information Sources*. Detroit: Gale Research Co., 1983.

Gnarowski, Michael. *A Concise Bibliography of English-Canadian Literature*. Rev. ed. Toronto: McClelland & Stewart, 1978.

Harbert, Earl N., and Robert A. Rees, eds. *Fifteen American Authors Before 1900: Bibliographical Essays on Research and Criticism*. Madison: Univ. of Wisconsin Press, 1971. Rev. ed., 1984.

Harmon, Maurice. *Modern Irish Literature, 1800–1967: A Reader's Guide*. Dublin: Dolmen Press, 1967.

Harris, Richard H. *Modern Drama in America and England, 1950–1970: A Guide to Information Sources*. Detroit: Gale Research Co., 1982.

Heninger, S. K., Jr. *English Prose, Prose Fiction, and Criticism to 1660: A Guide to Information Sources*. Detroit: Gale Research Co., 1975.

Hoffman, Daniel, ed. *Harvard Guide to Contemporary American Writing*. Cambridge, Mass.: Belknap Press of Harvard Univ. Press, 1979.

Holman, C. Hugh, and Richardi, Janis. *The American Novel through Henry James*. Arlington Heights, Ill.: AHM Pub., 1979.

Houtchens, Carolyn Washburn, and Lawrence Huston Houtchens. *The English Romantic Poets and Essayists: A Review of Research and Criticism*. Rev. ed. New York: Modern Language Association of America/New York Univ. Press, 1966.

Hubbell, Jay B. *Where Are the Major American Writers?: A Study of the Changing Literary Canon*. Durham, N.C.: Duke Univ. Press, 1972.

Jahn, Janheinz, and Claus Peter Dressler. *Bibliography of Creative African Writing*. 1971; Millwood, N. Y.: Kraus-Thomson, 1973.

Jones, Joseph, and Johanna Jones. *Authors and Areas of Australia*. Austin, Tex.: Steck-Vaughn, 1970.

Jordan, Frank. *The English Romantic Poets: A Review of Research and Criticism*. 3rd ed. New York: Modern Language Association of America, 1972.

Kirby, David K. *American Fiction to 1900: A Guide to Information Sources*. Detroit: Gale Research Co., 1975.

Klinck, Carl F., and Reginald E. Watters. *Canadian Anthology*. 3rd ed. Toronto: Gage Educational Pub., 1974.

Knight, Elizabeth, Jacqueline Bardolph, and Angus Calder. "A Bibliography of East African Literature in English, 1964–1981." *Journal of Commonwealth Literature* 17.1 (1982): 182–205.

Kramer, Leonie. *The Oxford History of Australian Literature*. Melbourne: Oxford Univ. Press, 1981.

Leary, Lewis. *American Literature: A Study and Research Guide*. New York: St. Martin's Press, 1976.

Lecker, Robert, and Jack David, eds. *The Annotated Bibliography of Canada's Major Authors*. Downsview, Ont.: ECW, 1979– .

Lewis, C. S. *English Literature in the Sixteenth Century, Excluding Drama*. Oxford: Clarendon Press, 1954.

Lievsay, John L. *The Sixteenth Century: Skelton through Hooker*. New York: Appleton-Century-Crofts, 1968.

Lindsay, Maurice. *A History of Scottish Literature*. London: Robert Hale, 1977.

Lock, Fred, and Alan Lawson. *Australian Literatures—A Reference Guide*. 2nd ed. Melbourne: Oxford Univ. Press, 1980.

Long, E. Hudson. *American Drama from Its Beginning to the Present*. New York: Appleton-Century-Crofts, 1970.

MacPherson, Margaret. "A Bibliography of East African Literature in English, 1964-1981, Part II: Drama." *Journal of Commonwealth Literature* 17.2 (1982): 163-7.

Matthews, William. *Old and Middle English Literature*. New York: Appleton-Century-Crofts, 1968.

McKenna, Brian. *Irish Literature, 1800-1875: A Guide to Information Sources*. Detroit: Gale Research Co., 1978.

Meserve, Walter J. *American Drama to 1900: A Guide to Information Sources*. Detroit: Gale Research Co., 1980.

Mikhail, E. H. *English Drama, 1900-1950: A Guide to Information Sources*. Detroit: Gale Research Co., 1977.

Miller, G. M., and Howard Sergeant. *A Critical Survey of South African Poetry in English*. Capetown: A. A. Balkema, 1957.

Nevius, Blake. *The American Novel: Sinclair Lewis to the Present*. Northbrook, Ill.: AHM Pub., 1970.

New Cambridge Bibliography of English Literature. Ed. George Watson. 5 vols. Cambridge: Cambridge Univ. Press, 1969-77.

New, William H. *Critical Writings on Commonwealth Literatures: A Selective Bibliography to 1970*. University Park: Pennsylvania State Univ. Press, 1975.

Nordloh, David J. "Aiming the Canon." *Scholarly Publishing* 16 (1985): 109-19.

Our English Heritage: South African English Literature. Cape Town: City Libraries, 1962.

Oxford History of English Literature. Ed. F. P. Wilson and Bonamy Dobree. Oxford: Clarendon Press, 1945- . (In progress.)

Patterson, Margaret. *Literary Research Guide*. 2nd ed. New York: Modern Language Association of America, 1983.

Penninger, Frieda Elaine. *English Drama to 1660 (Excluding Shakespeare): A Guide to Information Sources*. Detroit: Gale Research Co., 1976.

Press, John. *A Map of Modern English Verse*. London: Oxford Univ. Press, 1969.

Reiman, Donald H. *English Romantic Poetry, 1800-1835: A Guide to Information Sources*. Detroit: Gale Research Co., 1979.

Ribner, Irving, and Clifford Chalmers Huffman. *Tudor and Stuart Drama*. 2nd ed. Arlington Heights, Ill.: AHM Pub., 1978.

Rice, Thomas Jackson. *English Fiction, 1900-1950: A Guide to Information Sources*. 2 vols. Detroit: Gale Research Co., 1979-83.

Robinson, Fred C. *Old English Literature: A Select Bibliography*. Toronto: Univ. of Toronto Press, 1970.

Rollins, Hyder E., ed. *England's Helicon, 1600-1614*. Cambridge, Mass.: Harvard Univ. Press, 1935.

———, ed. *The Paradise of Dainty Devices (1576-1606)*. Cambridge, Mass.: Harvard Univ. Press, 1927.

———, ed. *Tottel's Miscellany (1557-1587)*. Rev. ed. 2 vols. Cambridge, Mass.: Harvard Univ. Press, 1965.

Rosa, Alfred F., and Paul A. Eschholz. *Contemporary Fiction in America and England, 1950–1970: A Guide to Information Sources.* Detroit: Gale Research Co., 1976.

Saint-Andre-Utudjian, Eliane. *A Bibliography of West African Life and Literature.* Waltham, Mass.: African Studies Association, 1977.

Schweik, Robert C., and Dieter Riesner. *Reference Sources in English and American Literature: An Annotated Bibliography.* New York: Norton, 1977.

Sisson, C. H. *English Poetry, 1900–1950: An Assessment.* London: Hart-Davis, 1971. Rev. ed. Manchester: Carcanet New Press, 1981.

Snyman, Jacobus Petrus Lodewicus. *The South African Novel in English (1880–1930): A Critical Study.* 2d ed. Potchefstroom: Univ. of Potchefstroom, 1952.

South Africa. University. Library. Subject Reference Department. *A Pilot Bibliography of South African English Literature (From the Beginnings to 1971).* Pretoria: Univ. of South Africa, 1976.

Spiller, Robert E., ed. *The Literary History of the United States.* 4th ed. 2 vols. New York: Macmillan, 1974.

Stevenson, Lionel, ed. *Victorian Fiction: A Guide to Research.* Cambridge, Mass.: Harvard Univ. Press, 1964.

Stone, Sue. "Humanities Scholars: Information Needs and Uses." *Journal of Documentation* 38 (1982): 292–313.

Stouck, David. *Major Canadian Authors: A Critical Introduction.* Lincoln: Univ. of Nebraska Press, 1984.

Stovall, Floyd, ed. *Eight American Authors: A Review of Research and Criticism.* New York: Modern Language Association of America, 1956. Rev. ed. Ed. James Woodress. New York: Norton, 1971.

Temple, Ruth Z. *Twentieth Century British Literature: A Reference Guide and Bibliography.* New York: Ungar, 1968.

Thomas, Clara. *Our Nature, Our Voices: A Guidebook to English-Canadian Literature.* Toronto: New Press, 1972.

Thomson, John. *New Zealand Literature to 1977: A Guide to Information Sources.* Detroit: Gale Research Co., 1980.

Tibble, Anne, ed. *African-English Literature: A Short Survey and Anthology of Prose and Poetry up to 1965.* New York: October House, 1965.

Tucker, Martin. *African in Modern Literature: A Survey of Contemporary Writing in English.* New York: Ungar, 1967.

Vinson, James, ed. *American Writers since 1900.* Chicago: St. James Press, 1983.

———, ed. *American Writers to 1900.* Chicago: St. James Press, 1983.

———, ed. *Contemporary Dramatists.* 3rd ed. New York: St. Martin's Press, 1982.

———, ed. *Contemporary Novelists.* 3rd ed. New York: St. Martin's Press, 1982.

———, ed. *20th Century Fiction.* Chicago: St. James Press, 1985.

———, and D. L. Kirkpatrick, eds. *Contemporary Poets.* 4th ed. New York: St. Martin's Press, 1985.

Waggoner, Hyatt H. *American Poets from the Puritans to the Present.* Rev. ed. Baton Rouge: Louisiana State Univ. Press, 1984.
Watt, Ian. *The British Novel: Scott through Hardy.* Northbrook, Ill.: AHM Pub., 1973.
Wells, Stanley, ed. *English Drama (Excluding Shakespeare): Select Bibliographical Guides.* London: Oxford Univ. Press, 1975.
―――, ed. *Shakespeare: Select Bibliographical Guides.* London: Oxford Univ. Press, 1973.
Wiley, Paul L. *The British Novel: Conrad to the Present.* Northbrook, Ill.: AHM Pub., 1973.
Wilson, Harris W., and Diane Long Hoeveler. *English Prose and Criticism in the Nineteenth Century: A Guide to Information Sources.* Detroit: Gale Research Co., 1979.
Woodress, James. *American Fiction, 1900-1950: A Guide to Information Sources.* Detroit: Gale Research Co., 1974.
Wright, Andrew. *A Reader's Guide to English and American Literature.* Glenview, Ill.: Scott, Foresman, 1970.
Zell, Hans M., Carol Bundy, and Virginia Coulon, eds. *A New Reader's Guide to African Literature.* New York: Africana Pub. Co., 1983.
Zesmer, David M. *Guide to English Literature from Beowulf through Chaucer and Medieval Drama.* New York: Barnes & Noble, 1961.

Serials
Robert Hauptman

Few selectors have the opportunity to create a collection *ab ovo*. Instead, they usually inherit developing or mature collections at institutions whose histories may go back hundreds of years. In such instances, serials collection development is not a particularly onerous task, especially in times of financial constraint. For untutored generalists who happen to select in English and American literature, the important titles are quickly learned. For the knowledgeable bibliographer, virtually all of the important titles are already familiar, and many of them are found even in the small college library. Despite the multiplicity of little literary magazines and the not unusual advent of a new and potentially influential review or scholarly journal, literary studies are unlike computer science, a discipline in which new journals proliferate at a most frightening rate. In fact, while the total periodicals population tends to increase almost geometrically, with each new edition of *Ulrich's International Periodicals Directory* containing four to five thousand new titles, only a handful of these will be of intense interest to English specialists. And if limited budgets and space are problems, they may not be able to add even a single title.

Journals are often a burden. Consider Donald Davinson's apt assessment:

This essay is for Lenore Clark, who taught me so much.

> Periodicals are expensive to buy, difficult to store, awkward to use, inefficient as a vehicle for transmitting information and, particularly, uneven in their patterns of bibliographic control. Despite this they continue to be perhaps the most important element in the system of recorded knowledge other than books themselves [p. 65].

Important they are, but their value must be put in perspective. It is certainly true that in the hard sciences significant and sometimes even revolutionary news is published in periodicals immediately upon discovery. This was the case, for example, when Watson and Crick announced their findings on the structure of DNA in *Nature*. Fewer extraordinary discoveries take place in the social sciences, and very few indeed in the humanities. The lag time between submission and publication, especially in prestigious journals like *PMLA*, can be excessive, and may often be measured in years. On the other hand, once the material appears, it is not necessarily outdated, as is the case, say, in chemistry, a discipline in which ten-year-old materials can usually be discarded.

In contrast, previously published humanistic essays collected in monographic form have value for many subsequent years. Indeed, and of utmost importance, the reputations of humanists generally rest on monographic publication. Consider the following: Erich Auerbach, *Mimesis*; Martin Buber, *I and Thou*; Martin Heidegger, *Being and Time*; Arthur O. Lovejoy, *The Great Chain of Being*; Margaret Mead, *Coming of Age in Samoa*; Alfred North Whitehead (with Bertrand Russell), *Principia Mathematica*. Even anthropologists and mathematicians can produce their seminal studies in monographic form. What this means is that new scientific ideas are typically communicated quickly in periodicals, whereas influential contributions in the humanities are less likely to take serial form. Journals, therefore, are more central in the sciences than other fields. Nevertheless, literary periodicals are, of course, useful and important, and they continue to play an essential and at times primary role in the communication of creative work and scholarly knowledge. They are cheaper, more efficient, and often aesthetically superior to both monographs and such new technological formats as on-demand, microform, and electronic publication (National Enquiry, *Scholarly Communication*, especially chapter 2, "Scholarly Journals").

In order to establish workable parameters for serials within a collection development policy, the English bibliographer must begin by considering the size of the collection and the population that it serves. An inherently small collection, additionally constrained by budgetary problems, will remain fairly constant, particularly if it exclusively serves an undergraduate clientele. A total of perhaps seventy-five literary reviews, scholarly journals, author newsletters, and little magazines would be adequate for a small to medium-size college library. Universities where a master's degree in English and American literature is offered would of necessity require an expanded collection. Here a total of 150 periodicals might serve. Any institution supporting the doctorate would have to increase the size of these holdings considerably. In times of financial exigency, when subscriptions are cut, collections can easily become inadequate, incapable of sustaining dissertation work. Furthermore, the quality of faculty research may diminish as material becomes less available. According to *ARL Statistics 1982-83*, Princeton University receives 32,910 serials, the University of Texas at Austin, 61,133, the University of Illinois, 93,913, and the University of California at Berkeley, 101,584 (Mandel and Lichtenstein, p. 37). It is clear that most academic institutions cannot compete with these giants.

This is not meant, however, to imply that more is automatically better. Bradford's Law of Scattering indicates that although many insignificant articles are dispersed throughout a multiplicity of journals, the most important pieces are published in a limited number of periodicals. And it is precisely for this reason that smaller academic libraries can serve their patrons effectively with fewer subscriptions. On the other hand, it is the avowed purpose of a research library to maintain large stores of materials, including less-used and even esoteric publications. But when one realizes that between 1960 and 1975 English studies journals increased by 192 percent, that the *MLA International Bibliography (MLAIB)* cited 1500 periodicals in 1970 and 2877 in 1980 (Winkler, p. 21), it is clear that bibliographers, even at large and prestigious institutions, are forced to make some difficult choices.

One of the problems which English specialists encounter is that very little work has been done in the field of serials evaluation. Additionally, the analyses that do exist may be marred by such physical constraints as the unavailability of journals for review as well as by the subjective predilections of the evaluator. This caveat noted, there are fifteen factors useful for guiding periodicals selection:

1. Authoritative sources, like Katz's *Magazines for Libraries*, may be consulted.
2. Whether a journal is widely indexed should be considered. (This is taken into account and noted in *Magazines for Libraries*.) But it ought to be remembered that new journals are not picked up by indexing services until a few issues have been published.

3. Consulting the *Arts and Humanities Citation Index* to determine which journals are cited most frequently can be informative. But just as there may be something specious about the use of citation analysis to evaluate the worth of an author's scholarship, so may its use to determine the merits of a specific journal be questionable. Katz's comments are especially germane here:

> Citation studies are a heated territory, particularly of vested interests, (financial and otherwise), in the myth of their importance. I'm not suggesting they be dismissed outright, although used in isolation for selection they are no more valuable than other bibliometric measurements which discount significant limitations of human action and reaction. I'm inclined to rank them with television ratings and polls which at least indicate, though do not ultimately predict public taste and trends. ["Joining Art," p. 11.]

Even Eugene Garfield, founder of the Institute for Scientific Information, asserts that because scientific and humanistic research methodologies differ, citation studies may be more applicable in the former than in the latter.[1]
4. Cost is a definite factor that ought to be closely evaluated.
5. The proximate availability in local or regional libraries could be considered.
6. The number of subscribers can indicate value. *Magazines for Libraries* and *Ulrich's International Periodicals Directory* provide subscription statistics, but many journals with small circulations (e.g., *Salmagundi*), have large reputations, which are based on influential publication records. In this regard, bibliographers should always be wary of plausible but misleading selection criteria.
7. Support for specific academic programs is of paramount importance, and faculty suggestions, especially as they relate to the individual's specialized research needs, must be carefully weighed.
8. User studies (both national and local) as well as in-house usage records (despite their costly nature) can be helpful.
9. Because of the general tendency to avoid non-English language materials, foreign language serials should be rigorously scrutinized.
10. Demand, which can be monitored through suggestions and interlibrary loan requests, is also useful in identifying serial titles of local interest.

11. Future research value is an important factor, though it is easily ignored when short-term goals take precedence.
12. Comparisons with similar collections can indicate weaknesses as well as strengths.
13. The publisher's reputation might be evaluated.
14. Format is an increasingly important consideration: hardcopy, microform, on-line, or exclusive electronic availability may influence decisions.
15. The overall goals of the library itself can aid in guiding collection developers. A physically small institution may nonetheless choose to create an extensive specialized collection of, for example, regional little magazines. A research library's *a priori* objective is to collect widely and diversely.

It is probably impossible to practice serials collection development in a purely bibliometric fashion. Some of the basic statistical data suggested under the fifteen preceding headings derive, in fact, from subjective opinion. In any case, a rigorously bibliometric method would certainly entail heavy reliance on and faith in two Institute for Scientific Information publications: *Arts and Humanities Citation Index* and *Journal Citation Reports*. How problematic this could prove is illustrated by Garfield's own analysis of science citations, which concluded that an effective multidisciplinary science collection would require only 500 titles, or a maximum of one percent of the 50,000 to 100,000 available (quoted in Bensman, pp. 17–18). Extrapolated to the approximately 3000 journals listed in *MLAIB*, this means that a good core collection for world literature would consist of a mere 30 periodicals. Though the sciences and humanities are not direct analogues, this result suggests the need to temper quantitative measurements by considerations of quality.[2]

SELECTION

The bibliographer's task is to establish, build, and maintain serials collections through judicious selection and weeding. Even in the worst of times, subscription changes in response to the publication of important new items or restructured academic programs may be necessary. When money is forthcoming and the physical space is available, there may be occasion to celebrate the initiation of tens (or even hundreds) of new subscriptions (with auguries of cancellation always imminent on the horizon). Serials, of course, encompass more than just journals. Simply put, a serial is any numbered publication issued on an ongoing basis, at regular or irregular intervals, with the intention of continuing indefinitely. Annuals (*Shaw*), monographic series (Twayne's English

Authors), indexes (*MLAIB*), directories (*Directory of American Poets*), continuing sets (*Contemporary Literary Criticism*), proceedings or transactions (*Transactions of the Philological Society*), and periodicals (*Parnassus*) are all serials. Second and subsequent editions of books (even of such regularly revised reference tools as St. Martin's *Contemporary Poets*) are not. Most types of serials have a potentially unlimited publication run; others, like monographic series, ultimately may end.

Serials Other Than Periodicals

The selection of serials outside of journals is simply described. There are, first of all, massive compilations like the *Union List of Serials in Libraries of the U.S. and Canada, New Serials Titles*, and Bowker's *Irregular Serials and Annuals*. These are all of extremely limited use. Since only the barest bibliographical data is presented, there is nothing substantive upon which to base a decision. *Irregular Serials*, for example, devotes many pages to literary materials, some of which are of interest to English bibliographers. But once a title is selected, reviews must still be sought, or a sample copy requested. The same holds true for the far more germane *MLA Directory of Periodicals: A Guide to Journals and Series in Languages and Literatures*. This consists of 3102 entries dealing with all aspects of world literature. Though its audience is potential contributors rather than librarians, the bibliographer can certainly skim it to identify appropriate titles. Since a high percentage of serials are either reference books or monographic studies in series, reviews can typically be found for even individual titles. By far the most useful source of information is the "Language and Literature" section in Joan K. Marshall's *Serials for Libraries*. Lamentably, it contains only fifty-seven entries, some of which are not relevant to English and American literary studies.

Journal selection presents a much greater challenge. The following discussion covers literary reviews, scholarly journals including author newsletters, poetry periodicals, and little magazines, and is divided among retrospective, current, and new titles.

Retrospective Selection of Journals

While such tools as the *Union List of Serials* and *New Serial Titles* record the existence of titles, they provide little further information. Extremely helpful for purposes of evaluation, however, are a number of bibliographies issued fairly recently. Jayne K. Kribb's *An Annotated Bibliography of American Literary Periodicals, 1741–1850* is a superbly indexed compilation of 940 journals. Decisions can be made with confidence based on her annotations. Four volumes—Robert B. White's *The English Literary Journal to 1900*, Michael N. Stanton's *English*

Literary Journals, 1900-1950, Edward E. Chielens' *The Literary Journal in America to 1900*, and Chielens' *The Literary Journal in America, 1900-1950*—provide something of a general bibliographic overview of English and American literary periodicals from their beginnings to 1950. They vary in usefulness, though. Only Stanton's excellent volume consists of a list of individually evaluated titles. The other three note the journals, but instead of commenting on them, provide citations to articles and books concerning them. Chielens does, however, annotate the contents of the cited works, though for selection purposes, a brief evaluation would have been preferable. Chielens may have reached a similar conclusion, since he is currently engaged in editing *American Literary Magazines: The Eighteenth and Nineteenth Centuries*, with a second volume on the twentieth century in the offing. The first contains 1500-word profiles, by diverse hands, of some 150 journals. Alvin Sullivan has undertaken a similar project: *British Literary Magazines* is a four-volume set that includes *The Augustan Age and the Age of Johnson, 1698-1788, The Romantic Age, 1789-1836, The Victorian and Edwardian Age, 1837-1913*, and *The Modern Age*. The first three volumes are now available, and they are excellent tools for retrospective selection. Each entry even indicates availability on microform. Walter Houghton's unusual three-volume *Wellesley Index to Victorian Periodicals, 1824-1900* contains tables of contents for many of the important journals of the period.

An astonishing array of these older journals titles is currently available in either original, reprint, or micro format. Dealers like Kraus Periodical can sometimes provide original hard copy for those libraries that still have empty shelves. Kraus, AMS, Johnson, and other reprint publishers maintain stocks of individual journals as well as constructed sets of majestic proportion. They frequently publish comprehensive serial catalogs for the librarian's convenience and will even prepare tailored lists for esoteric areas. For serials in micro format, *Guide to Microforms in Print* is an especially useful tool. Also important is University Microfilms International's (UMI) *Serials in Microform* which lists 13,000 items. Further, *UMI Research Collections* contains a wealth of appropriate sets, only two of which can be noted here: *Focus on English Literature, 1708-1907* features forty journals, including the *Tatler, Spectator, Guardian, All the Year Round, Germ*, and *Savoy*, while the outstanding *American Periodicals, 1741-1900* covers more than 1000 journals, many of which are relevant to literary studies. The latter is divided into three series, each of which can be purchased separately: Series I: 1741-1800, Series II: 1800-1850, and Series III: 1850-1900. There is no denying these massive microform projects are quite expensive, but they are often mandatory items for large university libraries, and excellent choices for smaller universities and large colleges.

Currently Published Journals

These can be selected from a number of different sources. The *MLA Directory of Periodicals* serves as a master list. Evan Farber's *Classified List of Periodicals for the College Library* contains excellent annotations, but it is limited in scope and sufficiently dated to be partially misleading. Also dated but occasionally useful is Donna Gerstenberger and George Hendrick's *Fourth Directory of Periodicals Publishing Articles on English and American Literature and Language*. Like the *MLA Directory*, it is geared toward potential contributors, and therefore offers no evaluative comments. Margaret C. Patterson's *Author Newsletters and Journals* is a wonderful compilation that contains annotated entries for 435 authors and 1129 titles. Some writers obviously merit more than one journal. There are, in fact, fifty-two devoted to Arthur Conan Doyle! Much of the important scholarship on such figures as Chaucer, Blake, Whitman, and Pound is published in these specialized and often excellent periodicals. Patterson helps to cull out the required material. The only general, annotated, and up-to-date lists are the present author's "Literary Reviews" and "Literature," and Noel Peattie's "Little Magazines" in Katz's *Magazines for Libraries*. The more than 300 annotations are both descriptive and evaluative (including strict recommendations in the best instances). Many of the volume's other sections, like "Abstracts and Indexes," "Bibliography," "Fiction," and "Women," also contain items of interest to English and American literary studies.

Journals occasionally publish discussions or bibliographies of current material. The most unusual and stimulating of these is Michael West's "Evaluating Periodicals in English Studies," a sarcastic diatribe concerning the *MLA Directory*, scholarly communication, and related matters. West concludes with three lists in which he grades the reputations of 175 journals: sixteen are distinguished, fifty-eight strong, and 101 average. A fourth list of more than fifty marginal titles was excluded by the editor of *College English*, where the essay appeared. Despite the grating truth of West's discussion, these lists are not very useful for selection purposes. The distinguished periodicals (e.g., *American Literature, ELH, PMLA, Speculum*) are found in virtually all collections; so, too, are most of those in the strong group (e.g., *Critical Inquiry, Georgia Review, Modern Fiction Studies, Shakespeare Quarterly*); and although the third group is termed "average," many of its journals are respected and important publications, hardly ripe for weeding: *American Scholar, Contemporary Literature, Genre, Journal of Modern Literature, Mosaic*. B.

90   Robert Hauptman

Bogg's briefly annotated "English Language and Literature Periodicals" is only slightly better, especially since it is sixteen years old. *Serials Review* is always an excellent place to locate useful information: for example, Virginia Seiser discusses book review coverage by twenty-three English literature periodicals, including *Journal of English and Germanic Philology, Shakespeare Quarterly,* and *Journal of Modern Literature,* and Kent Ekberg's article covers forty-six "Literary Periodicals" in lengthy and helpful comments. *Literary Magazine Review* is devoted exclusively to critical appraisals of journals.

New Titles

The Library of Congress's monthly *New Serial Titles—Classed Subject Arrangement* may be marginally useful, since coverage of new titles seems to be improving. Most issues of *PMLA* have a journals column, in which descriptive announcements of new periodicals can be found. Every issue of *Library Journal* contains Katz's "Magazines" column. He and other contributors often comment on new literary journals, which serves to keep *Magazines for Libraries* up-to-date. *Choice* and *Serials Review* provide some coverage. Further, Katz's chapter on periodicals in his *Collection Development* explains the use of lists of new materials published by subscription agents like Faxon and Ebsco. And even advertising brochures, despite their self-serving intentions, can alert the bibliographer to new and potentially important journals that should be made available immediately to library patrons. Recent examples include *Conjunctions, John Donne Journal, American Journal of Semiotics, American Poetry,* and the reborn *Kenyon Review*—all of which were reviewed in *Library Journal.* Also, pertinent articles do appear from time to time. Birgit Justen's "Neuere anglistische Zeitschriften" covers a plethora of new items, but it is just a list. Margaret C. Patterson's "Author Newsletters and Journals: Supplement 1" and "Supplement 2" update her volume cited above. This will be an annual feature in *Serials Review* from now on.

Much of the foregoing is equally applicable to little magazines, journals that are generally privately produced and that quite frequently emphasize poetry. Originally, little magazines were aimed at a limited audience, published material sometimes iconoclastic and usually unacceptable to commercial firms, did not pay contributors, and had a circulation of less than one thousand. Today these journals may compete favorably with commercial or academic publications in all of these categories. Some may have as many as 2000 or more subscribers, for example. Their physical and substantive quality varies tremendously—from shoddily reproduced pamphlets to extremely beautiful letterpress productions. Because both innovators and influential authors publish in them, it is necessary for most collections to acquire at least the basic titles. Larger libraries will, of course, expand their coverage, but only a few highly specialized collections, such as the University of Wisconsin-Madison and the New York Public Library, will be able to emphasize this aspect of literary publication. Collections of little magazines can be general, but it is usually better for smaller libraries to delimit in some way (e.g., geographically, substantively, or chronologically).

Little magazines present a number of special problems. They are difficult to trace because bibliographical control is limited, and they may cease publication after a few issues. Those that continue are often mercurial and change title, size, format, and frequency. Both Frederick Hoffman's *The Little Magazine* and Elliot Anderson's *Little Magazine in America* are superb historical overviews that additionally contain annotated listings of many jounals; these are useful for retrospective collection development. Len Fulton and Ellen Ferber's *International Directory of Little Magazines and Small Presses*, now in its twenty-first edition, contains thousands of publishers and journals, and is the master list for this specialized area. It does not, however, offer any evaluative comments. New listings in *Small Press Review* keep the *International Directory* updated. Robert Peters has published two *Black and Blue Guides to Current Literary Journals*. Although some mainstream material is included among their fifty-one entries, there are any number of journals like *Bluefish, Contact II,* and *Abraxas* carefully evaluated, according to Peter's unusual criteria. Further compilations may be forthcoming. The best source of evaluative commentary is Christine C. Rom's ongoing column in *Serials Review*. Rom writes well-developed critiques and also solicits contributions from others. Sometimes the columns are eclectic, but they can also hone in on specific topics (e.g., Ohio or Wisconsin little magazines). And occasional special features in this same journal include Geoffrey Soar and R. J. Ellis's "U.K. Little Magazines: An Introductory Survey" with about twenty-five lengthy reviews of both well-known (*Agenda, Stand*) and obscure (*Vanessa, Granta*) journals. This is an indispensable guide.

DESELECTION

Despite the farewell Daniel Gore and others have bid to Alexandria and the attempt to collect everything published, the first impulse concerning weeding is to say, "Don't do it." In the face of encroaching reality, an unrelenting Alexandrianism, especially in large research institutions, probably remains best. Smaller colleges may not need complete runs of *Scribner's Magazine* or *The Cornhill* but Yale, Texas, and Illinois do. Furthermore weeding classic literary serials only creates more room for ephemeral computer magazines. The deselection of currently received titles, on the other hand, often becomes mandatory, when budgeted monies run out. In this exigency, one should consult Stanley J. Slote's *Weeding Library Collections—II*, which is helpful even though concentrating on the book collection. Deselection is a painful and onerous process at best, but when necessary, the bibliographer should use the same criteria that are mandated for selection: authoritative opinion, indexing, citation analysis, cost, availability, number of subscribers, relationship to curricula, faculty input, use, circulation, language, demand, future research value, comparisons with other collections, publisher's reputation, format, and the library's general goals. Even after these criteria are considered, there are many items that simply cannot be cancelled.

First to go should be all duplicates, even those in branch libraries. Because deselection is typically prompted by financial problems, next to be cut are the exorbitantly priced items. Journal publishers often charge what the market will bear, and as Richard De Gennaro has suggested, it is up to purchasers to refuse to pay when the pricing is out of line. Deselection is a good way to do this. Once duplicates and burdensomely expensive items have been eliminated, the bibliographer will have to weigh all of the other criteria. Supporting academic programs is extremely important. Graduate work in Old English cannot be done, if all of the relevant serials are cancelled. Conversely, if a course of study is eliminated, then supporting resources can be as well. Faculty suggestions should always be considered carefully. Faculty members know what their students require, which specialized journals are important, and in which areas they are doing their own research. But frequently there will be a divergence of opinion even within a department; thus, it is no surprise that Jeffery Broude found that teaching faculty and librarians compiled different cancellation lists.

Networks, consortia, resource sharing, complementary collections, and interlibrary loan are all highly touted solutions to individual purchasing. Local groups like Minnesota's Minitex or national giants like OCLC or RLG can help provide needed materials. Nevertheless, availability can be a misleading criteria. Interlibrary loan is sometimes unreliable and untimely, and once a recent journal provides five articles to a given institution during a one year period, it may not be called upon again. Cancelling *Partisan Review* based on availability at other institutions would be foolish indeed. Availability may be a significant factor only when the other collections are physically proximate, and the patron can pay a personal visit. Tangentially, consider that the University of Pittsburgh, Carnegie-Mellon, and Duquesne universities as well as Carlow and Chatham colleges are all within a mile or so of each other, yet they just could not bring themselves to build one gigantic, nonduplicating, and shared library facility. Pride and cooperation make dissenting bedfellows. Nevertheless, when all of the negative aspects have been elaborated, it is still necessary to consider availability, and Karen Brewer and her colleagues have some excellent suggestions for bibliographers. Occasional disagreement notwithstanding, the anti-Alexandrians currently hold sway (and for good pragmatic reasons). Herbert S. White admonishes that the library is "a tool to be used" rather than "a scholarly collection of materials" (p. 29). Of course, library resources are collected for their current usefulness, but to ignore future research value (which White is, perhaps, not advocating) cannot be defended at the university level, large or small. All of this suggests that deselection ought be done with great care.

BASIC JOURNALS

The process of compiling core lists of journals is analogous to selecting titles for a particular collection. In the former case, needs are extrapolated to fulfill the requirements of similar institutions. Thus, the theoretical considerations and criteria discussed above in relation to individual collections are equally applicable to the compilation of these general lists. Specific collections may deviate considerably from the suggested titles, but there can be little doubt that such lists are helpful selection aids, particularly for less-experienced bibliographers. One would be as foolish to ignore completely these compilations as to rely solely on them, since as Richard Heinzkill observes: "Very few journals can be identified as being centrally important to this field [English literary scholarship]" (p. 355). Furthermore, Steward Saunders indicates that students do not emphasize core monographs in their reading. While book collections are obviously different from their journal counterparts, nonetheless, one might fairly deduce that students do not rely on core journals either.

The foregoing caveats noted, below are the basic journals that institutions should maintain in support of English and American literary studies. These are minimum suggestions. Additional periodicals are welcome, and virtually nothing is sacrosanct, although any collection lacking *PMLA, Speculum*, or *Hudson Review*, for example, certainly would be deficient. Each of the three lists is divided into four alphabetic sequences: literary reviews, scholarly periodicals, author journals, and little magazines. (This arrangement deliberately maintains the organization of *Magazines for Libraries*.) The lists do not include film, linguistics, theater, or interdisciplinary periodicals.

PRIMARY GROUP: SMALL COLLEGE (BA IN ENGLISH)

Literary Reviews

American Poetry Review
American Scholar
Antaeus
Boundary 2
Chicago Review
Georgia Review
Hudson Review
Iowa Review
Massachusetts Review

Ohio Review
Paris Review
Partisan Review
Poetry
Salmagundi
Sewanee Review
Southern Review
TriQuarterly

Scholarly Periodicals

American Literature
Black American Literature
  Forum
Bulletin of Research in the
  Humanities
Canadian Literature
Comparative Literature
Comparative Literature Studies
Contemporary Literature
Critical Inquiry
Diacritics
ELH
Extrapolation
Journal of English and
  Germanic Philology
Journal of Modern Literature
Melus
Medium Aevum
MLN
Modern Fiction Studies
Modern Language Journal

Modern Language Quarterly
Modern Philology
Mosaic
New Literary History
New York Review of Books
Notes and Queries
Novel
Parnassus
PMLA
Representations
Science Fiction Studies
Speculum
Studies in English Literature
Studies in Short Fiction
Studies in the Novel
Sub-Stance
Twentieth Century Literature
Victorian Studies
World Literature Today

Author Journals

Chaucer Review
Dickensian
James Joyce Quarterly

Johnsonian Newsletter
Milton Quarterly
Shakespeare Quarterly

Little Magazines

Calyx
Chelsea
Contact II
Crosscurrents: A Quarterly
Field
Greenfield Review
Hyperion: A Poetry Journal
IO

Open Places
Ploughshares
Samisdat
Small Press
Small Press Review
The Spirit That Moves Us
Stand

SECONDARY GROUP: LARGE COLLEGE, SMALL UNIVERSITY (MA IN ENGLISH)

All of the primary journals plus:

Literary Reviews

Antioch Review
Bennington Review
Blue Cloud Quarterly
Callaloo Review
Centennial Review
Credences
Conditions
Conjunctions
Dalhousie Review
Encounter

Grand Street
Kenyon Review
Minnesota Review
Missouri Review
New England Review and
    Breadloaf Quarterly
North American Review
Queens Quarterly
Virginia Quarterly Review
Yale Review

Scholarly Periodicals

American Journal of Semiotics
American Poetry
Anglia
American Notes & Queries
Bibliographical Society of
    America: Papers
CLA Journal
College English
Contemporary Poetry
ESQ
Early American Literature
Eighteenth Century Life
Eighteenth Century Studies
English Literary Renaissance

Genre
Journal of Pre-Raphaelite
    Studies
Language and Style
The Library
Modern Language Review
Nineteenth Century Fiction
Obsidian
Papers on Language and
    Literature
Philological Quarterly
Poetics Today
Review of English Studies
Seventeenth Century News

Studies in American Fiction
Studies in Bibliography
Studies in Romanticsm
Tulsa Studies in Women's
 Literature
University of Toronto
 Quarterly
Victorian Poetry
Women and Literature

Author Journals

Blake: An Illustrated
 Quarterly
Byron Journal
Faulkner Studies
Hemingway Review
Keats-Shelley Journal

Paideuma
Walt Whitman Quarterly
 Review
The Wordsworth Circle
Yeats Annual

Little Magazines

Abraxas
Barat Review
California Quarterly
December Magazine
Durak
Gargoyle
Invisible City
Ironwood

Modern Poetry in Translation
Poetics Journal
Poetry East
Poets On
Pulpsmith
Stony Hills
Wormwood Review

TERTIARY GROUP: UNIVERSITY (Ph.D. IN ENGLISH)

All of the primary and secondary journals plus:

Literary Reviews

Agenda
Arizona Quarterly
Capilano Review
Critical Quarterly
Denver Quarterly
Event
Kansas Quarterly
Literary Review
Meanjin
Michigan Quarterly Review
New Letters
New Orleans Review
Northwest Review

Ontario Review
Poet Lore
Prairie Schooner
Quarterly Review of
 Literature
Raritan
Shenandoah
Sing Heavenly Muse
South Dakota Review
Southern Humanities Review
Sulfur
Webster Review
Western Humanities Review

Scholarly Periodicals

Ariel
Biography
Bucknell Review
Bulletin of Bibliography
Cambridge Quarterly
Christianity and Literature
Criticism
Eire/Ireland
English Language Notes
Essays in Criticism
Harvard Library Bulletin
*Library Chronicle (*University of Texas)
Literary Research Newsletter
Oxford Literary Review
Poetics
Review of Contemporary Fiction
Scriblerian and the Kit-cats
South Atlantic Quarterly
Studies in Philology
Studies in the Literary Imagination
Style
Texas Studies in Literature and Language
Western American Literature
World Literature Written in English

Author Journals

The Arnoldian
Bronte Society Transactions
Flannery O'Connor Bulletin
Henry James Review
Hopkins Quarterly
John Donne Journal
Marianne Moore Newsletter
Mark Twain Journal
Tennessee Williams Review
William Carlos Williams Review

Little Magazine

Bluefish
Bravo
Cape Rock
Cut Bank
Gravida
Hanging Loose
Hiram Poetry Review
Kaldron
Milkweed Chronicle
Panjandrum Poetry Journal
Pig Iron
Precisely
Scree
Unspeakable Visions of the Individual

It appears subscriptions to any one group may be had for the price of the *Journal of Chromatography* (about $1000); all three groups (225 journals) can probably be purchased for the single subscription cost of *Nuclear Instruments and Methods* ($1776)! If the library has something tangible to offer, exchange programs can be worked out. If the institution sponsors a journal, the editor may be willing to donate exchanges that he receives; the number of important periodicals arriving at the local publication's office can be considerable. Effective serials collection development can be a challenge, but that is what makes librarianship rewarding.

NOTES

1. For a concise but excellent summary of current thinking on citation analysis as a selection criteria, see Anna H. Perrault's lengthy essay, "Humanities Collection Management—An Impressionistic/Realistic/Optimistic/Appraisal of the State of the Art," *Collection Management* 5.3/4 (Fall/Winter 1983): esp. 6-9.

2. One type of formulaic methodology is outlined by Andrew Peters in a brief piece that includes cost benefit considerations: "Evaluating Periodicals," *College & Research Libraries* 43.2 (March 1982): 149-51.

WORKS CITED AND RELATED MATERIALS

Anderson, Elliott, and Mary Kinzie, eds. *The Little Magazine in America: A Modern Documentary History*. Yonkers, N.Y.: Pushcart Press, 1978.

Arts and Humanities Citation Index. Philadelphia: Institute for Scientific Information, 1976- .

Bensman, Stephen J. "Journal Collection Management as a Cumulative Advantage Process." *College & Research Libraries* 46.1 (January 1985): 13-29.

Bogg, B. "English Language and Literature Periodicals." *International Library Review* 1.3 (July 1969): 379-401.

Brewer, Karen, et al. "A Method for Cooperative Serials Selection and Cancellation through Consortium Activities." *Journal of Academic Librarianship* 4.4 (September 1978): 204-8.

Broude, Jeffrey. "Journal Deselection in an Academic Environment: A Comparison of Faculty and Librarian Choices." *Serials Librarian* 3.2 (Winter 1978): 147-66.

Cauchi, Simon, and Roderick Cave. "Citations in Bibliography: Characteristics of Reference in Selected Journals." *Journal of Librarianship* 14.1 (January 1982): 9-29.

Chielens, Edward E. *American Literary Magazines: The Eighteenth and Nineteenth Centuries*. Westport, Conn.: Greenwood. (Forthcoming.)

———. *The Literary Journal in America, 1900-1950*. Detroit: Gale Research Co., 1977.

———. *The Literary Journal in America to 1900*. Detroit: Gale Research Co., 1975.

Davinson, Donald. *Bibliographic Control*. London: Clive Bingley; Hamden, Conn.: Linnet Books, 1975.

De Gennaro, Richard. "Escalating Journal Prices: Time to Fight Back." *American Libraries* 8.2 (February 1977): 69-74.

Ekberg, Kent, ed. "Literary Periodicals." *Serials Review* 6.3 (July-September 1980): 13-36.

Farber, Evan Ira. *Classified List of Periodicals for the College Library.* 5th ed. Westwood, Mass.: Faxon, 1972.
Fulton, Len, and Ellen Ferber, eds. *The International Directory of Little Magazines and Small Presses.* Paradise, Calif.: Dustbooks, 1965- . Annual.
Gerstenberger, Donna, and George Hendrick. *Fourth Directory of Periodicals Publishing Articles on English and American Literature and Language.* Chicago: Swallow Press, 1974.
Gohdes, Clarence Louis Frank. *Bibliographical Guide to the Study of the Literature of the U.S.A.* 5th ed. Durham, N.C.: Duke Univ. Press, 1984.
Graham, Walter James. *English Literary Periodicals.* New York: Octagon Books, 1966.
Guide to Microforms in Print. Westport, Conn.: Microform Review 1978- . Annual.
Heinzkill, Richard. "Characteristics of References in Selected Scholarly English Literary Journals." *Library Quarterly* 50.3 (July 1980): 352-65.
Hoffman, Frederick John, and others. *The Little Magazine: A History and a Bibliography.* 2nd ed. Princeton: Princeton Univ. Press, 1947.
Houghton, Walter E., ed. *Wellesley Index to Victorian Periodicals, 1824-1900.* 3 vols. Toronto: Univ. of Toronto Press, 1966-79.
Irregular Serials & Annuals: An International Directory. New York: Bowker, 1967- . Annual.
Journal Citation Reports. 3 vols. Philadelphia: Institute for Scientific Information. 1973.
Justen, Birgit. "Neuere anglistische Zeitschriften." *Zeitschrift fur Bibliothekswesen und Bibliographie* 26.1 (January-February 1979): 13-27.
Katz, William A. *Collection Development: The Selection of Materials for Libraries.* New York: Holt, 1980.
_____. "Joining Art and Technics at the Serials Desk." *Serials Librarian* 1.1 (Fall 1976): 7-11.
_____, and Linda Sternberg Katz. *Magazines for Libraries.* 5th ed. New York: Bowker, 1986.
Kribbs, Jayne K. *An Annotated Bibliography of American Literary Periodicals, 1741-1850.* Boston: G. K. Hall, 1977.
Machlup, Fritz, and Kenneth Leeson. *Information through the Printed Word: The Dissemination of Scholarly, Scientific and Intellectual Knowledge.* Vol. 2: *Journals.* New York: Praeger, 1978.
Mandel, Carol A., and Alexander Lichtenstein. *ARL Statistics 1982-83.* Washington, D.C.: Association of Research Libraries, 1984.
Marshall, Joan K. *Serials for Libraries.* Santa Barbara, Calif.: ABC-Clio, 1979.
MLA Directory of Periodicals: A Guide to Journals and Series in Languages and Literatures. New York: Modern Language Association of America, 1984.
Montag, Tom. "Stalking the Little Magazine." *Serials Librarian* 1.3 (Spring 1977): 281-303.
Mott, Frank L. *A History of American Magazines.* 5 vols. Cambridge, Mass.: Harvard Univ. Press, 1938-68.
National Enquiry into Scholarly Communication. *Scholarly Communication:*

The Report of the National Enquiry. Baltimore: Johns Hopkins Univ. Press, 1979.

New Serial Titles. Washington, D.C.: Library of Congress, 1953- .

New Serial Titles—Classed Subject Arrangement. Washington, D.C.: Library of Congress, 1973- .

New Serial Titles, 1950-1970, Subject Guide. New York: Bowker, 1975.

Patterson, Margaret C. *Author Newsletters and Journals.* Detroit: Gale Research Co., 1979.

_____."Author Newsletters and Journals: Supplement 1." *Serials Review* 8.4 (Winter 1982): 61-72.

_____. "Author Newsletters and Journals: Supplement 2." *Serials Review* 10.1 (Spring 1984): 51-59.

Perrault, Anna H. "Humanities Collection Management—An Impressionistic/ Realistic/Optimistic Appraisal of the State of the Art." *Collection Management* 5.3-4 (Fall-Winter 1983): 1-23.

Peters, Andrew. "Evaluating Periodicals." *College & Research Libraries* 43.2 (March 1982): 149-51.

Peters, Robert. *The Peters Black and Blue Guide to Current Literary Journals.* Silver Spring, Md.: Cherry Valley, 1983.

_____. *The Peters Second Black and Blue Guide to Current Literary Journals.* Silver Spring, Md.: Cherry Valley, 1985.

Saunders, Stewart. "Student Reliance on Faculty Guidance in the Selection of Reading Materials: The Use of Core Collections." *Collection Management* 4.4 (Winter 1982): 9-23.

Seiser, Virginia. "Review Sources." *Serials Review* 6.2 (April-June 1980): 67-73.

Serials in Microform. Ann Arbor: UMI, 1984.

Slote, Stanley J. *Weeding Library Collections—II.* Littleton, Colo.: Libraries Unlimited, 1982.

Soar, Geoffrey, and R. J. Ellis. "U.K. Little Magazines: An Introductory Survey." *Serials Review* 8.1 (Spring 1982): 15-28.

Stanton, Michael N. *English Literary Journals, 1900-1950.* Detroit: Gale Research Co., 1982.

Sullivan, Alvin, ed. *British Literary Magazines.* 4 vols. Westport, Conn.: Greenwood, 1983- . (In progress.)

Taylor, David C. *Managing the Serials Explosion: The Issues for Publishers and Libraries.* White Plains, N.Y.: Knowledge Industry Publications, 1982.

Ulrich's International Periodicals Directory. New York: Bowker, 1932- . Annual.

UMI Research Collections. Ann Arbor: UMI, 1984.

Union List of Serials in Libraries of the United States and Canada. Ed. Edna Brown Titus. 3rd ed. 5 vols. New York: Wilson, 1965.

Vann, J. Don, and Rosemary T. Van Arsdel, eds. *Victorian Periodicals: A Guide to Research.* New York: Modern Language Association of America, 1978.

Vesenyi, Paul E. *An Introduction to Periodical Bibliography.* Ann Arbor, Mich.: Pierian Press, 1974.

West, Michael. "Evaluating Periodicals in English Studies: Tell it in *Gath* if Ye

Must, Young Men, but Publish It Not in *Askelon*." *College English* 41 (April 1980): 903-23.

White, Herbert S. "Strategies and Alternatives in Dealing with the Serials Management Budget." In *Serials Collection Development: Choices and Strategies*. pp. 27-42. Ed. Sul H. Lee. Ann Arbor, Mich.: Pierian Press, 1981.

White, Robert B. *The English Literary Journal to 1900*. Detroit: Gale Research Co., 1977.

Winkler, Karen J. "When It Comes to Journals, Is More Really Better?" *Chronicle of Higher Education* 14 (April 1982): 21-22.

Wortman, William A. *A Guide to Serial Bibliographies for Modern Literatures.* New York: Modern Language Association of America, 1982.

Contemporary Literature

Charles W. Brownson

The selection of contemporary literature for library collections is notably vexing and controversial. Selection policy is frequently uncertain and disagreements are often heated by great differences in taste. Selection itself is complicated by the considerable bulk of published material and the dearth of selection tools that might be used to sort it. The frequent inability to say just what sort of book is wanted inhibits current and retrospective purchasing alike, requiring the detailed attentions of an expert when other disciplines can use more routine methods. The most important and desirable works, moreover, are frequently the most obscure, a state of affairs the reverse of the usual and one which creates both selection and procurement difficulties. And finally, the way in which contemporary literature is published does not consort well with library acquisition practices developed to cope with scholarly publication.

Each of these matters will be considered in turn, beginning with the initial policy decision to acquire contemporary literature.

SELECTION AND SELECTION POLICY

Though there are libraries which do not collect contemporary literature at all, the usual policy issue concerns the aggressiveness, and not the existence, of a collecting effort. That there should be a question here seems absurd. One no longer objects to collecting contemporary physics or history. Indeed, literature must be the last discipline to display a marked wariness of the contemporary. This is due to the unusual weight given in literature to taste.

Contemporary is, of course, a relative term. Joseph Conrad might be considered contemporary but will not be here for two reasons. The first is simply that the literature of Conrad's time does not present selection problems that the bibliographer of Sir Walter Scott or Charles Dickens is unprepared for. The second reason is that hostility to the contemporary grows with proximity to the present, and the problem of selection policy ought to be confronted in its most intransigent form.

The biggest difference, from the selector's point of view, between Conrad's time and our own, is that for the early part of the century it is generally agreed who the important authors are: a canon has emerged. Where the canon begins to fail, there fails also the supply of authoritative bibliographies and other tertiary reference works which so much simplify the selection process.[1] But there is another point, yet more contemporary, at which the secondary sources fail also: this is the living literature of our time, which truly deserves to be called contemporary. The paucity of independent judgment on currently active authors dictates a different selection strategy, and thus a different use of selection tools, from that appropriate to less contemporary literature. This is the point at which taste enters as a major selection criterion and with it all the well-known and unresolvable difficulties of policy.

The situation is not actually this neat, for there is always a period of several decades in which critical judgment, not yet solidified to the point of a standard reference work, has nevertheless produced an informal, fluid canon. This consensus, essentially a type of invisible college, appears to grow with participation in the college. Someone who samples a wide variety of literature and attempts to keep up with trends will have firmer views on who is collectible and will make confident (if not necessarily correct) decisions on more recent literature. But this clarification simply pushes the difficulties of taste further into the contemporary.

These difficulties will exist so long as literature is selected with reference to its quality: so long as the library attempts to obtain *good* books rather than representative ones. Of course, there are books whose importance to the collection is not in doubt: a new novel by Saul Bellow comes to mind. Everyone will buy these, though selectors will differ in the reasons they give for the books' importance. In the case of Bellow, it is of no consequence why there is consensus. But with less and less obvious material, this agreement collapses and the underlying conflict emerges: what are the terms on which a judgment of importance is to be based? Sensible selection practice would be to acquire the relatively obvious material by some expeditious means (an approval plan driven by an author list, perhaps) and to turn the selector's attention to less obvious material. It is here, after all, that selection decisions can make a difference, can produce a distinctive collection. Time was when many collections, especially the smaller, felt able to dispense with distinction in contemporary literature. Increased academic interest in this material, especially the popular genres, has made that position untenable, or at least unwise. At the same time, agreement on what is obvious has almost vanished (along with shared culture generally), and the buyer of good books is increasingly disadvantaged by a method not suited to the problem at hand.

The question of good and bad books may be clarified by examining it in the light of the conventional collecting levels.[2]

Minimal Support (Levels D-E)

Since only the most obvious books are pursued here, there is usually little controversy. Selection tools are chosen for their obviousness also: esoteric tools produce esoteric literature. The whole matter can be left to an approval plan by providing the vendor with a list of authors to be collected. The vendor's decisions are then value-free and easily monitored, and the occasional oversight does no harm when one is barely sampling the literature to begin with. (Note that the process itself is not value-free; only the decisions are. The application of values has been shifted to the construction of the list, where they are more under control and more accessible to criticism and modification.) If the library does not use an approval plan, one can make an author list for oneself out of standard reference works (James Vinson's *Contemporary Novelists*, for example), supplemented with locally appropriate specialized sources (of ethnic or genre literature, for example), and keep the list up to date from reviews as new authors appear. One might then run the list against such sources of information about new work as *Choice*, *Library Journal*, the newspapers, publishers's catalogs, or even *Books in Print*. At a yet more casual level, one might not make any effort at all to locate materials, but simply use the author list to filter whatever comes to hand. The expertise is all in the creation of the list. If the list is written down, the rest of the process can be turned into an algorithm and executed by anyone.

Research Support (Levels A-B)

Here there is generally no controversy either. Since everything (or at least a great deal of it) is sought, selection decisions are infrequent and the success of the effort depends on one's ability to discover the existence of desirable publications. Since there is such a dearth of bibliographic aid for very current literature, the process comes down to a dogged attention to everything, big and little, and so succeeds in proportion to the amount of labor committed to the task. The bibliographer's attention is turned to developing resources: getting on mailing lists, meeting people in publishing and distribution and making the library's desires known, wide reading, and the constant pursuit of clues. Selection criteria are seldom based on the quality of the literature, so that statistical methods can be used. Wanting a sample of romances, for example, which the industry produces at the rate of about four a day, one might decide to buy those published on the first day of every month. They are all alike, after all (or rather, their differences are statistical). Less extreme examples of mechanical selection principles can easily be imagined.

Study Level Support (Level C)

It is the C-level bibliographer who will be most concerned with the question of *good books* and identifying sources of authority on which to base these judgments of quality. There will be much talk of what is literature and what is art and a continual adjusting of reputations: the bibliographer is in the thick of the process by which the canon is decided, anxiously concerned that his collection contain the smallest percentage of losers. To testify to the commonness of this approach one need only contemplate such books as Richard Kostelanetz's *Exhaustive Parallel Intervals*, which consists entirely of number patterns, or Luigi Serafini's *Codex Seraphinianus*, an encyclopedia of an imaginary world written in an imaginary language. Anyone can think of several reasons not to buy these books, all more or less rationalized versions of the contention that there are better things to spend money on. By contrast, the selector of representative literature would buy them without hesitation as particularly good examples of fairly common if still minor literary trends. Indeed, one wonders how the great collections of literature used to write such compendia of the apparently trivial as Leslie Fiedler's *Love and Death in the American Novel*, could ever be assembled by libraries which insist on buying only good books. And the answer is that they could not.[3] The C-level bibliographer who uses the criteria of taste is condemning the collection to a mediocrity very expensive and probably impossible to repair. This may be a rational decision, but it ought also to be conscious and explicit.[4]

Consider, for example, the case of romance novels (or crime novels, or some other popular genre). Such material presents no particular problems to criteria of representativeness. It is quite obvious what questions one needs to ask, and how they might be answered, and how one's decisions might be defended: What is this material representative of? How much representation is appropriate? Is a broad sample required, or are there identifiable subgroups of particular interest or disinterest? Dependence on criteria of taste is much more problematic. One's opinion and critical abilities are continually appealed to, and continually under scrutiny. Effective defense of selection decisions is dependent on a slowly accrued authority, and the decisions themselves are open to charges of inconsistency. Small wonder that buyers of good books so often prefer to base decisions on the canon (that is, to stay within the boundaries of common agreement) and to avoid the whole question of popular (or any other noncanonical) literature wherever possible.

The characteristic approach of the canonical selector is not restricted to C-level collections, but appears whenever basic policy comes under discussion. Even libraries collecting comprehensively may submit the collecting decision to C-level criteria. Reputedly, the Huntington Library, before deciding to buy Wallace Stevens, considered whether he was yet important enough to merit inclusion.[5]

The alternative strategy argues that one does not buy good books but representative ones, leaving the question of utility, intractable as it is, to the users.[6] The folly of building a collection entirely on faculty demand is well known, documented by J. Periam Danton two decades ago, based on thinking going back much farther. This was, in fact, one of the first conclusions of the drive to establish a collection development theory. My point is that a canon of good books is merely the judgment of a collective faculty, and no particular authority for selection. But the desire to weed out bad books is evidently overpowering and can be found in the unlikeliest places: for example, in Richard Bruce Warr's recent (and remarkably silly) attempt to use bibliometrics to rank publishers in degree of favorability based on reviews.

The buyer of good books will often choose differently from the buyer of representative ones, as in the examples already given. Even when the decisions are the same, the reasons are likely to be very different. And the buyer of good books is hampered everywhere by inflexibility and insecurity that are the consequences of an absence of authorities and authoritative ways to distinguish good from bad. Consider, for example, these questions: what is the selection utility of a review of *Exhaustive Parallel Intervals* (other than to inform one of the book's existence), and how meaningful is the absence of Kostelanetz from (or his presence on) a list of contemporary authors? To the buyer of representative books, an ignorant or unfavorable review has no power to affect a judgment of representativeness, a quality which will never be captured in the lists and pronouncements of individuals. The buyer of good books will never attain such certainty.

The buyer of representative books, meanwhile, escapes the vagaries of taste with no loss of collection quality. The collection is responsive to a wider variety of interests and ages more gracefully. The selector, freed of the necessity for the constant application of expertise, is able to give more attention to policy and to the research which informs policy.

SELECTION AIDS

What is a representative book, then, and how might it be captured? Considering the arguments advanced above, it is a puzzle what advice to give regarding selection aids. Since there is no true authority, "authoritative" lists are essentially pretenses. More importantly, the time spent polling lists is not well invested. Brenni illustrates this well. He proposes such anthologies as the *O. Henry Memorial Award Prize Stories* and *Best Short Stories* as constituting a current bibliography of the best short fiction in America, blithely ignoring (or ignorant of) the academic and mainstream bias of these collections. One could collect such opinions for years and be none the wiser. Buying books is not a matter of taking a vote.

In other words, selection tools for contemporary literature should not be used in the same way as tools for older literatures. They are actually more like the wood from which the doghouse is built than the hammer and saw used to build it. The crucial, and limiting, question is not whether the wood is pine or fir, but the design of the doghouse.

It would be quite impossible to describe all, or even more than a few, of the ways a group of selection aids might be used. Let us take for an example the bibliographer's most important task, which is to learn of the existence of new books, especially ones in odd corners, as these are less likely to enter the library by routine methods. Suppose a computer were used to regularly collect names from a sample of serial secondary bibliographies, or lists of books received which appear in poetry journals, or some other appropriate index of publishing activity. One could then arrange to be alerted to authors named more than twice; or the list could be matched to others (murder mysteries available on the approval plan, living poets already in the collection) to throw up candidates for purchase. In the same vein, jargon could be collected from issues of such journals as *Boundary 2* and used in a free-term search of the *Arts and Humanities Citation Index* to generate material for a test of the library's collection in critical theory. This is monitoring the literature for representative material. The quantitative outlook is characteristic, as is the absence of direct appeals to evaluative opinion. Notice that one does not, as in the case of book reviews, inquire what is *in* the review, but only that there be two of them—or eight, or whatever seems best.

The following list, then, consists of resources, current and retrospective, which are useful in creating and monitoring a representative collection, with a few notes to indicate what relevant information they contain. The composition of the list will change from time to time, as new resources are born and old ones die, or lose their utility. Individual bibliographers will wish to expand it in areas of particular interest, or contract it in areas of notable disinterest.

For literatures less commonly collected in the United States, only background sources that define a base of reference have been provided. For U.S. literature, trade publications and sources of industry information useful in creating a statistical base, in promptly learning of the winners of prizes, and so forth are included.

Because of their essential appeal to authority, reviewing media as such are excluded. Preference, instead, has been given to comprehensive and regular serial bibliographies, with reviews listed only in fields where these are absent. What is aimed at is bibliographic control with the fewest possible sources, a statistical base, and clues to trends. (For small press review sources *see* the entry for book reviewing in the *International Directory of Little Magazines and Small Presses*.)

Some selectors may wish to use indexes and citation analysis to resolve doubtful cases, and this can even be required by policy (e.g., subscribing only to magazines to which there is index access, or collecting only authors on whom there is secondary material). My article "Access to Little Magazines" contains a list of all sources of index access to primary contemporary literature.

United States and Canadian Literature

American Book Publishing Record. New York: Bowker, 1960- . *ABPR*'s Dewey order is an obstacle to its use in academic libraries, but the cumulation and the detail of bibliographic description render it preferable to either the *Weekly Record* or *Books in Print (BIP)*. Most valuable for generating test lists. Use in conjunction with the *Small Press Record of Books in Print (SPBIP)* (Paradise, Calif.: Dustbooks, 1969-). This is an invaluable annotated list by author, with title, publisher, and subject indexes, the latter including such headings as "fiction" and "poetry." I have not determined the overlap of *SPBIP* with *ABPR*, but the additional increment over *BIP* is about 60 percent. There is a small press trade catalog also, which appears every few years: *The Whole COSMEP Catalog* (Paradise, Calif.: Dustbooks, 1973) was in reverse alphabetical order and the *COSMEP Catalogue of Independent Press Publications* (San Francisco: Western Microfilm, 1982) was published on microfiche. The most recent is *The International Association of Independent Publishers'*

COSMEP Catalogue (San Francisco: COSMEP, 1984). The Canadian counterpart of these, *Literary Press Group Catalogue* (Toronto: Literary Press Group 1982), is distinctly more useful. Twenty-eight Canadian presses publish about 476 titles a year of fiction and poetry, making the Canadian industry about two-thirds that of Australia to New Zealand.

American Book Review. New York: Writers' Review, 1978- . 6/yr. Covers small press publications well, though not in great quantity.

American Poetry Review. Philadelphia: World Poetry, 1972- . 6/yr. The best resource for academic and commercial poetry, this magazine is much disliked in some quarters for its conventionality: see the review by Robert Peters in *The Peters Black and Blue Guide to Current Literary Journals*. Rochester, N.Y.: Cherry Valley, 1983.

Armchair Detective. New York: Mysterious Press, 1967- . 4/yr. The preferred source, regularly includes checklists and a column on collecting crime fiction as well as reviews.

Choice. Middletown, Conn.: Association of College and Research Libraries, 1964- . 11/yr. The best academic general review medium, though not notably good at primary literature: it overlooks a great deal and its reviewers have depressingly conservative taste. Supplement with the annual article on first novelists from *Library Journal. Booklist* (Chicago: American Library Association, 1905- . 22/yr.) provides thinner coverage with no improvement in judgment but *Kirkus Reviews* (New York: Kirkus, 1933- . 24/yr.) offers some additional leverage on popular literature.

Fine Print. San Francisco: Fine Print, 1975- . 4/yr. Academic articles, press profiles, and lists of recent books from the art presses which are significant producers of new literature as well as new editions.

Grants and Awards Available to American Writers. New York: PEN American Center, 1969- . Annual. The best American list, kept up-to-date and winners supplied by the notices and the calendar in *Coda*. (New York: Poets and Writers, 1973- . 5/yr.) The alternative *Writer's Handbook* is heavily commercial and not recommended. The utility of these lists is primarily to identify new writers of note, as well as to insure acquisition of notable titles, often quite obscure when first published.

Journal of Modern Literature. Philadelphia: Temple Univ., 1970- . 4/yr. Publishes the most wide-ranging serial bibliography of secondary sources, including regional and ethnic literatures. Supplementary ethnic sources are given under the appropriate headings below. Other useful serial bibliographies are:

> *Modern Fiction Studies*. West Lafayette, Ind.: Purdue Univ., 1955- . 4/yr.
>
> *Review of Contemporary Fiction*. Elmwood Park, Ill.: Review of Contemporary Fiction, 1981- . 3/yr.
>
> *Science Fiction Studies*. Montreal: McGill Univ., 1973- . 3/yr.
>
> *Studies in Short Fiction*. Newberry, S.C.: Newberry College, 1963- . 4/yr.

Studies in the Novel. Denton, Tex.: North Texas State Univ., 1969- . 4/yr.

Twentieth Century Literature. Hempstead, N.Y.: Hofstra Univ. Press, 1955- . 4/yr.

Unisa English Studies Pretoria: Univ. of South Africa, 1968- . 2/yr. Annual review of articles on literary theory, critical methodology, and literary aesthetics.

Locus. Oakland, Calif.: Locus, 1968- . 12/yr. The science fiction trade magazine, it publishes more news and smaller reviews than the rival *Science Fiction Chronicle* (New York: Algol Press, 1979- . 12/yr.). Supplement these with the table of contents of the *Science Fiction and Fantasy Book Review* (Vista, Calif.: Science Fiction Research Associates, 1982- . 10/yr.) to monitor the output of SF primary literature.

New York Review of Books. New York, 1963- . 22/yr. Coupled with the *New York Times Book Review, Times Literary Supplement, Choice, Publishers Weekly,* and *Quill and Quire,* forms a complex which will generate commercial, mainstream literature if one has the patience to assemble it from these sources.

Patterson, Margaret C. *Author Newsletters and Journals.* Detroit: Gale Research Co., 1979. Newsletters are generally the first manifestation of the birth of an academic critical industry. The newsletters of successfully established industries become academic quarterlies. One way to monitor this process is this list.

Rosenberg, Betty. *Genreflecting: A Guide to Reading Interests in Genre Fiction.* Littleton, Colo.: Libraries Unlimited, 1982. Author lists and secondary sources for romance fiction, westerns, crime fiction and thrillers, and science fiction (including fantasy and horror). A good beginning place.

Serials Review. Ann Arbor: Pierian Press, 1975- . 4/yr. In addition to its obvious use, this has always had an interest in the small press. Christine Rom's column on little magazines appears now in *Collection Building* (New York: Neal-Schuman, 1978- . 4/yr.), which also publishes occasional guidance on literary resources.

Small Press News. New Sharon, Maine, Small Press News, 1981- . 10/yr. Political watch, calendar of trade meetings and book fairs, reviews and lists of books received.

Small Press Review. Paradise, Calif.: Dustbooks, 1967- . 12/yr. The most prominent source in its field. Reviews both books and magazines, updates the *International Directory of Little Magazines and Small Presses,* with articles and columns on printing, legal issues, distribution, publicity. Monitors the life and death of sometimes elusive small presses. The annual library issue distributed at the ALA convention is essential. This is the only American source, commercial or otherwise, to show any interest in publisher-library relations.

United States and Canada: Industry Information

Anthology of Magazine Verse and Yearbook of American Poetry. Beverly Hills, Calif.: Monitor Book Co., 1980. Contains a "Yearly Record" listing anthologies, poetry magazines, organizations, and awards, with a small list of secondary materials, all done better but not quite so conveniently by other sources. Despite the title, there does not appear to be a successor to this.

Annual Survey of Manufactures. Washington, D.C.: U.S. Department of Commerce, Bureau of the Census, 1952- . Annual. Fills in the period between the 5-year censuses.

Association of American Publishers. *AAP Industry Statistics.* New York: The Association, 1971. Annual.

Book Industry Trends. Darien, Conn.: Book Industry Study Group, 1977- . Annual.

Bowker Annual of Library and Book Trade Information. New York: Bowker, 1955- . Annual.

CCLM Catalog of Literary Magazines. New York: Coordinating Council of Literary Magazines, 1975- . Annual. Adds nothing to the *International Directory*, except to identify some of the more prominent little magazines.

CCLM Newsletter. New York: CCLM, 1979- . 3/yr. Grant agency policies. The Coordinating Council of Literary Magazines is the most prominent source of U.S. grant funds.

Census of Manufactures. Washington, D.C.: U.S. Department of Commerce, Bureau of the Census, 1905- . Quinquennial.

Directory of Small Magazine/Press Editors and Publishers. Paradise, Calif.: Dustbooks, 1970- . Annual. The personal name index to the *International Directory*.

Fiction Writer's Market. Cincinnati: Writer's Digest Books, 1981- . Annual. (See *Writer's Market*)

International Directory of Little Magazines and Small Presses. Paradise, Calif.: Dustbooks, 1965- . Annual. The standard current directory, succeeding *Trace*. Has contained, since 1975, a subject index with headings for fiction and poetry, as well as a geographical index, lists of reviewing sources and a handy list of acronyms.

International Directory of Private Presses. Sacramento. Press of Arden Park, 1978- . Biennial. Art presses. Not to be confused with the other directory of similar name, with which it overlaps only partially.

LMP: Literary Market Place. New York: Bowker, 1972/73- . Annual.

MIMP: Magazine Industry Market Place. New York: Bowker, 1980- . Annual. Neither this nor the *LMP* are notably literary, and being resolutely commercial, they have increasingly little utility to the literature bibliographer.

Publishers Weekly. New York: Bowker, 1872- . 52/yr. The commercial counterpart to *Small Press Review*. As literature becomes less and less commercial, *PW* becomes less and less useful. No one should use this unsupplemented on a regular basis. Trade publishing seems dimly aware of its increasing isolation from contemporary literature, as witness Bowker's recent invention of *Small Press*.

Publishers Weekly Yearbook. New York: Bowker, 1983- . Annual. Trade statistics, contributing little to those available in the *Bowker Annual* or (preferably) *Book Industry Trends*.

Quill and Quire. Toronto: Key Publishers, 1935- . 12/yr. The Canadian counterpart to *Publishers Weekly.* Superior coverage of publisher-library relations; a model for other trade magazines.

Small Press; The Magazine of Independent Book Publishing. New York: Meckler, 1983- . 6/yr. Anyone supposing this magazine concerns the traditional small press will be misled into some peculiar views. Its existence is evidence of the ghettoizing of commercial literature into specialized, and therefore small, but still resolutely commercial presses. This is the Canadian pattern, but without Canadian advantages. The magazine's name is deeply resented by the traditional small press. See the reviews in *Small Press News* No. 17/18 and No. 21. In the latter, Diane Kruchkow comments: "How can a magazine owned by a conglomerate, edited by someone with no small press experience, and published by someone who has never heard of the *International Directory*, claim to serve and promote us?" (p. 1).

Strophes. Albuquerque, N.M.: National Federation of State Poetry Societies, 1964- . 4/yr.

Writer's Market. Cincinnati: Writer's Digest Books, 1929- . Annual. With the parallel *Fiction Writer's Market*, useful for monitoring the number and type of commercial literary outlets, an activity not recommended for its cheering effects.

British and General Commonwealth

British Book News. London: British Council, 1940- . 12/yr. Stands to the *British National Bibliography Weekly List* as *American Book Publishing Record* does to the *BIP* precursor *Weekly Record*, but with additional valuable survey articles.

Commonwealth Literature Periodicals. Comp. Ronald Warwick. London: Mansell, 1979.

Journal of Commonwealth Literature. Oxford: Hans Zell Publishers, 1965- . 2/yr. The annual bibliography by country is the dominant serial bibliography, both primary and secondary. Includes translations and anthologies.

Little Press Books in Print. London: Association of Little Presses, 1970- . Irregular. Resembles the COSMEP catalogs (q.v.) and the *Publishers Trade List Annual* more than the *Small Press Record of Books In Print*, which it duplicates with regard to presses but not, interestingly, in respect of titles listed.

London Review of Books. New York and London: 1979- . 24/yr. A clone of the *New York Review of Books*, unnecessary but for the donnish attitude of the *Times Literary Supplement.* This still leaves noncommercial British fiction somewhat untouched, for which there is no simple remedy. *PN Review* serves well for British poetry.

PN Review (Poetry Nation). Manchester: 1971- . 6/yr.

Times Literary Supplement. London: Times Newspapers, 1902- . 52/yr.

World Literature Today. Norman, Okla.: Univ. of Oklahoma, 1927- . 4/yr. Supplements the *Journal of Commonwealth Literature* for non-Commonwealth literatures.

World Literature Written in English. Guelph: University of Guelph, 1962- . 2/yr.

As the *WLWE Newsletter*, 1962-71. Supplements *World Literature Today* with regular checklists.
Writers' and Artists' Yearbook. London: Adam and Charles Black, 1907- . Annual. Lists non-U.S. literary prizes.

Black African, Black American, Caribbean

African Book Publishing Record. Oxford: Hans Zell Publishers, 1975- . 4/yr.
African Book World and Press: A Directory. Munich: K.G. Sauer, 1977- . Triennial.
Black American Literature Forum. Terre Haute: Indiana State Univ., 1967- . 4/yr. Book reviews and occasional bibliographic surveys.
Black Scholar. San Francisco: Black Scholar Press, 1969- . 6/yr. Publishes an annual list of black books, but not specifically literary.
Gorman, G. E., and M. M. Mahoney. *Guide to Current National Bibliographies in the Third World.* Munich: K. G. Sauer, 1983. This is the initial source for basic bibliography on Africa, the Caribbean, and South Africa. Can be supplemented by the *Bibliography of Neo-African Literature* by Jahn Janheinz (London: Faber & Faber, 1968). Specifically Caribbean resources are not extensive: Joan V. Feeney's, *Peasant Literature: A Bibliography of Afro-American Nationalism and Protest from the Caribbean* (Monticello, Ill.: Council of Planning Librarians, 1975, Exchange Bibliographies, 822) can be noted together with *Caribbean Writers: A Bio-bibliographical-Critical Encyclopedia* (Washington, D.C.: Three Continents Press, 1979) and Marjorie Engber's *Caribbean Fiction and Poetry* (New York: Center for Inter-American Relations, 1970). None of these last three is particularly complete: Engber, for instance, lists only two works by Jean Rhys and two by V. S. Naipaul. Most recent is Daryl Cumber Dance's *Fifty Caribbean Writers: A Bio-bibliographical Critical Sourcebook* (Westport, Conn.: Greenwood, 1986). The journal *Obsidian* (1975-82. Detroit: 3/yr.), now reorganized as *Obsidian II* (Raleigh, N.C.: Dept. of English, North Carolina State Univ.), though not especially bibliographic, covers African and Caribbean as well as black American literature. The most satisfactory way of acquiring Caribbean materials is, as with Latin American and other Third World materials, not from printed lists but from dealers in the area (for example, Caribbean Imprint Library Services).
Lindfors, Bernth. *Black African Literature in English.* Detroit: Gale Research Co., 1979. The largest retrospective list, but not coextensive with the older *Bibliography of Creative African Writing* by Jahn Janheinz and Claus Peter Dressler (New York: Kraus Thompson, 1975), which is an expansion, for Africa alone, of Janheinz's earlier *Bibliography of Neo-African Literature* (q.v.). These two lists might be supplemented with the information in Donald E. Herdick's *African Authors* (Washington, D.C., Black Orpheus, 1973).
Research in African Literatures. Austin: Univ. of Texas, 1970- . 4/yr. Edited by Bernth Lindfors, this is the standard academic resource for current information, supplemented with the African Studies Association's *ASA News* (1968- . 4/yr. *African Studies Newsletter*, 1968-80).

Amerindian

Jacobsen, Angeline. *Contemporary Native American Literature*. Metuchen, N.J.: Scarecrow, 1977. The only list of note. Analyzes collections and provides a title index to single poems, as well as an author index.

Littlefield, Daniel F., Jr., and James W. Parins. *A Biobibliography of Native American Writers 1772-1924*. Metuchen, N.J.: Scarecrow, 1981. [Native American Bibliography Series, 2] *Supplement*. Metuchen, N.J.: Scarecrow, 1985. [Native American Bibliography Series, 5] Useful separate section of authors known only by pen name. Contains short biographies, and also lists translations.

Marken, Jack W. *The American Indian Language and Literature*. Arlington Heights, Ill.: AHM Publishing, 1978. The most extensive list up to 1978. Primarily folklore, mythology, and linguistics.

Rock, Roger O. *The Native American in American Literature*. Westport, Conn.: Greenwood, 1985. [Bibliographies and Indexes in American Literature, 3] The most useful guide for collection development. Includes secondary works on Amerindians as literary characters. Author and subject indexes.

Studies in American Indian Literature: Newsletter of the Association for the Study of American Indian Literatures. New York: Columbia University Press, 1974- . 4/yr. The only current resource.

Chicano

Decade of Chicano Literature (1970-1979): Critical Essays and Bibliography. Santa Barbara, Calif.: Editorial La Causa, 1982.

Lomeli, Francisco A., and Donaldo W. Urioste. *Chicano Perspectives in Literature*. Albuquerque, N. Mex.: Parajito Publications, 1976.

Martinez, Julio A., and Francisco A. Lomeli. *Chicano Literature: A Reference Guide*. Westport, Conn.: Greenwood, 1985. Subject articles and biobibliographic essays in one alphabet. Includes a chronology, a glossary, and a list of general works, but lacks a survey of Chicano and Mexican-American periodicals.

The Americas Review. Houston: Arte Publico Press, 1986- . 4/yr. (formerly *Revista Chicano-Riqueña*, 1973-85.) Lists books received. The only current resource for Chicano-English literature.

Trujillo, Roberto G., and Andres Rodriguez. *Literatura Chicana: Creative and Critical Writings Through 1984*. Oakland: Floricanto Press, 1985. Updates and supersedes bibliographic sections of *Decade of Chicano Literature (1970-79)*.

Australia, New Zealand, Oceania

Australian Literary Studies. Hobart: Univ. of Tasmania, 1963- . 2/yr. Annual bibliography of secondary sources in the May issue.

Day, Arthur Grove. *Modern Australian Prose 1901-1975*. Detroit: Gale Research Co., 1980.

Journal of South Asian Literature. East Lansing: Michigan State Univ. Asian Studies Center, 1963- . 2/yr. Continues *Mahfil*, which was entirely primary material. This is still mostly primary, but made up of theme issues usually containing a survey article and a bibliography of some out-of-the-way literature.

Lock, Fred, and Alan Lawson. *Australian Literature: A Reference Guide.* 2nd ed. Melbourne: Oxford Univ. Press, 1980.

McDowell, Robert, and Judith M. McDowell. *Asian/Pacific Literatures in English: Bibliographies.* Washington, D.C.: Three Continents Press, 1978. Primary and secondary material, translations into English, for Sri Lanka, Philippines, Malasia/Singapore, Aboriginal, Papua New Guinea, and Hong Kong.

Poetry Australia. Berrima, New South Wales: South Head Press, 1964– . 3/yr. Occasional commentaries.

Westerly. Nedlands: Univ. of Western Australia, Department of English, 1956– . 4/yr. Occasional reviews of the Australian literary scene.

India

Indian Literature. New Delhi: Indian Academy of Letters, 1956– . 6/yr. This annual's survey is discursive and difficult to make efficient use of. Covers Indian language and non-English Indian literatures.

Karkala, John A., and Leena Karkala. *Bibliography of Indo-English Literature: A Checklist of Works by Indian Authors 1800–1966.* Bombay: Nirmala Sadanand Publications, 1974.

Singh, Amritjit, Rajiva Verma, and Irene M. Joshi. *Indian Literature in English 1827–1979: A Guide to Information Sources.* Detroit: Gale Research Co., 1981.

Warwick, Ronald J. *Indian Literature in English.* London: Commonwealth Institute, 1979. (Checklists in Commonwealth Literature, 5) More selective than Singh.

South Africa

Contrast. Cape Town. 1960 . 2/yr. English and Afrikaans. Primary material only.

Gorman, G. E. *The South African Novel in English since 1950.* Boston: G. K. Hall, 1977.

―――, and M. M. Mahoney. *Guide to Current National Bibliographies in the Third World.* Munich: K. G. Sauer, 1983. This would be the preferred initial source for basic South African bibliography.

SANB; Suid-Afrikaanse Nasionale Bibliografie; South African National Bibliography. Pretoria: State Library. 1959– . 12/yr., with annual cumulation. Continuation of the *Publications Received in Terms of Copyright Act #9 of 1916* (Pretoria: State Library, 1916–59). Dewey order.

PROCUREMENT

In the older function of the area specialist, selection and procurement were combined. The area specialist, however, rarely dealt with English language materials because these countries, having well-developed publishing industries and bibliographic control, were thought not to require the expensive procurement expertise of an area specialist. The newer concept of collection development utilizing subject specialists includes control of English language publication, but the subject specialist, unlike the area specialist, is almost never a part of the acquisitions department and is frequently isolated from procurement procedures, with little or no authority to change them. The specialist in contemporary literature will be particularly inconvenienced, because most of the modern primary literature as well as some of the secondary material present significant procurement problems.

This section and those which follow deal with procurement difficulties for contemporary literature.

It must be remembered that acquisitions departments, no matter how sympathetic to the needs of collection development, are organized to maximize efficiency (as distinct from effectiveness) by the use of routine. This is not undesirable: procurement is more easily routinized than selection, and it is often preferable, where possible, to replace selection with faster, cheaper, and more predictable procurement routines. This is the rationale for blanket-order plans, standing orders, and all the familiar acquisitions apparatus.

But it is also important for the literature selector to know when, and in just what way, procurement routines damage selection effectiveness. The difficulty may be simply wasting time: knowing, for example, that some literary magazines collect requests for sample copies (paid and unpaid) until there are enough to obtain bulk mail rates, the literature bibliographer will resist routine application of a rule requiring sample copies of periodicals before subscription.[7] Other rules defeat selection: the preference for vendors over direct orders (discussed below) often means that selected titles are never acquired. At the extreme, selection can be made so difficult and time-consuming as to be impossible: lack of services such as order card preparation or pre-order bibliographic searching, or the use of a badly designed or administered (and so, unpredictable) approval plan can have this result.

It is to be hoped that electronic ordering, automated acquisitions, and on-line catalogs will improve matters. Computers are capable of administering endless exceptions without a mistake, and can perform labor intensive tasks that a human acquisitions staff could never consider, both qualities valuable to a literature bibliographer. But experience so far is not encouraging. Acquisitions reports are seldom detailed enough to be as useful as they might be to collection development, and the expensive enhancements necessary for more precise reports, for the administration of exceptions, and for support of interactive investigation of the database, are often resisted. Literature selectors, with their formidable problems of bibliographic control, should be at the front in bringing these machines into the service of collection development.

Approval Plans

Blanket or standing orders (wholesale purchase of entire imprints, series, etc.) are generally not useful for less aggressive collecting of contemporary literature, since the results would be too mixed in type and format. Approval plans utilizing a custom collection profile and not simply permitting rejection of individual titles, do have utility for all collecting levels. But there has been a reluctance to use them for contemporary literature because of the difficulty of specifying just what is wanted.

There are two main types of profiles for contemporary materials. One is based on critical standards and attempts to select on the basis of quality. The other type of profile focuses on such characteristics as genre, reading level, and kind of publisher. The first best serves the small or medium-sized collection that is attempting to buy good books, while the second is more appropriate to a collection (a large or an ambitious one) engaged in building a representative collection. Both types of profiles may be modified by the use of author lists, specifications of acceptable price, format, type of press, content (first novels, reprints), and the like. Approval plan vendors employ experts to make critical judgments, so that one never escapes this source of uncertainty: the predictability, prevalence, and tenor of these critical opinions will be a major factor in the choice of a vendor for contemporary literature. Critical judgments should be applied to definable material and in predictable ways. The lists of specifications should also be as flexible as possible. For example, will the vendor accept additions to the author list? Lacking these characteristics, a plan will be hard to adjust to local needs and will be unpredictable and thus likely to conflict with other acquisition methods such as direct orders.

All approval plans have some safety mechanism for doubtful materials which involves the use of multipart forms or slips sent to the library instead of the book itself. For contemporary literature these forms are one of the greatest benefits of an approval plan because the vendor, in daily and direct contact with publishers, is much more efficient in gathering information about new university press and trade publications than the librarian could ever be. No approval vendor handles the small press well, of course, but the liberal, even lavish, use of these forms can do much to free the bibliographer's time for attention to this more difficult material.

Some of the distributors specializing in small press books will accept approval plans of a sort. A better way is to make inquiries to the presses already well represented in your collection and discover who their distributors are and how these might be combined with blanket orders or other arrangements to bring at least a definable part of the small press under control.

The evaluation of an approval plan is essentially a repetition of the selection process and depends on one's ability to create a statistical sample of titles that should have been received on approval. Lacking the ability to specify just what is wanted (usually the case with contemporary literature), one is unable to evaluate the plan. For this reason alone, D-level selectors may want to restrict their use of approval plans to an author list. However, the use of selection forms and the availability of actual books for examination before purchase makes an approval plan an attractive means of exploration outside the safety of the obvious.

Distributors and Jobbers

These wholesalers are a necessary evil. The unspecialized ones are no more capable of dealing with the small press than the unspecialized approval plan vendors, and for the same reasons: economies of scale and the often eccentric business practices of the small press. But the inutility of distributors and jobbers for contemporary literature is greater than that. Warehouses are stocked according to a prediction of demand. The library buying a single copy of a book of poems not in the warehouse already is not likely to be as well served as a bookstore ordering fifty copies of the latest best-seller. At the extreme, the library will not be served at all, and when it finally decides to turn elsewhere it finds the book out of print.

Again, there are specialized distributors for the small press which should be used wherever possible.

Direct Orders

Libraries typically resist placing orders directly with the publisher because it multiplies the invoices and all other paperwork. One of the tasks of the aggressive buyer of contemporary literature is to overcome this resistance. Of course, one does not want to spend the library's budget on six-part forms, but frequently a direct order is the only way to obtain a publication expeditiously. Prepayment, the use of a WATS telephone line instead of OCLC or some other bibliographic source to obtain publication information, a looser preorder verification process, less reliance on sample copies and more on standing orders, less rigid definitions of pamphlet and ephemera all work to the benefit of the buyer of contemporary literature, and in the same way: these things gain time, and time is one of the bibliographer's scarcer commodities. One need only look at the publication statistics in the *Bowker Annual* to see that no subject is more awash in new publications. An aggressive library may acquire only *five percent* of all new fiction, and (for purely logistic reasons) less than half of what it deems buyable.

SMALL PRESSES AND LITTLE MAGAZINES

Much of the preceding assumes that the library is more or less committed to purchase small press publications. If this is not true, there is reason to think it should be. Literature (and especially that of interest to libraries) is increasingly the domain of what was once called the small press and the little magazine. (The terms "independent press" and "literary magazine" may now be more appropriate.)

In the last decade the mainstream conglomerate publishers have withdrawn from the market for middle-run books, editions of five to ten thousand, and this gap is being filled by the former small press (and by university presses as well, which have also increased their production of primary literature), for whom editions of five thousand are profitable.[8] The original small press continues, of course, to deserve its reputation as eccentric and anticommercial. But there is now little point in making a distinction, at least in the case of literature, between the small and the commercial press.[9] Contemporary poetry, as a glance at the credits of any poet will confirm, is now almost exclusively an affair of the small or independent press. A little money and some printing innovations have more recently placed fiction in a nearly parallel situation. Romance and crime fiction are the only genres that remain entirely commercial.

While most matters concerning the small press have, therefore, been incorporated in the general discussion, there remain a few points of special note.

Chapbooks are an important form of small press publication. Some libraries define these as pamphlets and make difficulties about cataloging them. This should be resisted.

The small press is rich in extracts, derivative editions, and broadsides. For example, one poem from a new or forthcoming collection is handset and separately published under a unique title. These are not intended for libraries, but to raise money from the carriage trade. They are often indistinguishable in catalogs and other lists from the desirable chapbooks, and vigilance is necessary to prevent acquiring them by accident. A lower limit of twenty-four pages, and an upper limit of $30, not

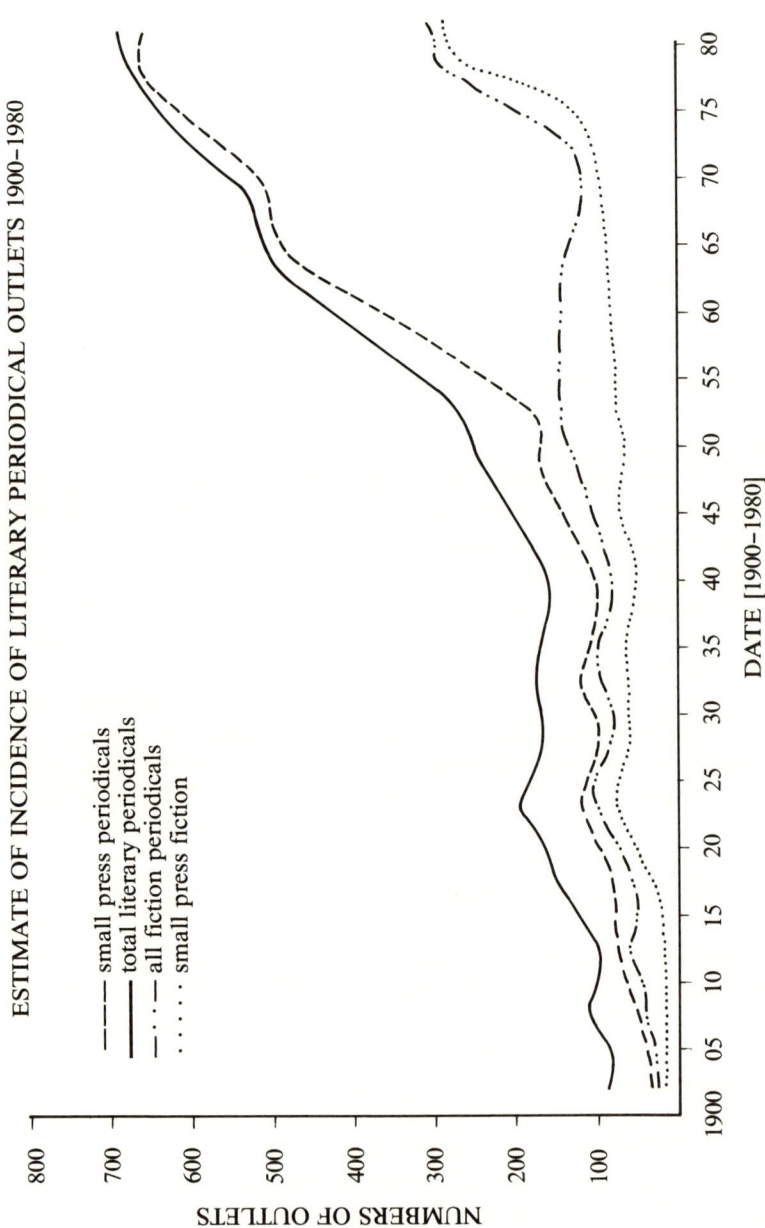

as a rigid policy but as guidance to clerical staff and approval plan vendors, seems to distinguish moderately well between the two forms.

Small presses and little magazines reveal the personalities of their editors. Time spent getting to know these people, their taste, and the character of their presses is time well spent, for then it is often possible to decide to purchase a new publication strictly on its provenance. This is an enormous savings in time. More importantly, knowledge of this sort makes possible controlled and reasonably safe experimentation with new authors and new styles. The collection is immeasurably enriched for a pittance (a small press novel costs half what a mainstream one costs), potentially great trouble is saved, and the library contributes to the support of literature. All this would be impossible if bibliographers could not rely on their judgments of a favorite group of editors. An equivalent sally into the mainstream press would cost more and accomplish less.

It should be remembered that small press knowledge is very perishable. As Roeming remarks, the average life of a little magazine is only seven issues (p. x), and that of a press just a few years. Age is thus a moderately good criterion to use in distinguishing the prominent presses and magazines. But the editor's name is better, for when a press dies, its editor usually founds a new one, bringing with him all the experience and personal contacts of the old.

Bibliographers who pursue little magazines are nearly bereft of selection strategies. The unknown, noncanonical authors who create so much anxiety are dominant here, indexing is erratic, samples are difficult to obtain. Press provenance, a few specialized sources (those not included here are cited in my article, "Access to Little Magazines"), and the bibliographer's own knowledge of the field are the extent of the means. A parallel situation, though perhaps not quite so difficult, pertains for the book output of small presses. Under the circumstances, it is all too easy to ignore this material as incorrigible. Given this, and the restructuring of the publishing industry underway, it is greatly to be feared that public access to the literature of our time has become discouragingly difficult. This can only work to further constrict budgets, damage collections, and leave literature a coterie activity and the property of specialists.

RETROSPECTIVE DEVELOPMENT

Ideally, all books are acquired when they are first published. This never happens, of course, particularly in contemporary literature where judgments are constantly revised. Retrospective development can be considered as anything that should have been done earlier and wasn't.

The notion of retrospective development of contemporary literature is a peculiar one, for it would seem that by the time a literature has come under retrospective scrutiny, it can no longer be called contemporary. And indeed, the systematic and large-scale retrospective development which takes place when a new course or program is approved is seldom attempted for contemporary literature, and for good reason. There are hardly any tools for selection, and hence just as few for surveying contemporary collections. Lacking these, system is absent, and the methodology of collection analysis is largely invalidated.

Retrospective development in a looser sense is, however, quite common. Let us say that an author previously unknown to me wins a prize or appears on the approval plan review shelves. Investigation reveals that this author has already published half a dozen novels. The two still in-print are ordered and the titles of the other four are submitted to the librarian in charge of out-of-print acquisitions. Or, in looking over the latest issue of *British Book News*, I find a review article on Australian poetry of the last decade. The list is checked against the library's holdings and lacking items ordered.

This sort of informal, *ad hoc* retrospective development is probably practiced by everyone. Its hallmark may be thought to be a lack of system, but it should be pointed out that in these examples is implicit a great deal of system. The approval plan brings an author to my attention because I have arranged matters so that it will, and the selection decisions and level of collecting against which the plan operates guarantee that material which it throws up will be of importance. I learn of a new prize author because I have a system to see to it that such things come to my attention, as for example, a regular schedule for reviewing a predetermined list of periodicals. I am able to make quick use of the lists I come across because I have previously assembled the information necessary: author lists, familiarity with presses and their editors, and a detailed understanding of my collection and its deficiencies. The knowledge, techniques, and bibliographic tools used for this casual activity are not different from those used every day. This, and the adventitious nature of the work, should not mislead anyone into underrating such continual testing of the collection. Though there is a paucity of bibliographic tools to aid the more formal surveys, publishers' backlists, dealers' catalogs, review articles (bibliographic essays, as distinct from book reviews), and other casual sources must be used when they are at hand. Later, they will be difficult or impossible to retrieve. It is a good plan to allocate time and assistance for this work.

The catalogs of out-of-print dealers are also frequently used for casual retrospective development. Some of this is necessary to maintain relationships with dealers and learn their stock, and a few dealers in contemporary literature even produce catalogs usable as bibliographies for collection review. But a great deal of time devoted to dealers' catalogs, particularly in contemporary literature, is a waste of time. One may check an author's whole oeuvre against the library's catalog thirty times before an uncommon work turns up. This is true generally, of course, but for contemporary literature the situation is worse because the only serious money to be made by a dealer is in modern firsts, preferably signed or with other significant provenance, and in manuscripts. Reading copies, which are what the buyer for the library stacks wants, are the stock of secondhand dealers, few of whom issue catalogs. Reading copies may certainly be acquired in this way, but the library which buys primarily from dealers' catalogs is paying more for its books than is necessary. Some dealers in contemporary literature handle reading copies all the time, but to get them it is necessary to give the dealer a want list. A library which is willing to invest resources in the preparation of want lists, and commit itself to buy the books on the lists when they are offered, is well on the way to a serious investment in a program of retrospective development. These resources can come in part from discontinuance of the repetitive, expensive, and largely futile checking of dealers' catalogs.

The other bar to the use of dealers' catalogs for contemporary literature is that only the most obvious authors are listed, because it is only these authors who have yet acquired collecting value. But these are just the authors most likely to be already in the library's collections. Experience suggests that more than two-thirds of the effort spent checking dealers' catalogs is wasted for this reason alone. Meanwhile, because of the reliance on catalogs, less obvious material never gets into the collection.

These strictures on dealers' catalogs do not have the same weight with dealers in small press materials for two reasons. First, such dealers are often also distributors, and their lists are amalgams of in-print and elusive material and casual stock. Second, there are probably fewer obviously collectible authors among those publishing with small presses (at least, obvious to the library) and so the effort spent checking catalogs of small press publications is likely to be more rewarding. Consult the distributor list at the back of the 1984-85 edition of the *International Directory of Little Magazines and Small Presses* (a feature regrettably absent from the 1985-86 edition), the listings in the *American Book Trade Directory*, or the advertisements in *AB: Bookman's Weekly*.

NOTES

1. The briefest scan of Vito Joseph Brenni's *The Bibliographic Control of American Literature 1920–1975* (Metuchen, N.J.: Scarecrow, 1979) will show how confused and tardy is bibliographic control of contemporary American literature. "Bibliographic control" does not mean that an item in question can be found in some bibliography, which is useless if the bibliography is itself obscure. One wants, for collection development purposes, large and easily accessible lists whose bibliographic characteristics are well known. Brenni lists a melange of sources which do not even add up to an American equivalent of the *New Cambridge Bibliography of English Literature*. The rest of the contemporary world's literature in English is hardly better off. Lest anyone suppose the situation cannot be better, let him try to replicate for literature a type of study common in the sociology of science (cf., Robert K. Merton, *The Sociology of Science: Theoretical and Empirical Investigations*, Chicago: University of Chicago Press, 1973), or run an on-line search of the ESTC. (See Symposium on the 18th Century Short-Title Catalogue, 1982. *Searching the Eighteenth Century*. London: British Library, 1983.)

2. Definitions of collecting levels may be found in section 1.8.1.2 of the American Library Association's *Guidelines for Collection Development*, edited by David L. Perkins (Chicago: American Library Association, 1979). Since current practice in ARL libraries has been influenced by the newer categories of the Research Libraries Group, some confusion may be avoided if ALA's alphabetic and RLG's numerical schemes levels are briefly characterized:

Level A [level 5]: comprehensive, including mss. and ephemera.
Level B [level 4]: research, doctoral support.
Level C [level 3]: study level, usually subdivided into two levels, one appropriate to master's programs and the other to undergraduate. Levels below 3 would be uncommon for literature as a whole except in special libraries, but support for contemporary literature only at lower levels is not uncommon at all.
Level D [level 2]: basic support, highly selective, sufficient to define a subject but no more.
Level E [level 1]: minimal. Level 0 is sometimes also used: not collected.

3. Fiedler was notable in his time for ransacking libraries for neglected popular literature. The more recent interest in quantitative studies of literature by critics, historians, sociologists, linguists, and others (given a boost by the microcomputer) merely extends the application of the omnivorous kind of scholarship which Fiedler and his predecessors have always engaged in. For a few suggestions of what can be done along this line in an appropriate collection, see the plans of the Sukov Collection of little magazines at the University of Wisconsin as outlined in a letter by Assistant Curator Deborah Reilly in *Small Press Review* 15.12 (December 1983):10.

4. One of the few articles to specifically discuss collecting contemporary literature is John Rutledge's "Collecting Contemporary European Literature for a Research Library," *Collection Management* 5.1–2 (Spring-Summer 1983):1–13. He writes correctly that on "the subject of how much literature should be bought, opinions range between the two extremes of exaggerated completeness and ascetic severity" (p. 3). Then, evidently frightened by the expense of the "inclusivist fantasy," he immediately abandons the middle position. This is the typical procedure and is not what is here intended by the term, rational. The inclusive policy which Rutledge sets up is a straw man. His rush to embrace a restrictive selection policy is reactionary, excessively timid, and dangerous to libraries and to literature.

5. Communicated to the author by the librarian, Daniel Woodward, in a lecture at Arizona State University, March 1984.

6. Innumerable decent, humane objections to this approach might be found in the literature. (See, e.g., Murray L. Bob, "The Industrialization of the Book," *Library Journal* 108.20 (November 15, 1983): 2127-29, or J. B. Miller, "Sublimity Versus Circulation," *Library Journal* 107.22 (December 15, 1982): 2309-14.) The common denominator of these arguments is the desire to preserve high culture from the inroads of the low. The point of any academic library, and especially a research library, engaging in such a defense is mysterious to me, while the danger of following intellectual fashions in high and low culture is very obvious. Frank J. Lepkowski gives other counter-arguments in a reply to Miller, "Saving Poetry," *Library Journal* 108.22 (December 15, 1983): 2304-6. The whole of Patrick Wilson's work might be interpreted as a caution against just such pretensions of librarians, and the cognitive authority of librarians is the explicit subject of the last chapter of his most recent *Second-Hand Knowledge* (Westport, Conn.: Greenwood, 1983).

7. Such matters are discussed by Noel Peattie in "Hatrack, Or How My Knowledge of Libraries Affects My Publishing," *Small Press Review* 14.6-7 (June-July 1982): 5-6. This is the annual library issue of *SPR* distributed at the ALA convention and usually contains a number of articles along these lines; also in this issue is a column by Celeste West, "The Library Beat" (pp. 11-12). *SPR* is the only American periodical that regularly takes up the subject of library-publisher relations, a matter on which *Publishers Weekly* is dismal (compare the Canadian *Quill and Quire*).

8. For a detailed analysis of the ills of the publishing industry, see Leonard Shatzkin's *In Cold Type: Overcoming the Book Crisis* (Boston: Houghton, 1982). Those unfamiliar with the workings of the industry might want to first read *Books: The Culture and Commerce of Publishing*, by Lewis A. Coser and others (New York: Basic Books, 1982).

9. In Canada, in fact, there cannot be said to be a small press as Americans understand it. The publication of literature in Canada is almost entirely the province of a group of presses allied to form the Literary Press Group. The output of these presses can hardly be called noncommercial, and they have the advantage of strong support of literature by the Canadian government. There is no distinction between these presses and their nonliterary counterparts which can be defined by terms not invidious to one or the other. The traditional small press thrives in the more divided countries of Great Britain, Australia, the United States, and (significantly) Quebec Province. The concept of a small press implies opposition, apparently. In Canada the publication of literature has simply been ceded to specialized presses, and the same process seems to be at work in the Unites States. Mainstream publishing in the United Kingdom and elsewhere, more committed to literature, is still competing for the territory.

WORKS CITED

Brenni, Vito Joseph. *The Bibliographic Control of American Literature 1920-1975.* Metuchen, N.J.: Scarecrow Press, 1979.

Brownson, Charles W. "Access to Little Magazines." *RQ* 22.4 (Summer 1983): 375-87.

Danton, J. Periam. *Book Selection and Collections.* New York: Columbia Univ. Press, 1963.

―――. "The Selection of Books for College Libraries." *Library Quarterly* 5.4 (October 1935): 419-36.

Fiedler, Leslie. *Love and Death in the American Novel.* Rev. ed. New York: Stein & Day, 1966.

Kostelanetz, Richard. *Exhaustive Parallel Intervals.* New York: Future Press, 1979.

Roeming, Robert F. *Catalog of Little Magazines: A Collection in the Rare Book Room, University of Wisconsin-Madison*. Madison: Univ. of Wisconsin Press, 1979.

Serafini, Luigi. *Codex Seraphinianus*. New York: Abbeville, 1983.

Vinson, James, ed. *Contemporary Novelists*. 3rd ed. New York: St. Martin's, 1982.

Warr, Richard Bruce. "Bibliometrics: A Model for Judging Quality." *Collection Building* 5.2 (Summer 1983): 29-34.

Textual Studies and the Selection of Editions

Joseph Natoli

"Any critic or historian," Fredson Bowers writes, "would prefer to discuss a literary work on the basis of a sound text" ("Textual Criticism," p. 23). A slight variation of this statement would suit my purposes here: "Any literary bibliographer would prefer to add a sound text to the library's collection." But though both critic and bibliographer would choose sound texts, their establishment is neither simple nor straightforward. The determination of textual reliability is the problematic task of textual studies, and to select editions wisely a bibliographer should know the different processes by which editions are developed.

This proposal that the bibliographer base the choice of editions not on mechanical selection procedures but on a thorough understanding of the disputant field of textual criticism parallels a situation within the discipline itself: the New Bibliography, championed by Fredson Bowers and following the Lachmann-Greg tradition, has attempted to reduce the production of a "sound" text to a procedural matter, while others such as James Thorpe, Philip Gaskell, and Jerome McGann have argued for a vastly more relative, subjective and collaborative process.

Though the so-called New Bibliography is a crucial point of beginning, it is actually *in medias res* with respect to the course of modern textual studies. Bowers maintains that an author's intentions are decisive in establishing the text and that through the aid of the grammar of textual studies these intentions can be exactly determined. Bowers builds on Walter Greg's modification of the Lachmann tradition of editing classical texts, which presupposed a "pure" original that could be extricated from its various lines of ancestral corruption. (See Pasquali for a critical account of the Lachmann method.)

Greg and Bowers inherited from this tradition the idea of a pristine original and its ever-increasing corruption. Greg's classic theory of the copy-text, the text upon which a critical edition is to be founded, is based on this search for a purified textual source. When an author's manuscript survives, it should become the copy-text but in the absence of the manuscript, an editor should select as copy-text the edition chronologically closest to the manuscript. By this means corruptions which occur during subsequent transmissions and productions of the work are avoided. In order to preserve the reliability of accidentals (spelling, punctuation, capitalization, and division), the manuscript is preferred because it has not gone through the erring hands of compositors, and in order to preserve the intended meaning of words, the substantives, only those revisions which can be proven to be authoritative are chosen.

Bowers argues that "scientific" collation of variant editions can identify both substantive and accidental variants and in large measure adjudicate among them. His "scientific" methods are bibliographical, and thus analytical or textual bibliography does, in fact, serve as the foundation of Bowers' view of textual criticism. An author's words are not to be interpreted in an effort to discover meaning but are thought of as "simple inked shapes" and texts themselves are "impersonal and nonconceptual inked prints" (Dunkin, pp. 95-96). When the holograph, the manuscript in the author's own hand, does not itself become the copy-text and the copy-text that is chosen proves not authoritative regarding substantives, then an eclectic text is formed. The edition emerging from this is not one that was ever previously produced by the author. It may, indeed, be very different from previous versions, especially when it is difficult to determine what changes in the first and subsequent editions were actually made by the author. Even if a holograph exists, the presence of authoritative, variant published editions leads to the creation of an eclectic text. Throughout, such collating efforts by the New Bibliographers are directed toward achieving "scientific" authoritativeness.

An eclectic edition is constructed by the editor. When there is disagreement regarding the choice of variants, the text produced may be considered the editor's version of a particular author's work. But Bowers himself admits that bibliography alone can resolve only a limited number of editorial questions:

Occurrences in which the bibliographical analysis can supply the whole answer to textual cruxes are fairly limited. For every example like *shortly* versus *thereby* in *Hamlet*, or *sullied* versus *solid flesh*, where an immediate bibliographical basis for decision can exist, there are hundreds that can rely only on the general guidance of bibliographical findings that have established the derivation and relationship of the texts as a whole. [*Bibliography*, p. 57]

However, even those few cases that Bowers finds indisputable are, indeed, questionable. Thorpe, speaking of the famous sullied/solid crux in *Hamlet*, observes that "every conclusion reached by one bibliographer is disputed by another." In his view, "there is a good deal of argument among bibliographers as to what constitutes a bibliographical fact" (*Principles*, p. 97). Thus, the grammar of Bowers' textual criticism is hardly a secure foundation, and his eclectic text, despite its scientism, can only be arguably, not absolutely, definitive.

Whether or not the New Bibliography provides an unshakeable "mechanical explanation for all mechanically produced phenomena" (Dunkin, p. 96) or represents rather another entrance into values and opinion is a dilemma that has reemerged with the establishment of the Center for Editions of American Authors (CEAA), now called the Center for Scholarly Editions (CSE) of the Modern Language Association of America. Philip Gaskell in *From Writer to Reader* takes on the CEAA. Focussing on Bowers' CEAA edition of Hawthorne's *The Marble Faun* as exemplary of the Center's strengths and weaknesses, Gaskell concludes that CEAA editions are not and never can be definitive. Their main editorial principle is flawed, coming aground where both manuscript and first printing are available but there is no record of whether substantive differences between the two were made with the author's consent. In these cases, he concludes:

> The editor cannot normally say that this version or that comes closest to the author's intentions. All he can say is that this version is to be preferred to that on other—perhaps critical—grounds. [p. 191]

In his review of the CEAA, Tom Davis reiterates Gaskell's point and extends a caution:

> I do not intend to argue that anyone's guess in textual matters is as good as the editor's; only that anyone who reads an edited text should be made aware that this is what he is doing; not reading Crane, but Fredson Bowers' edition of Crane. CEAA texts, it seems to me, do not fulfill this function, in spite of (because of) their forbidding panoply of textual material. ["CEAA" p. 74]

Gaskell consequently calls for a recognition that editing is as much criticism as it is bibliography and that it cannot be regimented and inflexible. Editors should "always consider the why and the wherefore and the how of their work according to the circumstances and the needs of each individual case" (p. 195). In a similar vein, F. W. Bateson cites what he calls Bowers' "trumpet-call against the critics"—the assertion that textual evidence will establish whether or not "Hamlet's father's bones were interred' as in Q2, or 'inurned' as in the Folio"—and concludes that the "bibliographical evidence is quite indecisive" and the matter can "only be finally determined from the internal evidence of style" (p. 123).

Thus, the imprimatur of definitiveness, which would render selection a pro forma operation, is not truly available. The vision of a scientifically constructed text rests on the shaky ground of a theory that falsely assumes that the author's final intentions can be objectively ascertained. In contrast to this conception of autonomous intentionality is Thorpe's collaborative view:

> The work of art is thus always tending toward a collaborative status, and the task of the textual critic is always to recover and preserve its integrity at that point where the authorial intentions seem to have been fulfilled. [*Principles*, p. 48]

The idea that intentions are a collaborative, social enterprise is very revolutionary. On the simplest level, it excises the notion of a fixed point of origin for authorial intentions and spreads them throughout an author's continued interaction with the world in which his texts are produced. Authority does not rest with the writer alone, but in his or her interaction with the publishing world, reviewers, commentators, editors, and printers. As Jerome McGann explains:

> Authority is a social nexus, not a personal possession; and if the authority for specific literary works is initiated anew for each new work by some specific artist, its initiation takes place in a necessary and integral historical environment of great complexity. [p. 48]

The notion of the definitive edition thus dissolves before the collaborative view of intentionality. Textual reliability becomes a relative matter, contingent upon complex social and historical circumstances. McGann uses Byron to point to the authority of ever-changing intentions:

> ... the case of Byron's works can stand as an exemplary one for a host of others; that is, many works exist of which it can be said that their authors demonstrated a number of different wishes and intentions about what text they wanted to be presented to the public, and that these differences

reflect accommodations to changed circumstances, and sometimes to changed publics. [p. 32]

Indeed, McGann takes Thorpe's collaborative notion a step further, arguing that a text continues after an author's death to collaborate with its audience. Textual soundness hence lies partially in the eye of the beholder, to the degree that one variant edition may prove more accessible to a particular class of readers than another. Tom Davis summarizes Gaskell's position:

> In this model a text is not a message in a medium, a ghost in a machine, but a book, made by the labour of many, by writers, and printers, and, indeed, readers, who collectively provide its final and most important realization. ["Textual Criticism," p. 389]

Or as Lorene Pouncey states it:

> Each poem said, each story read, and each drama played attains renewed perfection, in this last sense, every time it is said, read, or played. [p. 118]

We have, thus, proceeded from the classicist view of the "lost original" through the notion of a "finally intended text" (which is an eclectic creation) and then to the sense of the text as cultural product, its identity and authority extending beyond the author into the world and time.

Classicist, intentionalist, and collaborative views of the text are actually grounded in the issue, "Where is the text?" This question places literary theory secondary to textual criticism and bibliography—a proposition lately reaffirmed by Herschel Parker (p. xiv). Bowers' approach is an amalgam of two very different responses to the problem. On one hand, he adheres to Shelley's notion that the poem in the mind loses power in actualization, that the poet's unspoken, unprinted intentions are the locus of meaning. But to this Shelleyan-Crocean tenet, Bowers adds the pseudoscientism of the New Criticism with its belief that objective methods can establish subjective intentions. In contrast, such collaborationists as Thorpe, Gaskell, and McGann relate to the hermeneutics of Hans Georg Gadamer. Here the discernment of the best text lies in the convergence of the author's intentions, the institutions of publishing, and the reader. Since all three change over time, the notion of best is completely relative. The idea of "definitive" thus approximates the concept of "classic" in Gadamer's hermeneutics: it is that edition which enables a reader in the present to make real connections with the work. This concept that creation proceeds dually, both from the author's dialogue with the world and from the reader's dialogue with the work is grounded in the contention that the text, like meaning, exists temporally in the world.

The "best" text is, therefore, a choice among available variants based on present requirements. The proper question to ask is, "What text is most likely to be accessible given a particular audience?" Stated differently, we have moved from an expressionist view of the author as illuminating lamp to a reader or audience response view. The challenge is not to recover the author's primal intentions in a "definitive" text but to measure the reader's response in establishing, for a specific historical epoch, the most accessible text. Since "best" is relative to audience, editors of either a critical or uncritical edition must situate it "clearly in terms of its present orientation and set of purposes (McGann, p. 100).

The subjectivity that the New Bibliography hoped to erase has now returned very prominently and renders the task of the literary bibliographer highly indeterminate, since there can be no formula for selecting editions. But this indeterminacy also creates the conditions of meaningful choice among texts: some editions are not only to be preferred to others depending upon the context of one's own collection but, more importantly, the purchase of one edition does not preclude the purchase of others. Thus we return to the fact that the problematic nature of textual studies demands a detailed knowledge of textual histories on the bibliographer's part. How such knowledge affects the process of selecting editions is our next concern.

THE SELECTION OF EDITIONS

In the absence of a simple formula for identifying definitive editions, the literary bibliographer must learn the transmission histories of particular texts, from holograph to modern edition. And these textual "stories" cannot be confined to standard editions but should extend to all editions, since everyone is a product of a battle of forces. Tom Davis sees these forces as basically three: the editor who wishes to retreat into "bibliographical self-absorption," the publisher who looks "longingly at out-of-copyright photolitho reprints," and the reader who thinks of money and "second-hand bookshops." Davis concludes:

> It is an uneasy truce, and any editorial labors that actually emerge into print should be welcomed. Each, however, will bear the marks of compromise. ["Textual Criticism," p. 392]

The English selector must understand precisely the nature of the compromise made by each edition.

If the Clarendon edition of Thomas Hardy's *Tess of the D'Urbervilles*, fifteen years in the making, is inhospitable to simple reading, then we can see the compromise heavily favoring the editor in search of a definitive, scholarly version. The edition's role is essentially as a reference tool to be consulted for Hardy's revisions. In contrast to this editorial style, Edmund Wilson has argued for lightness and convenience as primary assets, and he was apparently first to propose an American equivalent of Gallimard's *Bibliothèque de la Pléiade*. Bowers chided Wilson for his preference, but ironically many see the Library of America editions as the equivalent of Gallimard, and Bowers has been very active in that enterprise.

Two publishers, Penguin and Vintage Books, consistently put the reader at the forefront. The latter produced a very approachable edition of *Ulysses*, yet the 1984 Garland synoptic version of that text places its errors at around seven a page. Penguin usually offers reliable texts that combine "scholarship, accessibility and mass production." The Penguin version of Browning's poetry represents "the first attempt at a fully annotated and complete edition" and the New Penguin Shakespeare, while not up to the New Arden and New Clarendon Shakespeares, is competently done (Davison, p. 348).

But there is no publisher rule to follow here. The Penguin edition of George Eliot's *Felix Holt* is based on the Cabinet edition of the work, which Fred C. Thomson, editor of the Clarendon *Felix Holt*, rejected because Eliot did not review its proofs. Thomson chooses instead the first edition because it was the last for which Eliot read proof. However, Bowers has pointed out that even when it is known that an author read proof, it is impossible to determine if all variants were approved, if, in fact, the author collated proof and manuscript or even reviewed the proofs closely. Does, in short, the presence of one or more authorial revisions make the entire edition a uniformly reliable one? Thus, even though a new edition may dismiss a prior one, as Thomson does here, and as Bowers did with his editions of *Tom Jones* and *The Scarlet Letter*, it is essential to know the specific arguments involved, the grounds upon which an edition is erected. For the deficiencies of one may be rectified in another.

Deficiencies may be quite real, and their consequences for interpretation very dramatic. According to one reviewer, Finneran's new edition of Yeats lacks reliability, since the editor failed to examine the archive documenting earlier aborted attempts to publish the poems (see Gould). This history of the transmission of a text is a necessary ground from which any new edition should emerge. The contemporary audience demands a dialogic engagement of the text and its history. A new edition of Eliot's *Selected Poems* continues to print "world" instead of "word" in "Ash Wednesday," thus hopelessly confusing the poem. And of course, there is the classic example of F. O. Matthiessen's ingenious interpretation of Melville's "soiled fish of the sea," a reading based on a misprinting of the word "coiled." Minor textual deficits can lead to major interpretive deficits.

The strengths and weaknesses of each edition are ultimately like those same qualities in the library's collection as a whole. The bibliographer's grasp of the latter is finally dependent upon understanding the former. Whether or not to make a particular edition now long out-of-print an advertised desideratum follows from knowledge about that edition in relation to other editions of the author's work as well as in relation to the local collection and demands made on it. Here Richard Hooker is a good example. In the compromise among scholarship, reader, and publisher, the Folger edition of Hooker opts emphatically for the first, so decidedly that anyone wishing simply to read Hooker, without being overwhelmed by the textual apparatus, must put the Folger edition aside and pick up the two-volume, modernized Everyman edition. Where and when a collection can do without the Folger Hooker is an assessment the bibliographer must make, but there will be both times and places where only the Everyman would be on the shelves. Of course, under different circumstances the Folger may be the only edition on the shelf, or both may be there. Knowledge of editorial compromises as well as of one's own collection and readership is determinative here.

Enforcing the importance of such detailed knowledge is the example of Jack Stillinger's two admirable editions of Keats. The earlier (1978) is aimed at textual critics and scholars and is unique in Stillinger's view because "it is the first in the history of Keats scholarship to be based on a systematic investigation of the transmission of the texts" (p. v). The later (1982), at one third the price and much more portable and accessible (thus satisfying Edmund Wilson's requirements) is "intended to be an all-purpose reading edition" (p. v). Stillinger's comments on other editions of Keats—including Miriam Allott's, which remains the most fully annotated, and Harry Buxton Forman's, which still features unique inclusions—is the sort of editorial introduction which McGann has called for. McGann's introduction to his edition of Byron not only describes its own strengths but also points out the ways in which E. H. Coleridge's previous great edition will never be superseded. Such introductions conveniently summarize textual histories and strike a middle ground between the brief notices of *Choice* and review-essays of *The Library*, although the bibliographer may seek on different occasions either the brevity or the detail of these representative journals.

Familiarity with textual histories encourages skepticism about all claims to editorial finality. But there are series that are justifiably respected. The Norton Critical Editions are consistently readable and reliable, always referring to themselves not as "the" but "an" authoritative text. In a review of classroom editions of *Moby-Dick*, Hershel Parker concluded that all except the Norton Critical Edition failed Joseph Katz's "four simple tests" for judging a practical edition ("*Red Badge of Courage*" p. 302). Katz defines practical editions as:

> ... those texts which are intended for the use of students, teachers, and the general reading public—of works that are read by Americans or that represent America abroad. They, even more than critical editions prepared for a scholarly audience, are the most significant means of transmitting our national culture. ["Practical Editions," p. 283]

Like Penguin texts, Norton editions sometimes turn out to be our closest approximation to "definitive" editions, as in the case of Dickens' *Bleak House*. Thus, "practical" may not always exclude "scholarly."

In the absence of critical editions of an author's work and often—depending upon the textual histories involved—even in their presence, first editions should be collected and made available as reading copies, even if this entails purchasing two copies, circulating and noncirculating. While first editions are not necessarily more authoritative nor fully collaborative with contemporary audiences, they nevertheless stand at the beginning of that text's history of transmission. Origin does not assure unchanging definitiveness, but it does inevitably shape and explain all future collaborations.

Often, appearance of an edition, especially its layout and typography, are qualities sought in reading copies. Thus a Heritage Press edition ranks high. Similarly, Oxford Paperbacks, such as the 1984 edition of Fanny Trollope's *Domestic Manners of the Americans*, usually possess readable typeface, flexible binding, and true *vade mecum* proportions. But finally, both personal preferences and objective scholarly credentials must be subject to the bibliographer's review of the nature of each edition's textual compromise and the current as well as future demands upon the local collection.

Because of these considerations, a bibliographer at one library may be searching antiquarian catalogs daily, while elsewhere one may instead regularly rely on reading copies identified through *Books in Print*. The editions sought can be variously small press, limited, rare, expensive, or cheap—none of these automatically fall into reputable or disreputable categories. Selection is always relative to individual contexts, both with respect to the text itself and the collection for which it is chosen.

The tools a literature bibliographer uses in selecting editions amount to those resources employed in acquiring knowledge of their particular textual compromises and transmission from past to present. There is no work presently available that narrates textual histories, detailing the establishment of an author's work and pointing out the strengths and weaknesses of each edition. Such a tool would have to be in a loose-leaf format. F. W. Bateson and Harrison Meserole's *A Guide to English and American Literature* and Valmai Fenster's *Guide to American Literature* are perhaps closest to this nonexistent source, although Bateson offers only simple designations—definitive, standard, fullest, critical, best, scholarly—with no grounds stated for these judgments. Given the fact that editions serve different purposes and often base themselves on competing views of what constitutes the best representation of an author's work, it is difficult for a bibliographer to rely solely on such unequivocal evaluations. Fenster furnishes more information about the specific qualities of editions than does Bateson.

An unannotated record of what editions have been published is provided by the *New Cambridge Bibliography of English Literature (NCBEL)*. But this finding list is already dated and gives only the names of the cast, not the stories they are involved in. The bibliography volume of Spiller's *The Literary History of the United States* is presently the closest American equivalent to *NCBEL*, although the *Gale Bibliography of Literature in America* aspires to match the *NCBEL*'s achievement. Blanck's *Bibliography of American Literature* not only covers the canon but also describes editions, which enables a bibliographer to verify editions in hand. Bruccoli's *First Printings of American Authors* is also valuable for confirming first editions.

But more useful than such reference tools are editorial introductions in the latest editions of an author's work. Supplementing these are the bibliographic surveys in the various reviews of research published by the Modern Language Association of America. Such volumes as Frank Jordan's *The English Romantic Poets,* Joel Myerson's *The Transcendentalists*, and George H. Ford's *Victorian Fiction: A Second Guide to Research* furnish excellent discussions of editions. What is always needed is the most up-to-date narrative account of the published history of a writer's work, one that includes a comparative treatment of different editions. Such an account may be the focus of book-length studies like Stillinger's *The Texts of Keats's Poems*, Bowers' *On Editing Shakespeare and the Elizabethan Dramatists*, or Langford's *Faulkner's Revision of Sanctuary*. Annual reviews such as *Year's Work in English Studies* and *American Literary Scholarship* can be very useful for both current and retrospective evaluations. The *MLA International Bibliography* now has a subject index with headings "Textual Criticism" and "Textual Editing." Howard-Hill's *British Bibliography and Textual Criticism* lists textual studies but unfortunately omits review essays, which are often most important for bibliographers. In this context, *Index to Reviews of Bibliographical Publications* is helpful. The best reviews are in the quarterly, *The Library*, although one can also refer to *The Papers of the Bibliographical Society of America, Review, Pages*, and the annual volumes of *Proof* (1971-77) and *Studies in Bibliography*. Journals other than those specifically concerned with textual criticism but also excellent sources for reviews and articles are: *Journal of English and Germanic Philology, Resources for American Literary Study, Studies in the Novel* (see its special issue, "Textual Studies in the Novel," 7.3, Fall 1973), *Bulletin of Research in the Humanities* (formerly *Bulletin of the New York Public Library*), *Scholar and Publisher, Harvard Library Bulletin, Direction Line, Modern Philology, Review of English Studies*, and *American Literature*. To this list can be added journals with a more specialized focus—author, period, movement—all of which vary in importance, depending upon local collection emphasis. The more general reviews that should also be read are the *Times Literary Supplement, New York Review of Books, London Review of Books, Small Press Review*, and *Women's Review of Books*.

When thorough knowledge has guided selection, and an item has been purchased, much of the job is done. But often the desired edition is out-of-print, like Thomas Wharton's 1785-91 edition of Milton's *Poems Upon Several Occasions*. In these cases, not only must the library decide whether and how to enter the antiquarian book market, but questions about the expense and physical location of the materials must also be addressed.

Some editions properly belong in the special or rare book collection. But since the circulating copies will be the principal agents for transmitting culture, they ought to be the best. Purchasing duplicate copies resolves this dilemma, but because this is costly, the definition of textual superiority must be precise. It requires knowledge of the collaboration between collection and user, for nothing is culturally transmitted which is untranslatable to the present cultural code. That text, therefore, which transmits itself most completely within a cultural context as well as within the parameters of it's historical evolution can be defined as "best."

It should also be noted that rare editions are not necessarily old, and new editions are neither necessarily inexpensive nor always easily available. A first edition, first impression of Thornton Wilder's *The Cabala* may sell for more than an early Francis Bacon; a limited edition from a private or fine press of a work—sometimes new but occasionally previously published—may be both rare and expensive. Indeed, first appearances of an author's work in limited editions by private presses generally represent a problematic group for selection. If the writer is established, such work will very often appear later in collections. But perhaps not, since poets are famous for offering only selective versions of their collected work. Also, later printings may be in variant form, so that the original publication possesses independent scholarly value. The reissuance of a previously published work in a deluxe format—handmade paper, handsewn, hand-set—is also an edition of an author's work, but because its scholarly and reading value may be nonexistent, its acquisition must be made on other grounds. Certainly the book and all matters pertaining to its production and transmission are a notable concern, and such an edition does reveal the interrelationship of artistic, literary, bibliographic, and historical factors. Furthermore, who can deny that a perusal of the Kelmscott Chaucer could not whet anyone's appetite for Chaucer? As with other editions, the decision to purchase will depend on the directions of local collections and resources along with the bibliographer's own judgment of the edition's merit.

CONCLUSION

The effective choice of editions depends on thorough knowledge of the process of textual studies. In McGann's view, "the best scholarly editions establish their texts according to a catholic set of guidelines and priorities whose relative authority shifts and alters under changing circumstances" (p. 94). In the same fashion, any selection of literary works is a collection in a particular world, created and utilized within a changing intellectual environment, just as each edition is itself a compromise of circumstances and values.

Just as there is a plethora of editions of different qualities and effects, so is there an abundance of literature collections existing variously. This is one side of the dialogue. On the other is the argument that collections and editions should seek to be ideal and definitive. Harvard's *Widener Library Shelflist*, along with the catalogs of such libraries as the Folger and Huntington represent this possibility.

While neither the One nor the Many seems particularly disastrous and much can be said in favor of both, we usually display a decided preference for the unity of the One over the plurality of the Many. The concept of a single, ideal collection on which every bibliographer draws is to some extent a carryover from the very successful practice of all libraries sharing uniform cataloging. But sometimes local institutions modify this ideal cataloging copy to suit their own circumstances. While the notion of definitive collections and editions promises all the efficiency and effectiveness of the uniform catalog, it unfortunately neglects the collaborative nature of scholarship as well as of texts. There is real loss when a particular collection replaces its own requirements with generalized ideals. Individualized differences should be respected and cultivated, and uniformity not established as a goal in itself.

Unless a literature bibliographer understands that active knowledge of distinctions, both in texts and in collections, are at the core of selection, then it is unlikely that a viable dialogue between the collection and user will exist. In this dialogue, opposing voices ought to be encouraged and the conflicts that emerge never effaced.

The identity of a collection derives from the texts it contains, but these dwell in the realm of consciousness, their essence residing not in physicality but in the interchange between words and the reader who seeks meaning contextualized within a present world. The literature collection is only superficially related to its physical presence and to develop it as if it were a purely physical enterprise is to violate its nature. It follows that conscious cultivation of a collection demands the active, persistent intercession of the bibliographer as a knowledgeable agent searching for literary meaning. To comprehend and locate that meaning both within the academic institution of letters and the local collection is what is involved in the apparently simple matter of selecting an edition. In the view of Blake, enough here is synonymous with too much.

WORKS CITED AND RELATED MATERIALS

American Literary Scholarship. Durham, N.C.: Duke Univ. Press, 1965-   .

Bateson, F. W. *The Scholar-Critic: An Introduction to Literary Research.* London: Routledge & Paul, 1972.

———, and Harrison T. Meserole. *A Guide to English and American Literature.* 3rd ed. New York: Gordian Press, 1976.

Blanck, Jacob. *Bibliography of American Literature.* New Haven: Yale Univ. Press, 1955-   . (In progress.)

Bowers, Fredson. *Bibliography and Textual Criticism.* Oxford: Clarendon Press, 1964.

———. *Essays in Bibliography, Text, and Editing.* Charlottesville: Published for the Bibliographical Society of the Univ. of Virginia by the Univ. Press of Virginia, 1975. (Contains a checklist of Bowers' publications.)

———. *On Editing Shakespeare and the Elizabethan Dramatists.* Philadelphia: Univ. of Pennsylvania for the Rosenbach Foundation, 1955.

———. "Textual Criticism." In *The Aims and Methods of Scholarship in Modern Languages and Literatures,* pp. 23-42. Ed. James Thorpe. New York: Modern Language Association of America, 1963.

Brack, O. M., and Warner Barnes, eds. *Bibliography and Textual Criticism: Eng-*

lish and American Literature, 1700 to the Present. Chicago: Univ. of Chicago Press, 1969.

Browning, Robert. *The Poems.* Ed. John Pettigrew and Thomas J. Collins. 2 vols. Harmondsworth, Eng.: Penguin Books, 1981.

Bruccoli, Mathew J., ed. *First Printings of American Authors: Contributions Toward Descriptive Checklists.* 4 vols. Detroit: Gale Research Co., 1977-79.

Byron, George Gordon Byron, Baron. *The Complete Poetical Works.* Edited by Jerome J. McGann. New York: Oxford Univ. Press, 1980- .

―――. *The Works of Lord Byron.* New rev. and enlg. ed. Ed. E. H. Coleridge. 13 vols. London: J. Murray, 1898-1905.

Carter, John. *ABC for Book-Collectors.* 5th ed. rev. New York: Knopf, 1981.

―――. *Taste and Technique in Book-Collecting: A Study of Recent Developments in Great Britain and the United States.* New York: Bowker, 1948.

Conference on Editorial Problems, 6th, University of Toronto, 1970. *Editing Seventeenth Century Prose.* Ed. D. I. B. Smith. Toronto: Hakkert, 1972.

Conference on Editorial Problems, 7th, University of Toronto, 1971. *Editing Texts of the Romantic Period.* Ed. John M. Baird. Toronto: Hakkert, 1972.

Conference on Editorial Problems, 8th, University of Toronto, 1972. *Editing Canadian Texts.* Ed. Francess G. Halpenny. Toronto: Hakkert, 1975.

Conference on Editorial Problems, 9th, University of Toronto, 1973. *Editing Eighteenth Century Novels.* Ed. G. E. Bentley. Toronto: Hakkert, 1975.

Conference on Editorial Problems, 10th, University of Toronto, 1974. *Editing British and American Literature, 1880-1920.* Ed. Eric W. Domville. New York: Garland, 1976.

Conference on Editorial Problems, 11th, University of Toronto, 1975. *Editing Renaissance Dramatic Texts, English, Italian, and Spanish.* Ed. Anne Lancashire. New York: Garland, 1976.

Conference on Editorial Problems, 12th, University of Toronto, 1976. *Editing Medieval Texts: English, French, and Latin Written in England.* Ed. A. G. Rigg. New York: Garland, 1977.

Conference on Editorial Problems, 13th, University of Toronto, 1977. *Editing Nineteenth-Century Fiction.* Ed. Jane Millgate. New York: Garland, 1978.

Conference on Editorial Problems, 14th, University of Toronto, 1978. *Editing Correspondence.* Ed. J. A. Dainard. New York: Garland, 1979.

Davis, Tom. "The CEAA and Modern Textual Editing." *The Library* 5th ser. 32.1 (March 1977): 61-74.

―――. "Textual Criticism: Philosophy and Practice." *The Library* 6th ser. 6.4 (December 1984): 386-97.

Davison, Peter. Rev. *The Poems*, by Robert Browning. Ed. John Pettigrew. *The Library* 6th ser. 4.3 (September 1982): 347-53.

Dickens, Charles. *Bleak House: An Authoritative and Annotated Text.* Ed. George Ford and Sylvère Monod. New York: Norton, 1977.

Dunkin, Paul S. *Bibliography: Tiger or Fat Cat?* Hamden, Conn.: Archon, 1975.

Editorial Conference, 1st, University of Toronto, 1965. *Editing Sixteenth Century Texts.* Ed. R. J. Schoeck. Toronto: Univ. of Toronto Press, 1966.

Editorial Conference, 2d, University of Toronto, 1966. *Editing Nineteenth Century Texts*. Ed. John M. Robson. Toronto: Univ. of Toronto Press, 1967.
Editorial Conference, 3d, University of Toronto, 1967. *Editing Eighteenth-Century Texts*. Ed. D. I. B. Smith. Toronto: Univ. of Toronto Press, 1968.
Editorial Conference, University of Toronto, 1969. *Editing Twentieth Century Texts*. Ed. Francess G. Halpenny. Toronto: Univ. of Toronto Press, 1972.
Eliot, George. *Felix Holt, The Radical*. Ed. Peter Coveney. Harmondsworth, Eng.: Penguin Books, 1972.
———. *Felix Holt, The Radical*. Ed. Fred C. Thomson. Oxford: Clarendon Press, 1980.
Fenster, Valmai Kirkham. *Guide to American Literature*. Littleton, Colo.: Libraries Unlimited, 1983.
Fielding, Henry. *The History of Tom Jones, A Foundling*. Ed. Fredson Bowers. Middletown, Conn.: Wesleyan Univ. Press, 1975.
Ford, George H., ed. *Victorian Fiction: A Second Guide to Research*. New York: Modern Language Association of America, 1978.
Gadamer, Hans Georg. *Truth and Method*. New York: Seabury Press, 1975.
Gale Bibliography of Literature in America: A Comprehensive Inventory of Publications by and about Writers of the United States. Ed. Mathew J. Bruccoli and Richard Layman. Detroit: Gale Research Co., 1984–   .
Gaskell, Philip. *From Writer to Reader: Studies in Editorial Method*. Oxford: Clarendon Press, 1978.
———. *A New Introduction to Bibliography*. New York: Oxford Univ. Press, 1970. (See especially "Reference Bibliography," 392–413.)
Gottesman, Ronald, and Scott Bennett, eds. *Art and Error: Modern Textual Editing*. Bloomington: Indiana Univ. Press, 1970; rpt. New York: Gordian, 1976.
Gould, Warwick. "The Editor Takes Possession." *Times Literary Supplement*, 29 June 1984: 731–33.
Greg, W. W. "The Rationale of Copy-Text." *Studies in Bibliography* 3 (1950–51): 19–36.
Hardy, Thomas. *Tess of the D'Urbervilles*. Ed. Juliet Grindle and Simon Gatrell. Oxford: Clarendon Press, 1983.
Harvard University. Library. *Widener Library Shelflist*. Cambridge, Mass.: Harvard Univ. Library, 1965–   .
Hawthorne, Nathaniel. *The Scarlet Letter*. Ed. Fredson Bowers. The Centenary Edition, vol. 1. Columbus: Ohio State University Press, 1962.
Hinman, Charlton. *The Printing and Proof-Reading of the First Folio of Shakespeare*. 2 vols. Oxford: Clarendon Press, 1963.
Hooker, Richard. *The Folger Library Edition of the Works of Richard Hooker*. Gen. ed. W. Speed Hill. Cambridge, Mass.: Belknap Press, 1977–   .
———. *Of the Laws of Ecclesiastical Polity*. 2 vols. Everyman Library. London: Dent, 1907; rpt. 1922–25.
Howard-Hill, T. H. *British Bibliography and Textual Criticism: A Bibliography*. Vols. 4–5 of his *Index to British Literary Bibliography*. Oxford: Clarendon Press, 1979–80.

Index to Reviews of Bibliographical Publications. Boston: G.K. Hall, 1976– .

Jordan, Frank, ed. *The English Romantic Poets: A Review of Research and Criticism.* 4th ed. New York: Modern Language Association of America, 1985.

Joyce, James. *Ulysses.* Corrected and reset. New York; Vintage, 1961.

———. *Ulysses: A Critical and Synoptic Edition.* Ed. Hans Walter Gobler. 2 vols. New York: Garland, 1984.

Katz, Joseph. "Practical Editions: A *Proof* Seminar." *Proof* 2 (1972): 283–84.

———. "Practical Editions: Stephen Crane's *The Red Badge of Courage.*" *Proof* 2 (1972): 301–18.

Keats, John. *Complete Poems.* Ed. Jack Stillinger. Cambridge, Mass.: Belknap Press, 1982.

———. *The Poems of John Keats.* Ed. Miriam Allott. Harlow: Longman, 1970.

———. *The Poems of John Keats.* Ed. Jack Stillinger. Cambridge, Mass.: Belknap Press, 1978.

Kenney, E. J. *The Classical Text: Aspects of Editing in the Age of the Printed Book.* Berkeley: Univ. of California Press, 1974.

Langford, Gerald. *Faulkner's Revision of Sanctuary: Collation of the Unrevised Galleys and the Published Book.* Austin: Univ. of Texas Press, 1972.

Maas, Paul. *Textual Criticism.* Oxford: Clarendon Press, 1958.

Matthiessen, F. O. *American Renaissance: Art and Expression in the Age of Emerson and Whitman.* London, New York: Oxford Univ. Press, 1941.

McGann, Jerome J. *A Critique of Modern Textual Criticism.* Chicago: Univ. of Chicago Press, 1983.

Melville, Herman. *Moby-Dick; or, The Whale.* Ed. Harrison Hayford and Hershel Parker. New York: Norton, 1976.

MLA International Bibliography of Books and Articles on the Modern Languages and Literatures. New York: Modern Language Association of America, 1922– .

Modern Language Association. "The Center for Scholarly Editions: An Introductory Statement." *PMLA* 92.4 (September 1977): 583–97.

———. *Statement of Editorial Principles and Procedures: A Working Manual for Editing Nineteenth-Century American Texts.* Rev. ed. New York: Modern Language Association of America, 1972.

Myerson, Joel, ed. *The Transcendentalists: A Review of Research and Criticism.* New York: Modern Language Association of America, 1984.

New Cambridge Bibliography of English Literature. Ed. George Watson. 5 vols. Cambridge: Cambridge Univ. Press, 1969–77.

Parker, Hershel. *Flawed Texts and Verbal Icons: Literary Authority and American Fiction.* Evanston, Ill.: Northwestern Univ. Press, 1984.

———. "Practical Editions: Herman Melville's *Moby-Dick.*" *Proof* 3 (1973): 371–78.

Pasquali, Giorgio. *Storia della tradizione e critica del testo.* 2nd ed. Florence: LeMornier, 1952.

Pouncey, Lorene. "The Fallacy of the Ideal Copy." *The Library* 5th ser. 33.2 (June 1978): 108–18.

Spiller, Robert E., ed. *The Literary History of the United States*. 4th ed. 2 vols. New York: Macmillan, 1974.
Stillinger, Jack. *The Texts of Keats's Poems*. Cambridge, Mass.: Harvard Univ. Press, 1974.
Tanselle, G. Thomas. *Selected Studies in Bibliography*. Charlottesville: Univ. of Virginia Press, 1979.
Thorpe, James. *Principles of Textual Criticism*. San Marino, Calif.: Huntington Library, 1972.
Trollope, Frances. *Domestic Manners of the Americans*. Ed. Richard Mullen. New York: Oxford Univ. Press, 1984.
Williamson, Hugh. *Methods of Book Design*. 3rd ed. New Haven: Yale Univ. Press, 1983.
Wilson, Edmund. *The Fruits of the MLA*. New York: New York Review, 1968.
Wilson, F. P. *Shakespeare and the New Bibliography*. Rev. ed. by Helen Gardner. Oxford: Clarendon Press, 1970.
Year's Work in English Studies. London: John Murray for the English Association, 1921– .
Yeats, William Butler. *The Poems*. Ed. Richard J. Finneran. New York: Macmillan, 1983.

Literature and Nonprint Media Resources

Peter V. Deekle

Nonprint materials can contribute significantly to the study and appreciation of literature. The spoken word recorded in audiotape and phonodisc formats enables the student of literature to hear works read aloud. In many instances authors have recorded selections from their own writing. Recordings also capture and preserve lectures, seminars, discussions, and interviews. Photographic media, such as slides or filmstrips, provide students and researchers with visual images which may illustrate or illuminate written or spoken texts. Film and video introduce the element of motion to visual images. New products such as computer software can assist with textual analysis and offer individualized instruction opportunities.

These audio, visual, and other nonprint media resources, however, need special attention by librarians responsible for literature because the primary sources of bibliographic and evaluative information are separate from most of the routine sources covering books and periodicals. Publishers and distributors of audiovisual materials also are distinct from the book trade. Finally, technical considerations command notice. But selecting these materials draws on the same kind of thinking as does selecting books: one considers the institution's objectives, the patrons' needs, the existing holdings, and the intrinsic qualities of the material.

There is no universal formula for allocating funds to purchase nonprint materials. Some libraries use a portion of the materials budget, others do not. Some give faculty and selectors considerable latitude with regard to nonprint selection, others do not. Each library must work out its own budgetary response to meet stated collection goals with regard to nonprint materials selection.

CHARACTERISTICS OF VARIOUS NONPRINT FORMATS

Each nonprint format offers distinctive potential enhancements to a library's collections. A selector should keep format characteristics in mind when reviewing titles for additions to a collection. Literature librarians should consider how the medium contributes to the message or content. Do not think of these media as translations or substitutes for books; films of literary works may shift attention from language or character to setting or camera angles. What can a teacher or student of rhetoric gain from hearing a recording of Martin Luther King's "I Have a Dream" speech? What do students experience in watching a televised performance of Shakespeare? Does one value the documentary quality of writers reading their own works, such as a recording of Robert Frost in recital, or does one also seek professional readers—actors—who dramatize a portion of a work of literature, such as James Earl Jones reading from Richard Wright's *Native Son*? Did the series of American short stories dramatized for public television provide a new cultural or aesthetic experience which should be available to library patrons? Librarians also must consider the question of formats as mere substitutes in contemplating the needs of those who would rather listen to books on cassettes than to the radio as they drive to work or clean their houses and who enjoy such "reading."

Works of literature in a nonprint medium form one category of resource. Two others are media about literature, such as a film on Hannibal, Missouri, intended to provide background on Mark Twain, and pedagogical products intended to substitute for or augment the work of the classroom teacher, such as a filmstrip on writing the research paper. In each case the librarian will consider, often in conjunction with patrons, the purposes of the library collection and the uses of the material, weighing such values as the aural aspects of poetry or the performance aspects of Shakespeare; the value of a group experience in hearing or seeing, and the entertainment and motivational factors.

Despite their comparatively high cost in relation to other nonprint formats, films record and visually document events in a realistic manner. Conversely, films also create their effects by stylized, surreal, visionary, and other manners, providing experiences distinctive to this medium. They provide a common experience for all viewers and are ideally suited for large group use. Because it records moving images as well as sound, film proves an effective way to acquire dramatizations. While video recordings still lack the visual clarity of film productions, this format offers many advantages over film. Students can easily use video recordings individually with minimal assistance. It is also a format suitable for group viewing if a classroom is appropriately equipped with a large screen video projector or television monitors. Video recordings allow for easy stop and start as well as rewind and repeat action. Video recordings are becoming increasingly available both for rental and purchase because of the home-market demand. In addition, costs for this format continue to decrease. If there are any problems to note for video recordings in addition to visual clarity, it is that group use can be difficult unless adequate playback equipment is available. Until recently the equipment has been difficult and time-consuming to deliver and set up, but this is rapidly changing.

Slides and filmstrips reproduce graphic or pictorial information. Easily used by groups or individuals, they require less care than some media. As commercial products, they are typically much less expensive than films or video recordings. Slide and filmstrip programs often have an audio component which enhances the visuals. Typically the audio program advances the visual automatically. Many slide programs also offer the benefit of easy updating or revision.

Phonodisc recordings preserve excellent sound fidelity and are simple to use, but they are often irreparably damaged if use is frequent and playback equipment is not maintained. Although open-reel tape recordings offer greater archival stability than tape cassettes, the latter format is extremely convenient, while open-reel tapes can be irritatingly troublesome, especially for the inexperienced user. The compact disc has an exciting future in libraries because of its sound quality, durability, ease of use, and reduced storage requirements.

The videodisc records still images, motion and sound. Playback quality is usually better than that of video. But this format remains untested in most libraries.

Computer software is the latest format of interest to the literature selector. New products that enable study of literary texts at computer terminals are already available. In addition, many educational packages offer self-paced individualized instruction.

Economic and technical reasons require that nonprint acquisitions be limited to specified formats because in each instance playback equipment is required. A library which introduces significant format diversity mandates a broad range of equipment purchases, increased staff commitment to user assistance and machine maintenance, and in most cases, less user self-service. Variations within a particular nonprint

Literature and Nonprint Media Resources 147

medium, such as videorecordings, further complicate selection. For instance, a library might decide to acquire videorecordings only in VHS (one-half inch) mode. When the occasional variant format selection or rental occurs (U-matic three-quarter inch mode or Beta), perhaps equipment can be borrowed. In some cases, material can be converted to another format within the library. Libraries must, however, obtain permission to carry out such conversions.

SELECTING NONPRINT MEDIA

Whenever possible, nonprint materials selection should be addressed in library collection development statements and other policy and procedure documents. Responsibilities of those involved in selecting, procuring, bibliographically controlling and servicing nonprint materials should be clearly delineated. In a setting where the media center is distinctly separated from the library, those responsible for library collection development should build sturdy bridges to connect the library with those who develop nonprint collections.

The following factors ought to influence nonprint selection decisions. They are interdependent. What is and is not important depends on the selector and the local situation.

1. *Appropriateness of medium to content.*
    For example, a costly film or videorecording of a lecture or panel discussion may be less appropriate than an audiotape cassette.
2. *Cost.*
3. *Technical quality of audiovisual elements.*
    Users have come to expect high-quality technical standards in all media. Materials should be previewed whenever possible.
4. *Ease of use.*
    If self-service is a primary requirement, certain formats such as film should be avoided.
5. *Durability.*
    At the time of purchase, a second copy may be acquired or produced for retention and preservation at minimal extra cost. One can also pay extra for the right to receive another copy at a later date when replacement becomes necessary.
6. *Correspondence to original literary version.*
    Is a work an adaptation, a summary, a selection, an interpretation, a variation on a theme? It is not always clear from print advertising and bibliographic information what the material really is. Investigate! Excerpted works are widely available in all formats of nonbook media.

Other factors may play a role in local decision-making or selection. Among these are cases where the material:

7. *Supports more than one discipline.*
   For instance, a literature title might become highly desirable if drama faculty and students are also likely users.
8. *Supports new faculty, new courses, or new areas of instruction.*
9. *Cannot be rented or borrowed locally.*
10. *Is of lasting value and has considerable prospect for use outside the classroom by individual users.*
    Libraries supporting film studies programs or courses may want, for example, to provide the resources to allow patrons to see a movie independently and on demand, just as they can read books individually and repeatedly.

PREVIEWING

Selectors should always relate the acquisition of nonprint titles to an assessment of probable use. In many, if not most academic environments, nonprint purchases remain faculty driven. Faculty typically request materials with specific pedagogical objectives in mind. In many institutions faculty must prepare a request which records their intended use of an item. Student opinion can be valuable if a committee selects or recommends media materials. In less formal circumstances, a selector should include both faculty and students in the preview process prior to selection. Previewing responses prove excellent indicators of likely use. The purpose of preview sessions is to assess content, production quality, and overall satisfaction of proposed objectives.

It is advisable to use a standard form which covers all topics to be evaluated. A written record of responses, even if anonymous, may prove more useful than verbal remarks. The use of standard previewing forms helps the library selector to insure the uniformity of elements treated by the preview committee members. Copies of preview forms are often available from libraries having large audiovisual departments. Sample forms are also printed in such texts as James Cabeceiras' *The Multimedia Library* (2nd ed.; New York: Academic Press, 1982).

Supplying preview copies for a librarian's individual assessment is a costly service for nonprint media vendors and distributors. Increasingly, they charge a rental fee. Although previewing prior to purchase remains an important operating principle for the selector, a "good faith" policy should be pursued; that is, a sincere interest in the product should always form the foundation of a preview request. Demonstrating "good faith" in dealing with vendors represents an investment in continuing cooperative business/client relations.

Literature and Nonprint Media Resources 149

SELECTION AIDS

Commercial vendor catalogs play a significant role in nonbook materials selection because bibliographic information tends to be sporadic and difficult to locate. Two well-established audio publishers whose catalogs the literature librarian will want to peruse are Spoken Arts (Dept. R86, P.O. Box 289, New Rochelle, N.Y. 10802) and Caedmon (1995 Broadway, New York, N.Y. 10023). At the same time, both the *National Union Catalog* and the bibliographic utilities are including more nonprint materials; they are increasingly useful as selection, verification, and acquisition aids. But a publisher's catalog description or bibliographic entry alone seldom should form the basis for a purchase decision. Typically publishers' advertisements do not supply enough information to allow an informed decision.

In this context critical reviews are essential. Journals publishing nonprint media reviews of special interest to the literature selector are:

American Film: The Magazine of the Film and Television Arts. Washington: American Film Institute, 1975- . This monthly (January-February and July-August issues are combined) contains discussions and reviews of most current domestic feature-length films and video programs.

Antioch Review. Yellow Springs, Ohio: Antioch Review, Inc., 1941- . This quarterly journal occasionally publishes reviews of spoken word recordings, including poetry readings.

Booklist. Chicago: American Library Association, 1905- . Published twenty-two times per year, this review publication identifies selected new titles in a variety of nonprint media.

Choice. Middletown, Conn.: Association of College and Research Libraries/American Library Association, 1963- . Nonprint selectors should consult this monthly's annual list of "outstanding" academic publications for critically acclaimed nonprint titles. Individual issues also include reviews of nonprint media titles.

Film Library Quarterly. New York: Film Library Information Council, 1967- . This journal reviews recent educational and feature films, some of which will be appropriate for consideration by selectors in literature.

High Fidelity/Musical America. New York: ABC Leisure Magazines, Inc., 1965- . Although this monthly publication is primarily concerned with recorded music, it treats some spoken word recordings. The December issue contains a useful directory of producers and distributors.

Home Video. New York: United Business Publications, 1979- . This monthly publication is intended primarily for use by the home consumer. Its reviews of available commercial videorecordings occasionally include titles of interest to the literary selector.

Journal of American Folklore. Washington, D.C.: American Folklore Society,

1888- . The quarterly contains a "Record and Film Review" section which treats recorded poetry readings, lectures, and other spoken word productions as well as 16mm films relevant to library study.

Landers Film Reviews. Escondido, Calif.: Landers Film Reviews, 1956- . This quarterly publication includes information on and reviews of many hard to identify cinematic treatments of literary works. While the primary focus is on elementary and secondary education, the academic or special collections bibliographer may well find information of interest. Reports of film festivals and a helpful directory of producers and film distributors are also included.

Literature/Film Quarterly. Salisbury, Md.: Salisbury State College, 1973- . With an annual circulation of about 700, this publication should receive greater attention. Lengthy and pertinent film reviews focus on film treatments of literary works.

Sight and Sound: The International Film Quarterly. London: British Film Institute, 1932- . The literary selector will find many feature-length films as well as television and video programming reviewed in this publication; its coverage is international in scope. Selectors are advised to consider the possible need for converting from the European video recording standard for use in the United States.

Sightlines. New York: Educational Film Library Association, 1967- . This quarterly publication reviews major feature films.

Stereo Review. New York: Ziff-Davis, 1958- . The selector will find reviews of a variety of spoken word recordings in this monthly publication, including poetry readings and sound tracks from productions of dramatic works. The focus is primarily on recorded music.

Tech Trends: For Leaders in Education and Training. Washington, D.C.: Association for Educational Communications & Technology, 1956- . Issued eight times a year, this publication emphasizes nonprint instructional media. All formats of audiovisual materials are reviewed.

Televisions. Washington, D.C.: Washington Community Video Center, Inc., 1973- . The reviews of current videorecordings focus on educational and instructional as well as artistic values.

Victorian Poetry. Morgantown, W. Va.: West Virginia University, 1963- . The literary selector will find occasional reviews of spoken word recordings in this quarterly publication.

Virginia Quarterly Review. Charlottesville: Univ. of Virginia Press, 1925- . This quarterly frequently comments on fiction and poetry recordings.

Yale Review. New Haven, Conn.: Yale Univ. Press, 1911- . Comments on new recordings associated with literature are often included in this important quarterly.

Indexes useful for locating reviews are:

Media Review Digest. Ann Arbor, Mich.: Pierian Press, 1971- . Annually includes approximately 40,000 entries for nonbook media reviews from 150 journals. The index is organized by format types (film/video, filmstrip, audio recordings, and miscellaneous). Some reviews are abstracted. The subject index will help selectors identify literary topics.

Film Literature Index. Albany, N.Y.: Filmdex, 1973- . Quarterly, with annual cumulations, this basic index in the field includes author and subject indexing to articles and reviews from over 300 periodicals. Selectors will appreciate the indexing by performer, director, and other collaborators.

International Index to Film Periodicals. Paris: International Federation of Film Archives, 1972- . This title indexes periodicals of importance in the research and study of film. Useful director, author, and subject indexes aid the selector. Although it lacks the frequency of publication enjoyed by *Film Literature Index*, it is an important tool in the critical assessment of film.

Record and Tape Reviews Index. Metuchen, N.J.: Scarecrow, 1972- . This annual index has a special section listing reviews of spoken recordings.

The National Information Center for Educational Media (NICEM) irregularly publishes the basic trade bibliographies for nonprint materials. While price and production dates are frequently omitted, contents descriptions are included. The volumes of most importance to the literature selector are:

Index to 16mm Educational Films. Index to 35mm Educational Films. Each index provides an alphabetical guide derived from the world's largest database for educational materials in nonbook formats. Included in the entries for all films are title, series, date of production, and other technical/bibliographic elements, which are also found in other indexes in the NICEM series.

Index to Educational Video Tapes. Includes a brief technical description of each listing as well as a synopsis of contents.

Index to Educational Audio Tapes. Records all educational audiotapes in the comprehensive NICEM database. The subject arrangement is complemented by a title index.

Index to Educational Slides. Contains approximately 26,000 listings; the selector is helped, as with other NICEM indexes, by a subject index.

Index to Educational Records. Lists all educational sound recordings in the NICEM database. The subject arrangement is complemented by a title index.

Index to Producers and Distributors. Selectors who use this index will find useful (but not necessarily the most current) directory information; the bibliographic information found in other NICEM titles is entered more briefly in this index. Selectors should also consult the current annual volume of *Audiovisual Market Place* for up-to-date directory listings of producers and distributors.

The "Schwann Catalog," officially entitled *The New Schwann* since 1983, lists phonodiscs, eight-track cartridges, audiocassettes, and compact discs for all recordings distributed in the United States. While the monthly issues focus on music, the Schwann-2 supplements (semiannual) identify available spoken word recordings. Lists stay current and do not cumulate. This tool is the equivalent of *Books in Print* for recordings in their various formats. There are no evaluations included. Some other basic bibliographical tools of interest to the literature specialist are:

On Cassette: A Comprehensive Bibliography of Spoken Work Audio Cassettes. New York: Bowker, 1985. This reference work lists 11,500 titles and contains six in dexes: title, author, reader/performer, subject, producer/ distribution, and producer-distributor/title. Most entries are briefly annotated.

Educational Film Locator. 2nd ed. New York: Bowker, 1980. This publication is a union list of over 40,000 films available from a 50-member consortium. Useful annotations based on screenings and critical reviews aid the selector in assessing the merit and appropriateness of individual films.

Feature Films on 8mm, l6mm, and Videotape. 7th ed. New York: Bowker, 1982. The seventh edition is a directory of feature films available for lease, rental, or sale in the United States and Canada. The literary selector will want to consult the bibliography of film reference sources. Helpful information concerning a film's history (release date, special technical data) is included in each entry.

North American Film and Video Directory: A Guide to Media Collections and Services. New York: Bowker, 1976. This is an index to institutions and nonprofit agencies which provide nonbook services. Information about the types of media collected and distributed by these institutions is provided. Unusual special collections found in museum or archival libraries are identified.

Directory of Spoken-Word Audio Cassettes. 3rd. ed. Guilford Conn.: J. Norton, 1983. Gerald McKee edited this edition of the directory which first appeared in 1972. Audio cassettes in all subjects are included.

Video Source Book. 7th ed. Syosset, N.Y.: National Video Clearinghouse, 1985. This latest edition includes over 30,000 entries in videotape or videodisc format, emphasizing instructional or general interest recordings. There are, however, also entries for programs in the fine arts and entertainment fields. A subject and main category index helps the selector who lacks title or production credits information.

New reference books and selection aids for nonprint materials appear regularly. Most tend to be published by small publishing houses and many have not been produced according to editorial standards of mainstay reference book publishers. As is the case with nonprint materials, nonprint reference books should be examined before purchase whenever possible.

Special film reference books are particularly valuable for the study of literature and film as well as for collection development. Notable examples are:

McCarty, Clifford. *Published Screenplays: A Checklist.* Kent, Ohio: Kent State Univ. Press, 1971. While dated, this title still proves useful for verification and collection development.

Langman, Larry. *A Guide to American Screenwriters: The Sound Era, 1929-1982.* New York: Garland, 1984. Published in two volumes, this title attempts to list all feature films under author. Volume two is a title index. While date of screenplay is given, no other publication details are supplied.

Enser, A. G. S. *Filmed Books and Plays 1928-1974.* Aldershot: Gower, 1982. This basic tool is supplemented by a volume which covers 1975-81. Film title and author/original title listings are supplied. No publication details on screenplays supplied.

Emmens, Carol A. *Short Stories on Film.* Littleton, Colo.: Libraries Unlimited, 1978. This tool, like Enser above, links original literary work with subsequent film. Brief synopses are supplied as are film title and short story title indexes. The entries are listed under author.

Welch, Jeffrey Egan. *Literature and Film: An Annotated Bibliography. 1909-1977.* New York: Garland, 1981. In his preface, Egan states his intention to list and annotate "all important books and articles published in North America and Great Britain having to do with the special relationship between films and works of literature" (p. ix). Items in the bibliography are listed chronologically; the volume is well indexed.

The basic guide to research on computer applications in literary analysis is John Abercrombie's monograph *Computer Programs for Literary Analysis* (Philadelphia: Univ. of Pennsylvania Press, 1984). Many of the programs discussed in Abercrombie's book are available on diskette. The quarterly journal *Computers and the Humanities* helps the selector stay informed of new literary research involving computer applications.

ORDERING NONPRINT MATERIALS

The nonprint selector in preparing an order needs to provide as much information as possible. This information, including a catalog reference number when available, will help the vendor supply the proper title in the desired format. Selectors or other acquisitions staff must minimally furnish the complete title, the designated format, and particular version for a nonprint order. This information should also be retained in the order file for reference on receipt of the product—to verify the accuracy of the shipment and to expedite the cataloging and processing of the piece. Nonprint materials will often be needed by users soon after previewing. Delays in acquisition and processing due to incomplete or inaccurate information are a continual concern. They should be avoided.

Often negotiations must occur between library and vendor if special use conditions, format conversions, or duplication requirements are identified by the selector for a given nonprint title. A librarian may have to request permission and specify conditions under which an original format (16mm film, for example) can be converted to another format (videocassette). It is always important to document such approved format conversions in a central and permanent acquisitions file. It is also essential to have an approved procedure and policy for nonprint use, particularly with regard to copyright. Complete records and licensing agreements between the library and any commercial or noncommercial source of materials must always be carefully maintained.

CATALOGING, STORING, AND USING NONPRINT MATERIALS

The nonprint selector often must work closely with the cataloger of library materials. Although *AACR2* standards for cataloging nonprint media are quite detailed, there are numerous elements of the bibliographic record which the selector may prescribe. In the case of nonprint materials associated with literary works, the description of the original literary work must be linked to the nonprint product derived from or related to that work. Furthermore, the catalog description of a given nonprint title should identify the original format as well as that of the derived conversion, if the library has acquired the rights to a converted format of the original. The patron should know that an original exists in another format.

It is important to provide bibliographic access to the nonprint resources at the site of use and loan, if this is separated from the library. It is now common to provide access through the central catalog facility. Integrated access to both print and nonprint holdings via a central catalog serves both users and all materials to full advantage. Such a commitment does, however, have an impact on cataloging assignments and workflow.

A variety of shelving options can be considered depending on physical space available, user and service objectives, security concerns, and other constraints. Typically, nonprint materials can be more effectively stored when separated from print media and shelved by standardized sequential numbering systems rather than subject-oriented classification.

It is necessary for most institutions to provide for the on-site use of nonprint materials. Playback equipment should be kept in good working condition. Faulty equipment means damaged materials and frustrated users. Both individual and group use should be feasible in a media center setting.

Staffing is a major issue with regard to equipment delivery and maintenance. Unlike most books and periodicals, nonprint materials need a machine or device employed before they can be used. And to reiterate:

machines must be maintained. In addition, special user needs for machine assistance often come into play for media center personnel.

While nonprint materials can greatly enhance a library's literature collections, they also demand departure from selection, acquisitions, processing, and servicing mechanisms and other routines libraries traditionally use. A library commitment to nonprint materials cannot be fully realized unless those factors which influence their selection and use are responsibly and creatively addressed.

Building Literary Reference Collections

Scott Stebelman

Selecting for the reference collection is often a key responsibility for the English and American literature bibliographer. The tools he or she chooses affect the quality of research at the institution—if the bibliographer chooses well, patrons will be able to locate research materials expeditiously; if he or she chooses haphazardly, these same materials may never be identified, or if so, inefficiently. At many libraries, the kinds of resources chosen for the reference collection are delimited by general collection development policy statements. Such policies address categories of materials—e.g., encyclopedias, indexes, dictionaries—and the role of the selector is to insure that materials published in these categories are acquired. If a collection statement does not exist, the librarian may work backwards and infer taxonomies from what already exists in the collection; or, concerned that certain materials may never systematically have been acquired in that library, the selector may review general reference texts to see what other librarians view as essential.[1]

Although preexisting collection statements are useful in identifying categories of important materials, they cannot—in and of themselves—be used to select individual titles. Such statements need to be supplemented by a clear understanding of how students and faculty conduct literary research, and by observing, over a period of months or years, how patrons actually use a collection. To provide a systematic framework for selection decisions, this chapter will discuss briefly the nature of literary research, then address three questions germane to the reference selector: What factors determine the inclusion of new titles in the reference collection? What categories of materials should be collected? Which resources are necessary to identify retrospective and current reference tools?

CHARACTERISTICS OF LITERARY RESEARCH

In an article analyzing the different manners in which scholars and librarians define research, Stephen Stoan makes the important point that scholars are less dependent upon bibliographic access tools than librarians realize. Through serendipity, the amassing of reprint files, contact with colleagues working in the same area, and the scanning of footnotes, scholars identify literature most germane to their subject. The latter method—the scanning of footnotes—is often the most important, for the footnotes exist in symbiotic relationship to the text: just as they frame the intellectual argument of the text, providing authority for assertions made therein, so the text acts as a gloss, or an annotation, for the footnotes, indicating their potential usefuless to scholars engaged in similar research. This leads Stoan to conclude "that to an extraordinary degree the primary literature [books/journal articles] indexes itself, and does so with greater comprehensiveness, better analytics, and greater precision than does the secondary literature [indexes/abstracts]" (p. 109). Although Stoan's analysis pertains primarily to social science research, similar statements have been made by those characterizing humanities research (Burchard, Stieg). This is not to say that the teaching faculty are oblivious to reference tools; it does explain, however, why so few of them can be found near the *MLA International Bibliography of Books and Articles on the Modern Languages and Literature (MLAIB)* or other serial bibliographies. National bibliographies, manuscript finding aids, and library catalogs often have greater importance to them, helping to verify incomplete citations or determine which libraries they must visit to study original documents.[2]

But if faculty are presumed to have mastered the research methods of their disciplines, this is certainly not the case with graduate students who, in a sense, are apprentice scholars. In a survey of 111 schools offering the Ph.D. in English and American literature, Mary George and Mary Ann O'Donnell found that 55 percent of the schools provided a course on methods of literary research or in the use of the library. The kinds of skills students acquire in these courses vary, but often they are different from what librarians might expect. For example, in addition to learning about the *Dictionary of National Biography (DNB), The New Cambridge Bibliography of English Literature (NCBEL)* and other reference tools, the preponderance of time may be devoted to analytical and descriptive bibliography. Part of the students' responsibility might be to edit a series of poems or letters, in the process justifying why one variant reading was chosen over another; or they might have to determine the accuracy of statements attributed to a writer. Commenting on the scholarly techniques graduate students must master, Harrison Meserole (who teaches the research methods course at Pennsylvania State University) says: "The point is, of course, that not only must one know what he is about in consulting reference sources, but also he must *verify* his sources" (p. 58). Although an undergraduate may use the biographical information found in the *DNB* to better understand his writer, a graduate student will be expected to validate its accuracy. Ironically, the graduate student becomes an expert on a subject by weaning himself from other experts—he knows a statement to be true, or false, because he has examined the primary documents upon which it is based.

The group that probably benefits the most from basic reference tools is the undergraduate student. Just as graduate students are expected to become authorities by the time they finish their dissertations, undergraduates rarely need to go beyond authorities in determining the facts surrounding an issue. These authorities may be their instructors or the books placed on reserve; on occasion they are the names cited in bibliographies. In undergraduate English courses, if the instructor assigns a library exercise, it is typically either a research paper on a contemporary issue, or it is an essay on some literary work that requires the student to become familiar with the writer's life and variant interpretations of the work under consideration. The instructor' primary objective is "to get the student into the library," to teach him basic skills in using the collection and ferreting out information. The most common tools recommended to the student are the *MLAIB* for secondary criticism, or a biographical encyclopedia to disclose the basic facts of a writer's life. Where graduate seminar papers or dissertations are expected to include extensive literature reviews, undergraduate papers are not; in many cases, student bibliographies of ten citations or less are deemed acceptable. To meet these more modest needs, selectors should consider purchasing retrospective bibliographies that group citations under a single work: they are more simply organized and hence easier to use than serial bibliographies, and they provide enough citations to meet the research needs of most undergraduates.

FACTORS DETERMINING THE INCLUSION OF NEW TITLES

If the reference department has a collection development policy statement, the factors considered below may already have been delineated and the reader might skip to the next section. However, if they have not, then questions that need to be asked when evaluating a title for inclusion in the reference collection are:

1. Is the tool so popular that, for the sake of accessibility, it should be housed in the reference collection? The *MLAIB* is exemplary, consulted probably more than any other literary reference work. Though heavily used, it is also bibliographically complex, at times requiring the interpretive assistance of reference staff—a secondary concern that itself should be factored into the location of new titles. Popularity ought to be gauged by staff knowledge as well as patron interest. For example, although few students may be aware of *Author Biographies Master Index* or Havlice's *Index to Literary Biography*, many reference librarians consult them frequently to determine where biographical essays may be found. The first question that must be asked of any candidate for the reference collection is: how much use will it get? For a list of some of the more popular sources that should form, at a very minimum, the basis of a literary reference collection, *see* Nancy L. Baker's *A Research Guide for Undergraduate Students: English and American Literature*.
2. Is the tool so important that, without its inclusion, research will be seriously impaired? Watt's *Bibliotheca Britannica* is not a popular book, but it is one of the few that provides subject access to Renaissance literature. Establishing the authorship of a pseudonymous work is also highly specialized, but the standard tool in that area is Horden's *Dictionary of Anonymous and Pseudonymous Literature*, and it too belongs in the collection. Many reference works exist not to identify materials on a given subject but to verify bibliographic citations, or to list additional editions of a work. The *National Union Catalog* and the British Museum's *General Catalogue* are the premier tools in this area; more limited chronologically and geographically but still central are the short-title catalogs of English books for the years 1475–1700, edited by Pollard and Redgrave, and Wing. Verification tools are also critical for the selector, who may need to determine whether a book offered for sale is a duplicate of one already held by the library.

Constituting another kind of important research source are guides to large microform collections for which libraries have not entered analytics into their catalogs. In an attempt to provide some access to such collections, these guides, typically supplied by the micropublishers, are placed in the reference collection. They indicate which titles the library owns, as well as the reel number works can be found on. As cumulative guidebooks are published, the earlier volumes are discarded or transferred to the general collection.

3. Is the tool one that the bibliographer often uses in library instruction presentations? For example, if every year the English specialist offers a workshop on early American literature, he may want students to be aware of Patricia Parker's *Early American Fiction*, Walter J. Meserve's *American Drama to 1900*, and other bibliographies of the period. One way of capitalizing on the presentation is to insure that most works cited in the workshop are going to be available in the reference collection. This may create conflict with whoever has overall management responsibility for the reference collection, since these titles can have a limited audience. An alternative way of guaranteeing access is to place the works on reserve, but the advantage of having them in the reference collection is to link them with other literary tools and underscore the research utility of the entire collection.

CATEGORIES OF MATERIALS TO BUY

Although some titles may not be easily classified, the majority of literary reference works may be assigned to the following categories:

1. *Anonymous and Pseudonymous Literature.* Until the middle of the nineteenth century, much literature was written by authors who remained unidentified. This creates special problems for scholars trying to establish the complete oeuvre of a particular writer; it also handicaps understanding of how a writer's literary or political values shifted over time. Works which disclose the authorship of anonymous or pseudonymous works are thus useful. Of first importance is John Horden's revision of Halkett and Laing's long standard *Dictionary of Anonymous and Pseudonymous English Literature*; the revision will add 80,000 entries to those from the original publication, and will provide extensive evidence for attribution. To date, only the first volume has been published, but subscriptions should be entered for the entire set.

   Horden's revisions are useful to patrons wanting to know who wrote a specific work. For those who are trying to identify the different pen names of an author, works such as the following are more apposite: Harold Sharp's *Handbook of Pseudonyms and Personal Nicknames*, Frank Atkinson's *Dictionary of Literary Pseudonyms: A Selection of Popular Modern Writers in English*, and Helen Force's ready reference tool, *Who Is Who*.

2. *Archival and Manuscript Finding Aids.* These are critical tools for graduate students and faculty seeking access to primary documents. Aside from general tools that belong in the reference collection, such as Robert Downs' *British and Irish Library Resources*, or *The National Union Catalog of Manuscript Collections*, bibliographers should locate guides to literary manuscripts here as well. This is easier to do than many other reference works, since there are fewer of them, among which are the *Index of English Literary Manuscripts* and Joanne Akeroyd's *Where Are Their Papers?* Those that are subject or genre specific, like Gisela Guddat-Figge's *Catalogue of Manuscripts Containing Middle English Romances* or record the holdings of a single library, such as the *Catalogue of Manuscripts in the Houghton Library, Harvard University*, are more often housed in the stacks.
3. *Author Bibliographies.* Bibliographies devoted to single authors can be divided into two groups: primary and secondary. Primary tools list books, essays, etc. published by writers, secondary ones record works written about them. Consulting these bibliographies can often be a highly efficient research strategy for students: in many cases, they allow the undergraduate to circumvent the *MLAIB*, and they provide a hefty corpus on which the graduate student may build. Because of the abundance of author bibliographies, a key decision that must be made is which of them warrant inclusion in the reference collection, and which should be located in the stacks. Knowing those authors most heavily weighted in the English Department's curriculum can guide decisions. Probably there will be courses devoted exclusively to Shakespeare, and perhaps to Chaucer and Milton. In American literature, Emerson, Melville, Twain, and Faulkner are among the primary writers. Whatever author bibliographies are not included in the reference collection can be assigned a noncirculation status in the stacks, to insure their on-going availability for research.
4. *Biographical Encyclopedias.* Almost as abundant as author bibliographies are biographical encyclopedias, whose scope can embrace the world (*Cassell's Encyclopaedia of World Literature*) or be limited to a single city (Michael True's *Worcester Poets*). It is presumed that the reference collection will already have the standard and most comprehensive of these tools—the *DNB* and the *Dictionary of American Biography*. To identify those that are specific to literature, the selector can consult works cited in the *Author Biographies Master Index* and Havlice's *Index to Literary Biography*: they direct the student to biographical tools that con-

tain essays on specific writers. Deciding which of those tools to house in the reference collection should be based on several factors:
  a. What other disciplines will also be served by their inclusion? *Contemporary Authors*, for example, is a favorite source because it includes not just literary figures but those writing in the areas of political science, history, sociology, etc.
  b. What tools are necessary to support regional research? A library located in Texas would want to include Florence Barns' *Texas Writers of Today*, whereas a library in the Midwest might not even purchase it for the general collection.
  c. Which tools are essential for supporting course content? If children's literature is taught in the English Department, the reference collection should have *Something about the Author*, Ann Commire's *Yesterday's Authors of Books for Children*, Norah Smaridge's *Famous Author-Illustrators for Young People*, and perhaps several other works in this area.
  d. Which tools provide bibliographies appended to their essays? Like literary handbooks, biographical encyclopedias have so many entries that they must necessarily be brief; students need to know sources for additional information, should their papers be more ambitious than book reports. Tools such as the *Dictionary of Literary Biography* are excellent in this regard, particularly for minor writers.
5. *Concordances.* Concordances are useful to scholars because they indicate not only how often a word appears in a corpus (and thus by inference its importance), but also the contexts. Like author bibliographies, concordances have proliferated in the last two decades and location decisions can be treated in a similar manner: if devoted to major writers, such as Chaucer, Shakespeare, and Milton, these tools belong in the reference collection, along with concordances of authors who have entire courses given to them in the English Department curriculum.
6. *Dictionaries.* In addition to English-language dictionaries, academic reference collections should also contain historical dictionaries, slang dictionaries, etymologies, and usage dictionaries. Aside from those listed in Sheehy and Walford, bibliographers ought to review the chapter on dictionaries in Katz's *Introduction to Reference Work*. Although intended for reference librarians selecting for public libraries, the advice is generally sound, and the discussion of prescriptive versus descriptive dictionaries is

important, especially since many educators expect prescriptive usage in student papers. Important supplements to Katz are Kenneth Kister's *Dictionary Buying Guide*, Robert Lewis Collison's *Dictionaries of English and Foreign Languages*, Sidney I. Landau's, *Dictionaries: The Art and Craft of Lexicography*, and Yakov Malkiel's *Etymological Dictionaries: A Tentative Typology*; these works either provide useful comparative data about dictionaries, or they discuss the criteria that must be decided in defining the boundaries of any national vocabulary. The obvious reasons for buying general dictionaries are to establish the meanings of specific words and to verify their spellings. Although Katz is critical of dictionaries having special features, such as the kind of factual information contained in almanacs, this supplemental information can be useful at a busy reference desk. For example, *Funk & Wagnalls New Standard Dictionary of the English Language* has a section entitled, "Glossary of Foreign Words, Phrases, Etc. Current in English Literature and Law," and *Webster's New Collegiate Dictionary* has one that phonetically transcribes geographical names. The former will be useful to law students and graduate English students; the latter, to undergraduates preparing oral reports.

7. *Grammar/Style/Term Paper Manuals.* Students frequently ask, "Does the library have any guides on how to write a term paper?" There is a plethora of such works; in fact, most of them are used as texts in composition courses. Because there are so many, libraries can refer students to the public catalog, which will ultimately lead them to the general collection; or they can keep a few standard titles (such as the *Prentice-Hall Handbook for Writers*) in the reference collection. Additional tools that assist students in writing papers are word usage books and style manuals. Fowler's *Dictionary of Modern English Usage* is the standard tool for usage questions; Gibaldi and Achert's *MLA Handbook* is the manual required by most literary journals (including *PMLA*, the official organ of the Modern Language Association of America) and is therefore the style manual of choice for most English professors. This trend appears to be changing, as more publishers recommend the *Chicago Manual of Style*, and instructors realize that students may very well be taught to use one style manual in an English class, only to be told to use another when taking classes in another department.

8. *Indexes to Anthologies and Reprint Collections.* When specific plays,

poems, or short stories are assigned to students, it soon becomes apparent that the library's few editions of a writer's work are insufficient to satisfy even a class of twenty students. This is when indexes to anthologies or reprint collections can be a godsend. The most famous of these are *Play Index, Ottemiller's Index to Plays in Collections, Granger's Index to Poetry,* and *Short Story Index.* The Chicorel Library Publishing Corporation has also published indexes for each of these genres, but they are less useful because they are not updated periodically. Another tool that is often not used to full advantage is *Essay and General Literature Index*; librarians usually consult it for essays about a person, not by them. But the latter feature can exhume popular essays that are hidden in general subject collections.

9. *Indexes to Dissertations.* Although *MLAIB* lists dissertations, it is an easy temptation to think its coverage is inclusive (after all, *MLAIB* seems to be comprehensive in its record of other publications). However, such is not the case, since *MLAIB* treats only dissertations which appear in *Dissertation Abstracts International (DAI).* A thorough investigation will require the scholar to consult several additional tools. The first of these is *Comprehensive Dissertation Index (CDI)*, searchable either online or in print. *CDI* lists North American dissertations treated by *DAI* as well as those which are not (e.g., the University of Chicago); it also records some foreign dissertations.

Because *CDI* is a key word in title index (though from 1980 to the present, users can search the abstracts as well as titles in the online database), it does not index the dissertations themselves; consequently, a dissertation can discuss a specific subject but if synonymous terms or subsets of it are not listed, relevant titles will not be retrieved. This is where indexed bibliographies can be quite useful. Among them are McNamee's *Dissertations in English and American Literature* (which also cites German dissertations), Altick and Matthews' *Guide to Doctoral Dissertations in Victorian Literature 1886-1958* (which includes French, German, and British dissertations), and Woodress' *Dissertations in American Literature 1891-1966* (which covers German, French, British, and some Commonwealth countries). Bibliographic control of foreign dissertations is still spotty, although *DAI* is trying to enhance coverage through Part C of its bibliography.[3]

10. *Literary Gazetteers.* Literary gazetteers are useful to scholars tracing the habitats of their authors, or for travelers visiting other countries and wanting to locate the key literary spots. In an ex-

cellent review article, Linda Keir Hinrichs evaluates the strengths and weaknesses of six different gazetteers, from Bidwell's *The Places of English Literature* (1924) to *The Oxford Illustrated Literary Guide to Great Britain and Ireland* (1981). Scholars usually approach gazetteers for three reasons: to determine all the places where an author lived, to ascertain which literary figures lived in a particular place, or to learn the background of a geographical allusion. Reference collections should include gazetteers that address these different needs. Two or three are usually sufficient; the remainder can be shelved in the general collection.

11. *Literary Handbooks*. These provide definitions of rhetorical, prosodic, critical, and compositional terms, and brief essays on literary periods, movements, and writers. The ideal handbook has three characteristics: its essays will be lengthy enough to provide a sufficient overview for the student; it will have bibliographies appended to the essays, enabling students to research a term more fully; and it will represent both old and new schools of literary criticism. Because no single handbook satisfies all these criteria, reference collections usually house several of them. At the very least, the handbooks indexed in Urdang's *Literary, Rhetorical, and Linguistics Terms Index* should be included, to eliminate the guesswork about which will index a specific term. Thomas Clayton's critical survey of literary handbooks also offers useful advice.

12. *Literary Research Guides*. These tools are the *sine qua non* of graduate study. They indicate which reference tools will satisfy a particular need, be it manuscript locations, biographical information, or secondary bibliographies. It is almost impossible to have enough of them in the reference collection, if not for the patron then at least for the literary bibliographer, who has to be familiar with a variety of tools to be an effective research consultant. A favorite among English instructors is Altick and Wright's *Selective Bibliography for the Study of English and American Literature*. It groups citations according to format (e.g., dictionaries, manuscripts) and country, and has a "Glossary of Useful Terms" that defines textual or bookseller terminology useful when selecting out-of-print materials. Despite the volume's popularity, it rarely annotates entries and is particularly weak on Commonwealth literature. Schweik and Riesner's *Reference Sources in English and American Literature* possesses three strengths other guides lack: it is well annotated, cites interdisciplinary tools important to literary scholarship, and provides chronological charts for the

national bibliographies of England and America (an especially useful aid for bibliographers teaching methods of scholarship courses, or providing workshops to graduate students). Particularly good for its coverage of Commonwealth literature, little magazines, and children's literature—and excellent as a selection tool—is Margaret Patterson's *Literary Research Guide*; its annotations are extensive, and as a guide to research it can be used by both undergraduate and graduate students. As James Rettig's review essay observes, some guides are actually bibliographies pointing students to the best bibliographies, editions, etc. Bateson's *Guide to English and American Literature*, Spiller's *Literary History of the United States*, Leary's *American Literature: A Study and Research Guide*, and Fenster's *Guide to American Literature*, fall into that category. Because no individual research guide will answer all questions, bibliographers should acquire new ones as they are published. Checking them against one's own knowledge of the field almost always reveals several new titles that can be added to one's repertoire of research tools.

13. *Microform Guides*. Usually only the oldest and most heavily funded American research libraries have extensive pre-nineteenth-century holdings. Within the last few decades smaller and newer libraries have been able to replicate these holdings, and thus enhance the research capabilities of their institutions, by buying large microform sets. Suzanne Dodson's *Microform Research Collections* is an excellent guide to these collections. Although it includes a subject index, readers should scan the entire contents to identify relevant cross-disciplinary titles. Guides to individual collections have also been published. Some are first-rate, such as the *American Culture Series*, while others are organized ineffectively. Though the quality of such access tools varies, the contents of these collections are so important to research that libraries supporting graduate programs must acquire the guides.

Whether all of them belong in the reference collection is, however, another question. Guides to large collections, such as *Early English Books*, most certainly do. Since the library often does not analyze the thousands of titles within these collections, reel guides (or annotated source bibliographies) frequently provide the only access available to users, and for that reason alone most belong in the reference collection.[4] Those that offer access to single author microform projects are usually readily available through the public catalog, and therefore can be shelved in the general collection.

14. *National Bibliographies.* Critical to literary research, national bibliographies seek to identify all works published during a specified period, and thus can serve as author bibliographies (for monographic titles), typically supplying information sufficient to distinguish one edition of a work from another. National bibliographies are easier to monitor than other reference tools, since they are fewer and better established. Many have already been published, such as Pollard and Redgrave's *Short-Title Catalogue*, and Evans' *American Bibliography*. In these instances, the major chore for the bibliographer is to insure that revised editions are acquired and to establish standing orders for supplemental volumes that are published serially. Incidentally, the increased storage of microforms in the reference collection has been in part prompted by the publication in this format of national bibliographies like the *National Union Catalog*, the British Museum's *General Catalogue*, and *The Eighteenth-Century*; the provision of microfiche readers for patrons is becoming a concomitant necessity.

Though national bibliographies covering several decades or centuries are essential to the reference collection, there are numerous bibliographies, many of them covering but a few years, which can be relegated to the stacks: only the most tenacious scholar will consult them. For a handy list of these tools, Schweik and Riesner should be consulted.

15. *Plot Summaries.* Reference librarians often abhor plot summaries, suspecting students rely on them exclusively, instead of reading the original work. Regardless of suspicions, many students and faculty find these works useful in refreshing faded memories of texts. Magill's *Masterplots* will probably already be in the collection; the supplementary *Magill's Literary Annual* should be placed on standing order. Also valuable is his *Survey of Contemporary Literature*, which is more period specific. When summaries are not found in these tools, reference staff can consult Kolar's *Plot Summary Index*, which will refer patrons to the correct tool.

16. *Quotation and Proverb Books.* Old war horses, such as Bartlett's *Famous Quotations* and Stevenson's *Home Book of Quotations*, will presumably already be in the reference collection. The relative merits of such standard sources are examined in Elaine McPheron's review essay. Unfortunately, these general tools rarely are successful in tracing down literary quotations, primarily because the quotations sought by scholars are often unmemo-

rable. For example, if a patron wanted to know which of Keats' poems began "Thou still unravish'd bride of quietness," most bibliographers would recognize its origin in "Ode on a Grecian Urn." More likely, however, is the question, "In which of Keats' poems do the lines 'It seemed an emerald in the silver sheen/Of the bright waters' appear?" Quotation books will not provide an answer, but a concordance (possibly shelved in the general collection) to his poetry will. Even more difficult is trying to find quotations in works for which there is no index or concordance. Someone doing biographical research on Keats' life may want to know the source of the statement: "My love for my Brothers from the early loss of our parents and for earlier Misfortunes has grown into an affection 'passing the love of women.'" In this case, the patron will have to comb his letters until the passage is found. Locating references of known authors is difficult enough, but a common problem is to be presented with a quotation and have to discover its author. For example, who said "Keats was a victim of personal abuse and the want of power to bear it?" Again, a quotation book will not disclose the answer; in this case, it can be found by consulting Moulton's *Library of Literary Criticism*. The important point is that more often than not patrons will have to go beyond quotation books and dig for their answers in primary documents housed in the general collection.

17. *Retrospective Bibliographies.* Retrospective bibliographies assemble, within a specified chronological period, the citations on a particular subject, genre, or author. Reference collections routinely include the *New Cambridge Bibliography of English Literature* and *Literary History of the United States*, primarily for the graduate students; even less general works, such as Jordan's *The English Romantic Poets* or Stanton's *Bibliography of Modern British Novelists*, should also be considered for the collection. In fact, any tool that represents a major literary period, genre, or methodology is appropriate to the reference collections of research libraries. Smaller academic libraries, if for no other reason than space, may restrict more severely the bibliographies added to reference.

Retrospective bibliographies are frequently the first place to send undergraduate students needing research materials. *Magill's Bibliography of Literary Criticism* and Pownall's *Articles on Twentieth Century Literature* often will satisfy their needs: these tools bring together under writers' names numerous citations, which are then conveniently grouped by individual works. Supplemental, more specialized tools are Kuntz's *Poetry Explication*, Walker's and Weixlmann's bibliographies for the short story, and Eddleman's for American drama. Salem Press, perhaps buoyed by the success of *Magill's Bibliography of Literary Criticism*, is producing biobibliographies at an alarming rate. Many academic libraries are purchasing them indiscriminately, but the value to undergraduates of such sets as Magill's *Survey of Modern Fantasy Literature* and *Survey of Science Fiction Literature* is not always apparent. The standardized format for this "Survey" series includes an author's principal works and collections, other literary forms, achievements, biographical analysis, principal publications other than the genre covered, and a bibliography. For major figures the bibliograpies are inadequate; for minor writers they include citations not readily found in other tools. In addition to the information about minor writers, perhaps their most useful feature is the genre essays. For example, Magill's *Critical Survey of Short Fiction* features excellent introductory essays on the popular novel, the picaresque novel, and the historical novel. Some of these subgenres are discussed in literary handbooks, but tersely in comparison to these Magill products. It is unfortunate, however, that no bibliographies append these essays, as they do with those treating individual authors.

Gale is another publisher whose retrospective bibliographies are uneven. Some—such as Lindfors' *Black African Literature in English*—are excellent regional guides; others, such as Penninger's *English Drama to 1600 (excluding Shakespeare)*, add little that is not easily found in other sources. Comparison of this latter work with its Goldentree counterpart, Ribner and Huffman's *Tudor and Stuart Drama*, yields several differences: although published within two years of each other, the Goldentree volume lists 261 secondary studies of Marlowe's work, while the Gale bibliography lists only 69. The latter does, however, include concordances, and references are briefly annotated, but it certainly lacks the organizational simplicity of *Magill's Bibliography of Literary Criticism*, and its selectivity makes it an inappropriate tool for graduate students or faculty members.

Gale is also publishing specialized bibliographies that excerpt criticism of writers from various literary periods. Modeled somewhat on Moulton's *Library of Literary Criticism*, these works are useful for readers attempting to refamiliarize themselves with the history of critical response. While experienced scholars will use these sources to direct them to the cited works, undergraduate students may never go beyond the excerpt. This is pedagogically questionable, because it discourages learning how to find materials in the library, a skill that is transferable to other research projects. Such misuse also makes the student dependent on one woefully fragmented tool for his view of the author. Bibliographers must determine, for the graduate student, whether a new tool supplies citations that have been heretofore uncollected as well as whether the citations reflect an exhaustive review of the literature; for the undergraduate, the most important consideration is how easy the tool is to use.

18. *Serial Indexes and Abstracts for Literary Studies.* Unlike retrospective bibliographies, serial bibliographies are published indefinitely and at specified intervals. Because of their popularity, every academic library should include the *Humanities Index (HI)* and *MLAIB* in its reference collection. With its simple alphabetic organization, *HI* is the best serial bibliography for undergraduates; *MLAIB*, with its comprehensiveness, is necessary for graduate and faculty research. Less exhaustive but indexing journals not contained in *MLAIB* is *Annual Bibliography of English Language and Literature*; it also has the distinct advantage of listing book reviews, a feature especially important for titles published before 1960, the year *Index to Book Reviews in the Humanities* began publication. (Also valuable in this regard is the *Combined Retrospective Index to Book Reviews in Humanities Journals, 1802–1974.*) A final major serial tool, in spite of its complex format, is *Arts and Humanities Citation Index*. Indispensable for scholars, its citation indexing and key-word-in-title access are unique features among literary bibliographies.

SELECTION TOOLS

Having discussed some strategies for building reference collections and the categories of materials that belong in them, we can now turn to those tools that will identify new reference books to be considered for acquisition. Essentially bibliographies, they can be divided into retrospective and serial classes.

RETROSPECTIVE SOURCES FOR REFERENCE SELECTION

Sheehy's *Guide to Reference Books* ought to be closely checked and, because of the increasing importance of interdisciplinary scholarship, not only the sections germane to literature. This project could be undertaken within the reference department with a list of all titles not held sent to the appropriate subject specialist. A tool complementary to

Sheehy is Walford's *Guide to Reference Materials*; it provides a more extensive survey of British publications, with reviews occasionally noted.

Literary handbooks, beyond their importance for graduate and advanced undergraduate students, are also valuable as selection tools, identifying works that expedite research and consequently belong in the reference collection. Their scope ranges from newspaper indexes and manuscript finding aids to universal bibliographies and national bibliographies. In many ways these handbooks serve as core bibliographies for literary research.

More reference oriented than these handbooks are Rogers' *The Humanities* and Stevens' *Reference Books in the Social Sciences and Humanities*. Not restricted to literature, they include works in other key disciplines (e.g., philosophy and theater) that all academic reference collections should contain. Rogers' introduction also provides an excellent, if brief, overview of bibliographic control in the humanities.

Reference collections at Harvard and the Library of Congress are the largest in America, but even smaller libraries can usefully consult Gardner's *Library of Congress Main Reading Room Reference Collection, Subject Catalog* and Harvard University's *Widener Library Shelflist*, volume 33 of which is *Reference Collections Shelved in the Reading Room and Acquisitions Department*. But both are so extensive that they contain many titles better located in the general collection. In many ways the Widener volume is easier to use, because its shelflist organization allows for broad subject groupings. Gardner's list, on the other hand, arranges titles according to Library of Congress Subject Headings, the reader needing to guess the appropriate heading to retrieve an item.

SERIAL SOURCES FOR REFERENCE SELECTION

Academic libraries, especially those that have limited or no approval plans, need to check the monthly issues of *Choice* for new titles. Its "Reference" section offers brief reviews of general as well as author and subject bibliographies that usually provide concrete recommendations on whether to purchase or avoid a title.

More inclusive than *Choice* is the *Weekly Record*. Most references are from Library of Congress records, with additional ones supplied by publishers. Monthly and annual cumulations group citations into broad Dewey categories, with a subject index appended for more precise access. By regularly scanning the *Weekly Record*, small press titles and works from other exotic publishers not reviewed by *Choice* can be identified. For librarians attempting to build research or comprehensive collections, this tool is essential. Also useful in this context are the *British National Bibliography, Canadiana*, the *Australian National Bibliography*,

African Book Publishing Record, and the *New Zealand National Bibliography*. Except for the last title, these works organize publications by Dewey Decimal numbers; author, title, and subject indexes are also provided.

But as helpful as such specialized bibliographies are for major research institutions, which often want to buy every scholarly title published in America, Britain, and the Commonwealth, most academic libraries must be more selective. In addition to *Choice*, *American Reference Books Annual (ARBA)* identifies major scholarly U.S. imprints. Reviews are similar to those in *Choice* but have the added advantage of citing notices published in other journals. Holte and Wynar's *Best Reference Books 1970–1980* identifies the most distinguished sources treated during *ARBA*'s first decade. Two other tools immensely valuable in selecting for the general collection are also moderately useful for reference selection: *Year's Work in English Studies* and *American Literary Scholarship*. Both lag several years between publication date and the year of coverage, and the number of reference books reviewed is small in comparison to other services, but titles listed are usually important. Librarians must not limit themselves to the "General Works" section, since many reference books are period specific and are found only in the chapters devoted to the different eras.

A modest biannual publication is *The Reference Book Review*. No recent issue has exceeded thirty pages; the reviews themselves are also brief, sometimes as short as 100 words. Early issues listed five or more reviewers, but lately only the editors—Cameron and Donna Northouse—are explicitly associated with the publication. Because notices are almost always positive, *The Reference Book Review* is a useful guide for what to buy, but unfortunately it fails to indicate what to avoid. Its brevity and infrequent publication also mean that only the most general reference works are treated.

RSR: Reference Service Review is a more substantial tool for selectors. Many of its essays are devoted to building collections in specific disciplines or genres. These pieces not only cite the important reference tools in each area but also make comparative judgments, indicating tools that remain useful despite their older imprints or that provide information not found elsewhere. Several essays have focused on literary topics, ranging from science fiction to children's literature. A "Books Received" section appends most issues, although its general scope limits the value to literary selectors.

RQ concerns itself exclusively with issues in reference service and library instruction and consequently includes reviews of new reference books. But because of its broad subject, the magazine treats fewer than five literary titles per issue. Ironically, sometimes more useful is its section entitled, "Books Received But Not Reviewed," which announces numerous new titles from publishers who produce literary series of interest to academic libraries, such as Garland, G. K. Hall, Gale, and Scarecrow.

Semiannually, *College & Research Libraries* features "Selected Reference Books." Although the byline is that of Sheehy, general editor of the authoritative *Guide to Reference Books*, the reviews are a joint effort of the reference departments of Columbia University's Butler and Lehman libraries. As with *RQ*, the scope is so multidisciplinary that only a few literary tools can be evaluated. The reviews of new titles are, however, followed by announcements of new editions and supplements, an important feature for libraries trying to have the most current reference tools.

Finally, in spite of their heavy emphasis on public library materials, *Booklist* and *Library Journal* must also be mentioned. The bimonthly *Booklist* includes "Reference Books Bulletin," which cites some works appropriate to academic libraries. The reviews are unique because they are the product of a subcommittee of the American Library Association's Publishing Committee. As a result, they register a collective consensus rather than the idiosyncratic preferences of single readers. Usually limited to a few paragraphs, the notices can be rather lengthy when a major reference tool is evaluated. The annual compilation would be more useful if the titles were grouped under broad subjects, but unfortunately they are arranged alphabetically, with no subject index.

The biweekly *Library Journal* reviews more reference books than other services, and identifies—with a star—those books judged to be of "outstanding quality, significance, or popular appeal." But this appraisal must be viewed cautiously, since the primary audience is public librarians. An added advantage *Library Journal* has over other services is its coverage, albeit quite selective, of small presses.

In conclusion, bibliographers, if they are to acquit their responsibility to the reference collection, must take into account a number of factors. They must work within guidelines which ideally have been codified in a reference collection policy statement. They must appreciate the different research needs of undergraduate students, graduate students, and English department faculty. They must work to understand the reference tool needs and expectations of other library personnel who staff the reference desk as well as help improve their library research skills. They must be aware of the diverse categories of literary reference aids, insuring that new works or revisions of older ones are acquired as published. They must monitor review services which not only announce new publications but which also cover the quantity of citations necessary to support the collection development intensity level established by their library. And they must attempt to keep the reference collection vital—titles outdated, superseded, and no longer appropriate should be reassigned to other collections or discarded. To do selection well, it must be done systematically: only this will provide continuity to the collection and satisfy the pluralistic research needs of scholars served by the library.

NOTES

1. Representative works include Marion V. Bell and Eleanor A. Swidan, *Reference Books: A Brief Guide*, 8th ed. (Baltimore: Enoch Pratt, 1978); Bohdan S. Wynar, ed., *Recommended Reference Books for Small and Medium-Sized Libraries and Media Centers*, 5th ed. (Littleton, Colo.: Libraries Unlimited, 1986); Eugene P. Sheehy, comp., *Guide to Reference Books*, 10th ed. (Chicago: American Library Association, 1986); and A. J. Walford, *Walford's Guide to Reference Materials*, 3 vols., 4th ed. (London: Library Association, 1980- .)

2. Of the importance of citation verification tools for faculty, see Elaine C. Clever, *Faculty Use of University Library Reference Facilities for Citation and Data Information*, U.S., Educational Resources Information Center, ERIC Document 041 613, March 1970.

3. More complete retrieval of French dissertations is available through *Catalogue des Thèses de Doctorat Soutenues Devant Les Universités Françaises* (Paris: Cercle de la Librarie, 1884/85-); of German dissertations through *Jahresverzeichnis der Deutschen Hochsculschriften* (Leipzig: VEB Verlag fur Buch-und Bibliothekwesen, 1885- .)

4. For a discussion of local access aids, *see* Scott Stebelman, "Bibliographic Control of Microforms: Suggestions for Improved Local Access," *Microform Review* 10 (1982): 162-65.

WORKS CITED

African Book Publishing Record. London: Hans Zell Publishers, 1975- .

Akeroyd, Joanne Vinson. *Where Are Their Papers?: A Union List Locating the Papers of Forty-Two Contemporary American Poets and Writers*. Storrs, Conn.: Univ. of Connecticut Library, 1976.

Altick, Richard D., and William R. Matthews. *Guide to Doctoral Dissertations in Victorian Literature, 1886-1958*. Urbana: Univ. of Illinois Pr., 1960.

―――, and Andrew Wright. *Selective Bibliography for the Study of English and American Literature*. 6th ed. New York: Macmillan, 1979.

American Culture Series, 1493-1875: A Cumulative Guide to the Microfilm Collection. Ann Arbor: University Microfilms International, 1979.

American Literary Scholarship. Durham, N.C.: Duke Univ. Press, 1963- .

American Reference Books Annual. Littleton, Colo.: Libraries Unlimited, 1970- .

Annual Bibliography of English Language and Literature. Cambridge: Modern Humanities Research Association, 1920- .

Arts & Humanities Citation Index. Philadelphia: Institute for Scientific Information, 1978- . (Earliest printed volume is 1976.)

Atkinson, Frank. *Dictionary of Literary Pseudonyms: A Selection of Popular Modern Writers in English.* 3rd ed. London: C. Bingley, 1982.
Australian National Bibliography. Canberra: National Library of Australia, 1961- .
Author Biographies Master Index. Ed. Barbara McNeil and Miranda C. Herbert. 2nd ed. 2 vols. Detroit: Gale Research Co., 1984.
Baker, Nancy L. *A Research Guide for Undergraduate Students: English and American Literature.* New York: Modern Language Association of America, 1982.
Barns, Florence Elberta. *Texas Writers of Today.* 1935; Rpt. Ann Arbor: Gryphon Books, 1971.
Bartlett, John. *Familiar Quotations: A Collection of Passages, Phrases, and Proverbs Traced to Their Sources in Ancient and Modern Literature.* 15th ed. Boston: Little, Brown, 1980.
Bateson, F. W., and Harrison T. Meserole. *A Guide to English and American Literature.* 3rd ed. London: Longman, 1976.
Booklist. Chicago: American Library Association, 1905- .
British Museum. *General Catalogue of Printed Books.* 263 vols. London: Trustees, 1959- . (Cumulative supplements published irregularly.)
British National Bibliography. London: Council of the British National Bibliography, British Museum, 1950- .
Burchard, John E. "How Humanists Use a Library." In *Intrex: Report of a Planning Conference on Information Transfer Experiments, September 3, 1965,* pp. 219-23. Ed. Carl F. J. Overhage and R. Joyce Harman. Cambridge, Mass.: MIT Press, 1965.
Canadiana. Ottawa: National Library of Canada, 1951- .
Cassell's Encyclopaedia of World Literature. Ed. S. H. Steinberg. 2nd ed. 3 vols. London: Cassell, 1978.
Catalogue of Manuscripts in the Houghton Library, Harvard University. Alexandria, Va.: Chadwyck-Healey, 1986- .
The Chicago Manual of Style for Authors, Editors, and Copywriters. 13th cd. Chicago: Univ. of Chicago Press, 1982.
Choice. Middletown, Conn.: Association of College and Research Libraries, 1964- .
Clayton, Thomas. "Literary Handbooks: A Critical Survey." *Literary Research Newsletter* 5.2 (Spring 1980): 67-87.
College & Research Libraries. Chicago: Association of College and Research Libraries, 1939- .
Collison, Robert Lewis. *Dictionaries of English and Foreign Languages: A Bibliographical Guide to Both General and Technical Dictionaries with Historical and Explanatory Notes and References.* 2nd ed. New York: Hafner Publishing Co., 1971.
Combined Retrospective Index to Book Reviews in Humanities Journals, 1802-1974. Woodbridge, Conn.: Research Publications, 1982-84.
Commire, Ann, ed. *Yesterday's Authors of Books for Children: Facts and Pictures*

about Authors and Illustrators of Books for Young People, from Early Times to 1960. 2 vols. Detroit: Gale Research Co., 1977-78.
Comprehensive Dissertation Index, 1861-1972. 37 vols. Ann Arbor: University Microfilms, 1973. (Annual supplements published since 1973.)
Contemporary Authors: A Bio-Bibliographical Guide to Current Authors and Their Works. Detroit: Gale Research Co., 1962- .
Dictionary of American Biography. 20 vols. New York: Scribner, 1928-37. (With supplements.)
Dictionary of Literary Biography. Detroit: Gale Research Co., 1978- .
Dictionary of National Biography. Ed. Leslie Stephens and Sidney Lee. 22 vols. London: Smith, Elder, 1908-1909.
Dissertation Abstracts International. Ann Arbor: University Microfilms, 1938- .
Dodson, Suzanne Cates. *Microform Research Collections: A Guide.* 2nd ed. Westport, Conn.: Meckler, 1984.
Downs, Robert B. *British and Irish Library Resources: A Bibliographical Guide.* Rev. ed. London: Mansell, 1981.
Early English Books, 1475-1640. Ann Arbor: University Microfilms International, 1937- .
Eddleman, Floyd Eugene, comp. *American Drama Criticism: Interpretations, 1890-1977.* 2nd ed. Hamden, Conn.: Shoe String Press, 1979. (With supplement.)
The Eighteenth Century: Title Listing. Woodbridge, Conn.: Research Publications, 1982- .
Essay and General Literature Index. New York: Wilson, 1934- .
Evans, Charles. *American Bibliography: A Chronological Dictionary of All Books, Pamphlets, and Periodical Publications Printed in the United States of America from the Genesis of Printing in 1639 Down to and Including the Year 1800.* 14 vols. Chicago: Blakeley Press, 1903-59.
Fenster, Valmai Kirkham. *Guide to American Literature.* Littleton, Colo.: Libraries Unlimited, 1983.
Force, Helen H., ed. *Who Is Who.* Santa Ana, Calif.: Professional Library Service, 1967.
Fowler, H. W. *A Dictionary of Modern English Usage.* 2nd ed. New York: Oxford Univ. Press, 1965.
Funk & Wagnalls New Standard Dictionary of the English Language. New York: Funk & Wagnalls, 1963.
Gardner, Katherine Ann, comp. *The Library of Congress Main Reading Room Reference Collection, Subject Catalog.* 2nd ed. Washington, D.C.: Library of Congress, 1980.
George, Mary W., and Mary Ann O'Donnell. "The Bibliography and Research Methods Course in American Departments of English." *Literary Research Newsletter* 4.1 (Winter 1978): 9-23, 38-39.
Gibaldi, Joseph, and Walter S. Achert. *MLA Handbook for Writers of Research Papers.* 2nd ed. New York: Modern Language Association of America, 1984.
Granger, Edith. *Granger's Index to Poetry.* 8th ed. New York: Columbia Univ. Press, 1986.

Guddat-Figge, Gisela. *Catalogue of Manuscripts Containing Middle English Romances*. Munich: W. Fink, 1976.
Halkett, Samuel, and John Laing. *Dictionary of Anonymous and Pseudonymous English Literature*. New and enlg. edition by James Kennedy, W. A. Smith, and A. F. Johnson. 9 vols. Edinburgh: Oliver & Boyd, 1926-62.
Harvard University. Library. *Widener Library Shelflist*. Vol. 33: *Reference Collections Shelved in the Reading Room and Acquisitions Department*. Cambridge, Mass.: Harvard Univ. Library, 1970.
Havlice, Patricia P. *Index to Literary Biography*. Metuchen, N.J.: Scarecrow Press, 1975. 2 vols. (Supplements to Havlice's work have been published.)
Hazlitt, William Carew. *A Manual for the Collector and Amateur of Old English Plays*. London: Pickering & Chatto, 1892.
Hinrichs, Linda Keir. "Where in the Dickens Is Gad's Hill? Or, A Comparative Review of Literary Guides to Britain." *RSR* 10 (Fall 1982): 55-59.
Holte, Susan, and Bohdan S. Wynar, eds. *Best Reference Books 1970-1980: Titles of Lasting Value Selected from American Reference Books Annual*. Littleton, Colo.: Libraries Unlimited, 1981.
Horden, John, ed. *A Dictionary of Anonymous and Pseudonymous Publications in the English Language*. 3rd ed. Harlow, Eng.: Longman, 1980- .
Humanities Index. New York: Wilson, 1974/75- .
Index of English Literary Manuscripts. London: Mansell, 1980- .
An Index to Book Reviews in the Humanities. Williamston, Mich.: Philip Thomson, 1960- .
Jordan, Frank, ed. *The English Romantic Poets: A Review of Research and Criticism*. 4th ed. New York: Modern Language Association of America, 1985.
Katz, William A. *Introduction to Reference Work*. 4th ed. 2 vols. New York: McGraw-Hill, 1982.
Kister, Kenneth F. *Dictionary Buying Guide: A Consumer Guide to General English-Language Wordbooks in Print*. New York: Bowker, 1977.
Kolai, Carol Koehmstedt. *Plot Summary Index*. 2nd ed. Metuchen, N.J.: Scarecrow Press, 1981.
Kuntz, Joseph M., and Nancy C. Martinez. *Poetry Explication: A Checklist of Interpretations since 1925 of British and American Poems Past and Present*. 3rd ed. Boston: Hall, 1980.
Landau, Sidney I. *Dictionaries: The Art and Craft of Lexicography*. New York: Scribner's, 1984.
Leary, Lewis. *American Literature: A Study and Research Guide*. New York: St. Martin's Press, 1976.
Library Journal. New York: Bowker, 1876- .
Lindfors, Bernth. *Black African Literature in English: A Guide to Information Sources*. Detroit: Gale Research Co., 1979.
McNamee, Lawrence F. *Dissertations in English and American Literature: Theses Accepted by American, British, and German Universities, 1865-1964*. New York: Bowker, 1968. (Supplements bring record to 1973.)
McNeil, Barbara, and Miranda C. Herbert, eds. *Author Biographies Master Index*. 2nd ed. 2 vols. Detroit: Gale Research Co., 1984.

McPheron, Elaine. "Dictionaries of Quotations: A Comparative Review." *RSR* 12 (Winter 1984): 21-31.

Magill, Frank N., ed. *Critical Survey of Short Fiction*. 7 vols. Englewood Cliffs, N.J.: Salem Press 1981.

_____. *Magill's Bibliography of Literary Criticism*. 4 vols. Englewood Cliffs, N.J.: Salem Press 1979.

_____. *Magill's Literary Annual*. Englewood Cliffs, N.J.: Salem Press, 1977- .

_____. *Masterplots: 2010 Plot Stories and Essay Reviews from the World's Fine Literature*. Rev. ed. 12 vols. Englewood Cliffs, N.J.: Salem Press, 1976.

_____. *Survey of Contemporary Literature*. Rev. ed. 2 vols. Englewood Cliffs, N.J.: Salem Press, 1977.

_____. *Survey of Modern Fantasy Literature*. 5 vols. Englewood Cliffs, N.J.: Salem Press, 1983.

_____. *Survey of Science Fiction Literature*. 5 vols. Englewood Cliffs, N.J.: Salem Press, 1979.

Malkiel, Yakov. *Etymological Dictionaries: A Tentative Typology*. Chicago: Univ. of Chicago Press, 1975.

Meserole, Harrison T. "The Design and Function of the 'Introduction to Research and Bibliography' Course in Graduate English Study." *Literary Research Newsletter* 1.2 (April 1976): 53-68.

Meserve, Walter J. *American Drama to 1900: A Guide to Information Sources*. Detroit: Gale Research Co., 1980.

MLA International Bibliography of Books and Articles on the Modern Languages and Literatures. New York: Modern Language Association of America, 1921- .

Moulton, Charles Wells. *Library of Literary Criticism of English and American Authors*. 8 vols. Buffalo: Moulton, 1901-1905. (Abridgment, with more current information, published by Ungar, 1966.)

National Union Catalog. Ann Arbor: Edwards, 1958- .

National Union Catalog of Manuscript Collections. Washington, D.C.: Library of Congress, 1962- .

New Cambridge Bibliography of English Literature. 5 vols. Cambridge: Cambridge Univ. Press, 1969-77.

New Zealand National Bibliography. Wellington: National Library of New Zealand, 1966- .

Ottemiller's Index to Plays in Collections: An Author and Title Index to Plays Appearing in Collections Published between 1900 and Early 1975. Ed. John M. Connor and Billie M. Connor. 6th ed. Metuchen, N.J.: Scarecrow Press, 1976.

Parker, Patricia L. *Early American Fiction: A Reference Guide*. Boston: G. K. Hall, 1984.

Patterson, Margaret. *Literary Research Guide*. 2nd ed. New York: Modern Language Association of America, 1983.

Penninger, Frieda Elaine. *English Drama to 1660 (Excluding Shakespeare): A Guide to Information Sources*. Detroit: Gale Research Co., 1976.

Play Index. New York: Wilson, 1949- .

Pollard, Alfred William, and G. R. Redgrave. *A Short-Title Catalogue of Books Printed in England, Scotland, and Ireland and of English Books Printed Abroad, 1475-1640.* 2nd ed. London: Bibliographical Society, 1976- .
Pownall, David E. *Articles on Twentieth Century Literature: An Annotated Bibliography, 1954 to 1970.* 7 vols. New York: Kraus-Thomson, 1973-80.
Prentice-Hall Handbook for Writers. Ed. Glenn Leggett and others. 9th ed. Englewood Cliffs, N.J.: Prentice-Hall, 1985.
Reference Books Bulletin (formerly *Reference and Subscription Books Reviews*). Chicago: American Library Association, 1968- .
The Reference Book Review. Dallas: Cameron Northouse, 1976- .
Rettig, James. "Beyond the MLA International Bibliography: Bibliographic Guides for English and American Literature and Dictionaries of Literary Terms in Print." *RSR* 7 (April-June 1979): 47-55.
Ribner, Irving, and Clifford Chalmers Huffman, comps. *Tudor and Stuart Drama.* 2nd ed. Arlington Heights, Ill.: AHM Pub., 1978.
Robbins, J. Albert, et al. *American Literary Manuscripts: A Checklist of Holdings in Academic, Historical, and Public Libraries, Museums and Authors' Homes in the United States.* 2nd ed. Athens, Georgia: Univ. of Georgia Press, 1977.
Rogers, A. Robert. *The Humanities: A Selective Guide to Information Studies.* 2nd ed. Littleton, Colo.: Libraries Unlimited, 1979.
RQ. Chicago: Reference and Adult Services Division, American Library Association, 1960- .
RSR: Reference Services Review. Ann Arbor: Pierian Press, 1973- .
Schmidt, Karlernst. *Anglistische Bucherkunde.* Tubingen: Niemeyer, 1953.
Schweik, Robert C., and Dieter Riesner. *Reference Sources in English and American Literature: An Annotated Bibliography.* New York: Norton, 1977.
Sharp, Harold S. *Handbook of Pseudonyms and Personal Nicknames.* 2 vols. Metuchen, N.J.: Scarecrow Press, 1972. (With supplements.)
Sheehy, Eugene P. *Guide to Reference Books.* 10th ed. Chicago: American Library Association, 1986.
Short Story Index. Ed. Dorothy Elizabeth Cook and Isabel Monro Stevenson. New York: Wilson, 1900- .
Smaridge, Norah. *Famous Author-Illustrators for Young People.* New York: Dodd, Mead, 1973.
Something about the Author: Facts and Pictures about Contemporary Authors and Illustrators of Books for Young People. Detroit: Gale Research Co., 1971- .
Spiller, Robert E., and others. *Literary History of the United States.* 4th ed. 2 vols. New York: Macmillan, 1974.
Stanton, Robert. *A Bibliography of Modern British Novelists.* 2 vols. Troy, N.Y.: Whitson, 1978.
Stevens, Rolland E. *Reference Books in the Social Sciences and Humanities.* 4th ed. Champaign, Ill.: Stipes Publishing Co., 1977.
Stevenson, Burton E. *The Home Book of Quotations, Classical and Modern.* 10th ed. New York: Dodd, Mead 1967.

Stieg, Margaret F. "The Information Needs of Historians." *College & Research Libraries* 42 (November 1981): 549-60.

Stoan, Stephen K. "Research and Library Skills: An Analysis and Interpretation." *College & Research Libraries* 45 (March 1984): 99-109.

True, Michael. *Worcester Poets, With Notes Toward a Literary History*. Worcester, Mass.: Worcester County Poetry Association, 1972.

Urdang, Laurence, ed. *Literary, Rhetorical, and Linguistics Terms Index*. Detroit: Gale Research Co., 1983.

Walford, A. J. *Walford's Guide to Reference Materials*. 4th ed. London: Library Association, 1980- .

Walker, Warren S., comp. *Twentieth-Century Short Story Explication: Interpretations 1900-1975, of Short Fiction Since 1800*. 3rd ed. Hamden, Conn.: Shoe String Press, 1977. (With supplements.)

Watt, Robert. *Bibliotheca Britannica: Or, A General Index to British and Foreign Literature*. 2 vols. Edinburgh: Constable, 1824.

Webster's New Collegiate Dictionary. Springfield, Mass.: Merriam, 1979.

Weekly Record. New York: Bowker, 1974- .

Weixlmann, Joe. *American Short-Fiction Criticism and Scholarship, 1959-1977: A Checklist*. Chicago: Swallow Press, 1982.

Wing, Donald. *Short-Title Catalogue of Books Printed in England, Scotland, Ireland, Wales, and British America, and of English Books Printed in Other Countries, 1641-1700*. 2nd ed. New York: Modern Language Association of America, 1972- .

Woodress, James. *Dissertations in American Literature, 1891-1966*. 3rd ed. Durham, N. C.: Duke Univ. Press, 1968.

Year's Work in English Studies. London: English Association, 1921- .

Special Collections

Michael T. Ryan

The term "special collection" is a relatively recent one in librarianship. It came into general use in the 1940s and 1950s when it was applied to departments within libraries charged with maintaining rare book, manuscript, and related format collections. Yet, special collections are ubiquitous in academic libraries, whether they are housed in departments dedicated solely to them or whether they are dispersed in the stacks or among the holdings of a branch library. Special collections are not necessarily bound by location; coherence of content may be as important as contiguity of shelving. Antiquarian books, codex manuscripts, and the papers of modern writers are indeed special, but so too may be holdings in other formats—maps, prints, films, photographs, artifacts, postcards—and in other subject areas—history, religion, the social sciences, popular culture, medicine, oenology, malacology, and artificial intelligence. If academic libraries are collections of collections, so too they are collections of special collections. For the selector of British and American literature, an ecumenical view of "special collections" will open up new aspects of collection development, new possibilities for collection building

CONTEXTS

Most college and university libraries, whatever their size and status, have identified collecting areas that are special to them—and often to other institutions as well. The range and scope of these are, however, sufficiently broad that if a library chooses to avoid competing for expensive items, it can still find an appropriate and meaningful niche. There is enough material for everyone. It is possible to follow Voltaire's advice and *cultiver nos jardins*.

What is special about special collections? The answers to this question are as varied as the collections themselves. They range from monetary value to research utility and include everything from the intellectual to the sentimental. The key is the institutional context: special collections reflect in their own ways the values of the larger institution, its priorities, research interests, faculty traditions, donor relations, and alumni involvements. But since institutions do not always know what they value, it is up to librarians to identify what is truly special in the collections and in the marketplace from both a local and a larger perspective. That is why the business of special collections should never exclusively be the province of the special collections librarian; it is potentially the charge of every subject and area selector. The subject bibliographer is uniquely positioned to identify and build special collections in an academic library, ideally in collaboration with colleagues in special collections departments. Through faculty contacts, knowledge of collections, and familiarity with the traditions of intellectual production, the subject selector has almost everything necessary to develop special collections. All that is missing from that list are imagination and persistence.

In the context of a research institution, special collections can be distinguished by at least four criteria. There are probably more and possibly fewer, but the following offer at least a shorthand definition:

1. *Intensity of focus*: the nature and scope of the subject/area to be documented are clearly and sharply defined.
2. *Comprehensiveness of coverage*: selectivity within the target area is often sacrificed for the attainment of a critical mass, developed through exhaustive—and deliberately uncritical—acquisitions.
3. *Documentary purpose*: where possible, the acquisition of primary source materials (e.g., manuscripts, notebooks, correspondence that are documentary in character) is a primary goal.
4. *The whole and the parts*: the whole should be greater than the sum of its parts. This argues in effect that the combination of resources together in a single setting produces a transcendent value, evident to scholars as well as to librarians. The relationships of the sources among themselves are capable of generating new perspectives and providing new vistas—a new sense of "the whole."

Many special collections departments in this country grew out of literature collections, and the traditions of philology, bibliography, and literary scholarship have had a dominant role in shaping the field of special collections librarianship. Indeed, it could probably be said that of all the areas in which one could build special collections, none has been so intensely cultivated as British and American literature. From collecting the "canon" in original issue, to acquiring materials by writers who might be something someday to someone—a canon of the future—special collections based on literature have dominated. And yet even in an area as well worked as literature, there are discoveries to be made, collections to be formed that will have some enduring significance. The precarious status of the canon together with the multidisciplinary context of most literary research today has presented new possibilities. For the bibliographer whose principal task is developing academic collections, the building of special collections will follow naturally enough.

ENDS AND MEANS

Developing and maintaining special collections is a programmatic activity which needs to be informed by self-knowledge and a clear sense of direction. More important even than knowing how to acquire materials is understanding the purposes and goals of the program to acquire them. The development of special collections usually requires the channelling of institutional resources—sometimes a relatively large amount of them—into comparatively small areas. It is thus crucial that the program have a clearly articulated set of goals.

A sense of purpose is particularly important in those cases where a selector inherits special collections begun years ago whose raisons d'etre have been lost in the mists of time or in the university's archives. Such collections may indeed have written policy statements— for example, the acquisition of all poetry published in Wiltshire between 1750 and 1850—but no real sense of purpose intelligible to the present; in other words, they have assumed lives of their own. While this may be acceptable when the policy is accompanied by an endowment that provides its own rationale, it may not be sufficient when operating funds are being allocated to the effort. In such cases, the selector needs to refocus the collections and their meaning for the institution to make them living concerns. Defining or redefining purposes may result in expanded programs of acquisition, or, conversely, in sharply curtailed efforts; it may involve a shifting of energy away from acquisition to interpretation or access. Whatever the result, the ends should be clearly in view: for special collections to be special they must fit the context in which they will exist. And this is a thoughtful, not a dogmatic process, one that grows out of discussion and dialogue with the library's many constituencies, especially the faculty.

In academic libraries, special collections are usually part of the effort to support research. Their definition and scope should follow from larger collection development policy statements or reflect shared understandings of research priorities within the institution. Where collection strengths parallel academic programs, it may be desirable to consider these areas "special" and target them for more intensive development. Alternately, a new commitment by the English Department to contemporary fiction may signal a need to pursue intensive programs of collection building that might include special collections. Where special collections are seen as part and parcel of the library's research collections, the essential concerns are scope, level, and depth. Developing special research collections to support the study of contemporary fiction can imply a willingness to collect comprehensively—but collect what? and how thoroughly? Defining the limits and degree of effort is therefore central to intelligent collection development.

In this as in several other areas relating to the development of special collections, archivists and manuscript curators have taken a lead which bibliographers can follow to advantage. They have elaborated the concept of "documentation strategy" and in doing so have changed the question from "what do I want to collect and why?" to "what do I want to document and why?"[1] Documentation strategy proceeds from a set of questions about the nature of research and moves to a consideration of sources, formats, and genres, rather than beginning with lists of names and categories which may or may not have any fundamental coherence or contribute significantly to the research potential of the collections. Posing the question in terms of documentation strategies is useful, since it opens up collection development to the interdisciplinary orientation fundamental to research in the humanities today.

For the selector in British and American literature the notion of a documentation strategy offers an alternative to the most traditional concept of all special collections, that of the author collection. The latter is essentially an outgrowth of the efforts of private collectors in the nineteenth and twentieth centuries to assemble comprehensive collections of printed and manuscript materials relating to individual authors. For better or worse, the author collection has long been a staple of many special collections departments in academic libraries. Though it has often resulted in the formation of truly outstanding holdings, the concept may beg fundamental questions about the nature of literary scholarship. It assumes that research value is implicit in the harvest, rather than first asking what type of research is being supported. If, for example, the basic bibliographic work on a writer has been done, what research purpose would be served by building yet another comprehensive author collection? While sets of author collections may be part of a documentation strategy, the latter will serve to keep in view the purposes and aims of such collections. A documentation strategy should, in other words, define a research context within which the selector can make fundamental decisions about the content and scope of author collections.

For modern and contemporary writers in particular, it is important to be clear in advance about what one wants to document simply because of the abundance of material potentially available and the costs of acquiring it. The evolution of the text from manuscript to print; the biographical and social context; the process of creation; the writer's relations with colleagues, editors, and publishers; the marketing and distribution of a work; the impact of the work; and the critical relationship of the text and/or author to literature past and present—all carry with them different though related collecting programs, each with its own costs and rewards. For example, questions of format are clearly implicit in each of these research areas. In an age in which a single text can exist in multiple media, the selector can be confronted by a dizzying array of offerings through which to make his or her way. The prudent selector should be able to evaluate offerings in terms of the research program and its documentary requirements.

There is no dearth of approaches to a documentation program. In addition to lists of authors whose appeal rests solely on their place in or proximity to the canon, there are special collections of schools (Black Mountain); groups (Fugitive writers, the Beats); styles (Imagist, Objectivist); regions (New York, Southern); genres (contemporary poetry, science fiction, mysteries, gothic romances); gender (women); ethnic groups (black, Mexican American, Native American, Jewish)—to name but a few possibilities. While there may be no shortage of topoi, it is important that whatever combination of categories is chosen (e.g., Jewish women writers in Minnesota in the nineteenth and twentieth centuries) has some evident coherence and integrity and reflects in some way the priorities of the institution. Faculty involvement in the process of planning is thus crucial, and indeed faculty contacts may be central to the success of the effort.

While special collections are often synonymous with a library's major research level collections, they serve other functions as well. Indeed, they can exist in several different contexts. In college libraries, for example, special collections are often assembled for instructional purposes. In such cases, comprehensiveness of coverage is less important than representativeness. It may be more desirable to have examples of the evolution of texts in different periods than to document the process intensively for several works. Thus, well-chosen interpretations of Milton from the seventeenth and eighteenth centuries may be more useful than a comprehensive collection of editions of Milton. It may be as important to have one set of corrected galleys by D. H. Lawrence as to have several. Developing special collections to serve curricular and pedagogical needs is possibly more challenging than building research collections, if only because the test is in the ability of the selector to identify and acquire examples which best make the point. Defining a field of usable examples requires not only a knowledge of the present curriculum but an ability to imagine possible curricula as well; for the examples will remain long after the curriculum has changed and its creators moved on. The research-level special collection can also—indeed should—function as a library of examples and thus will take its place in the curriculum as well. Defining contexts, actual and possible, is crucial to the work of developing special collections, since without them the collection has no point of reference outside itself. This is fine for private collectors but difficult to sustain in a university with limited resources and anything but limited needs.

Special collections can serve institutional functions beyond research and teaching. They help create a sense of identity, of particularity, of uniqueness; they can bestow character and personality on an institution, possibly even eminence and prestige, or at least the sense that they are within grasp. In this context, a library's special collections have a well-established symbolic role to play; they operate within a system of symbols which constitutes the university's attempts to define and promote itself. While this may be obvious, for the literature selector it is an important point to grasp, since special literature collections possess a totemic value all their own by virtue of their relative position in the culture as a whole. Literary manuscripts, corrected proofs, correspondence, even signed volumes with association value are recognized conveyers of status and prestige, and in the competitive world of higher learning they can be potent symbols indeed.

On the other hand, the quest for honors may be less important than university-related characteristics that reinforce the identity of institutional programs and traditions. Thus, it makes little sense for a school like Stanford to compete in the market place for the literary archives of authors not associated with the institution, when Stanford has had its important Creative Writing Program through which has passed a succession of distinguished writers as students and as faculty. Documenting that program and the work of those who have participated in it seems doubly appropriate: both as a contribution to research and as an archival responsibility. Other institutions with special programs in the humanities relating to regional developments, schools, and traditions may also have or wish to have special collections of books, manuscripts, correspondence, ephemera, photographs, and other material which serve to document regional traits and literatures. Most institutions have *some* special collections that are intimately tied to the place, however broadly or narrowly defined. Sometimes these may be the collections of record within their field; other times they are fortuitous assemblages of material maintained to bestow or communicate identity and distinctiveness.

For the literature selector whose charge includes the discovery, maintenance, and development of special collections, clarity of purpose and knowledge of institutional contexts are central to the task. It is never enough to know *what* materials you have; why you have them, how they got there, and what they mean are also parts of the program. If working with special collections at any level and in any capacity is a programmatic activity, then a sense of the whole is necessary to understand the organic relationships among the parts. Special collections which exist outside some identifiable context of institutional purpose or need may, in fact, be endangered species.

COLLECTION DEVELOPMENT POLICY

The general acceptance of the collection development policy statement as a necessary instrument of any program of collection building and maintenance has made it formally possible to situate special collections within a larger context of bibliographic activity. Indeed, there seems to be consensus among selectors and collection development officers about the need to make sure that special collections are not only represented in the policy statement but *integrated* into it. This consensus reflects in turn the view that special collections do not simply complement the general collections but in fact grow out of them, are intellectually if not physically a part of them, and represent special research strengths. For example, the Research Libraries Group (RLG) Task Force on Conspectus Analysis has wisely resisted the temptation to devise a separate special collections inventory tool which might erode the synthetic capabilities of the Conspectus. Rather, in RLG as among the institutions participating in the North American Collections Inventory Project, special collections are indicated primarily in the notes to individual segment lines as well as being reflected in the values for collection strength and current collecting intensity.[2] Although the Conspectus is hardly ideal for capturing the nature, scope, and complexity of many special collections, it at least provides a format for locating them in the larger context of collection development. Where the selector feels it is appropriate, it may even be desirable to create a more detailed policy statement which can record the special strengths of the collection in adequate detail for the selector as well as for the constituency served and the library administration.

A selector new to an institution which already possesses a collection development policy statement will, of course, want to review the document thoroughly for a variety of purposes. In combination with a systematic screening of the collections, such a review could, in fact, disclose the extent of "special collections" of literature not described by previous selectors. Research-level collections may contain pockets of special intensity or unique materials which constitute special collections or points of departure for developing special collections. Conversely, the new selector in an institution which lacks or is in the process of articulating its collection development policy has the perfect opportunity to describe and define policy that encompasses special materials from the start.

RELATIONSHIPS WITH SPECIAL COLLECTIONS DEPARTMENTS

Ideally, there should be a genuine partnership between the literature bibliographer and the special collections librarian. Given that most special collections departments began as and remain primarily collections of British and American literature, there would seem to be a natural meeting ground between them and literature bibliographers. And yet the historical isolation of special collections departments has made this partnership more difficult to achieve than to define, if only because it has tended to bifurcate the literature bibliographer's responsibilities. The latter are often described solely in terms of selecting from current publishing output, while the work of retrospective buying and intensive collection development is apportioned to the special collections librarian. However, there is much to be said for and more to be gained from an integrated approach in which the work of each proceeds along a commonly defined continuum of possibilities.

Integrating core selectors into special collections departments is a natural consequence of a shared policy statement and promotes a holistic rather than fragmented view of the library's literature collections. Without that holistic perspective, related collections tend to be developed in isolation from one another and so lack shared purpose and coherence. In practice, there are any number of ways in which the literature selector and the special collections librarian can work together. The literature selector's knowledge as a subject bibliographer or area specialist and familiarity with faculty interests and program requirements can complement well the special collections librarian's familiarity with the book trade, the donor pool, and the special holdings of other institutions. Cooperation between the two is generally most productive when it occurs at the beginning of a project, whether it involves acquiring antiquarian materials or the papers of contemporary writers. A new program in eighteenth-century studies, for example, may require an intensive collection development effort in a library which has never devoted much effort or money to that area. Given the proliferation of facsimiles, reprints, and microfilm sets, there is the possibility for substantial overlap between the work of the literature selector and that of the special collections librarian. A coordinated approach at the beginning of the project would husband resources more effectively by deciding basic issues of format and overall goals. Similarly, a program to acquire the papers of selected writers would benefit from coordinated planning since the bibliographic knowledge of the selector on the one hand, and the familiarity of the special collections librarian with the administrative requirements of the format on the other, are both necessary.

The literature holdings of special collections departments are sometimes less the result of policy and planning than of gifts and chance. This does not necessarily mean that they are irrelevant to the programmatic needs of the institution but rather that their acquisition proceeds along a different trajectory. For the literature selector, a working partnership with the special collections librarian will not only provide a better knowledge of the holdings of the department but also a firmer sense of the rhythm of acquisitions and donor behavior and of the fields of future development—in other words, the actual, the probable, and the possible. Some understanding of the nature of development opportunities is important since they may help shape an overall collection building program. A major gift or bequest expected within the next five years could bring with it opportunities or requirements for intensive collection development. At the same time, special collections departments often acquire materials from endowed funds which are restricted to certain types and/or periods of literature. A knowledge of the fund structure of special collections can obviously be useful to the literature selector who needs to husband funds and conserve resources. A coordinated approach to endowed and general funds is clearly to everyone's advantage.

THE LARGER SCENE

There are few institutions of any consequence without special collections of literature. The library contemplating the development of a new one might, therefore, do well to determine who has what and who is working on what. The competition for paper—even the humblest scrap—from a writer of any note is strong, and sobering. Plans to build a collection in an area already occupied by several major collections probably should be diverted along some other line; similarly unwise are thoughts of concentrating on a field in which a neighboring institution has been at work for years. However, access to information on holdings of repositories beyond one's backyard is imperfect at best. The British have done a better job than their American counterparts. The Library Association's *Directory of Rare Book and Special Collections in the United Kingdom and the Republic of Ireland* (1985) is a model of its kind, an eminently readable reference work providing generous orientation without being boring or overly mechanical. The Standing Conference of National Universities and Libraries (SCONUL) has begun a Location Register of Twentieth-Century English Literary Manuscripts and Letters which is headquartered in the library of the University of Reading. Lee Ash's familiar *Subject Collections* on this side of the Atlantic presents similar information in a different format, while Alice D. Schreyer's *Rare Books, 1983–84: Trends, Collections, Sources* provides a comprehensive view of the profession, the trade, and more than 300 repositories. Information about manuscript holdings is especially difficult to come by in one source. The National Historical Publications and Records Commission's *Directory of Archives and Manuscript Repositories* (1978) is a useful starting place, while those with more patience and stamina can try their hand at the multi-volume *National Union Catalog of Manuscript Collections*. The Research Libraries Group has recently implemented an automated Archives and Manuscripts Control (AMC) format in RLIN which may, in time, provide an easily accessible, consolidated database for nonprint materials in this country.

Other useful guides include:

Beal, Peter, et al., comps. *Index of English Literary Manuscripts.* London: Mansell; New York: Bowker, 1980– . Vol. 1, 1450–1625; vol. 2, 1625–1700; vol. 3, 1700–1800; vol. 4, 1800–1900; vol. 5, Indexes of titles, first lines, names, repositories. Authors represented are generally those included in the *Concise Cambridge Bibliography of English Literature.* Alphabetical by author's surname; for each author there is introductory material relating to the author's manuscripts, followed by descriptive list of locations of collections.

Foster, Janet, and Julia Sheppard. *British Archives: A Guide to Archive Resources in the United Kingdom.* Detroit: Gale Research Co., 1982. Alphabetical listing

of 708 entries by town. Lists of repositories, subject headings; general index.
Great Britain. Historical Manuscripts Commission. *Accessions to Repositories.* London: Her Majesty's Stationery Office, 1957- . Digest of "the more significant or unusual accessions to British libraries and record offices during the year. The large routine accessions of record offices are necessarily ignored and have still to be looked for in the annual published reports of the repositories themselves." Includes index to repositories.
Hamer, Philip M., ed. *A Guide to Archives and Manuscripts in the United States.* New Haven: Yale Univ. Press, 1961. Alphabetical listing by state, then by city and institution. Descriptive entries for 1300 depositories; index. Useful in conjunction with NHPRC *Directory,* entered below.
Ker, Neil Ripley. *Medieval Manuscripts in British Libraries.* Oxford: Clarendon Press, 1969- . Lists libraries and describes medieval manuscript holdings of institutions for which cataloging is minimal or nonexistent. Volume 1: London; volumes 2 and 3 are arranged alphabetically by name of library, from Abbotsford to York.
Robbins, John Albert. *American Literary Manuscripts: A Checklist of Holdings.* Athens: Univ. of Georgia Press, 1977. Alphabetical by author name; author name followed by library and format symbols.
Roberts, Stephen Andrew, et al. *Research Libraries and Collections in the United Kingdom.* London: Bingley; Hamden, Conn.: Linnet Books, 1978. In four categories: (1) national, specialist and public libraries; (2) university libraries; (3) polytechnic libraries; (4) Scottish central institutions. Descriptive entries arranged by name of library and/or institution. Collection, institution, and personal name index, subject index, geographical index of library locations.
Union List of Manuscripts in Canadian Repositories. Ottawa: Public Archives of Canada, 1976. Supplements for 1977-78, 1979-80. Descriptive lists of collections, alphabetical by name of person, corporate body, or government agency, in English and French. List of finding aids to collections; list of participating repositories; catalog of collections by repository; general index.

If nothing else, perusing these guides and indexes will communicate a sense of the extraordinary dispersal of primary source materials for literature among the various British and North American repositories. While the growth of multilibrary consortia has helped bring about some first steps towards collaborative collection development, cooperation has yet to extend, even rhetorically, to special collections. For reasons of prestige, identity, and donor relations as well as because of the limitations of restrictive covenants on many gifts of money and material, special collections have almost always tended to be driven by local needs rather than by larger agendas.

THE TRADE

In part, the question "what areas should we be developing intensively?" can be answered by turning to the market: what is, in fact, available and at what price? The sources of literary special collections are many and as diverse as the collections themselves, but they almost always intersect with the book trade at some point. And the market for literary manuscripts and printed works is one of the most extensive, well-developed, and expensive parts of the trade as a whole. There is a substantial body of work on the literary marketplace which the bibliographer can consult as necessary. This section will provide only a general orientation and perspective.

The booktrade is composed of a congeries of overlapping specialists who compete for customers and above all for stock. In generic terms, there is an antiquarian trade, itself with many subdivisions; an out-of-print trade; and a "modern firsts" trade, dealing primarily in twentieth-century literature. While a single bookseller may handle material from all three categories simultaneously, each dealer generally organizes his or her stock and approach to fit the conventions of one or another segment of the trade. The Antiquarian Booksellers Association of America (ABAA) embraces all of these categories, and its directory constitutes a convenient point of departure and orientation. The ABAA is a professional group that collects dues, monitors the trade, and sets standards; membership in it is by application and not automatic. Therefore, its members do not embrace everyone who deals in antiquarian materials or modern firsts; younger dealers, especially, and book scouts tend to fall outside the ranks. The antiquarian book trade includes dealers at every level, from a handful of relatively opulent and ostentatious firms to the legion of individuals living on the margin and working out of their homes.

In spite of this variety, the antiquarian book trade is reasonably well organized. Dealers know each other's stock and specialties, and there is a brisk and constant trade among them. And the steady stream of catalogs, lists, and quotes provides an abundance of more or less digestible information about the market. Selectors developing special literature collections can take some comfort in this since the specialized nature of their projects will ultimately allow them to winnow the pool of possible vendors down to a manageable number of sources. The variety of formal and informal channels of communication among dealers means that the trade itself is the best source of information about itself, something the selector will discover soon enough. While there is no substitute for fieldwork, there are sufficient guides and directories to the antiquarian book trade. Recent editions of some principal directories of antiquarian booksellers include:

ABAA Membership Directory 1986. Alphabetical listing by firm name; list of members emeritus; geographic, specialty, and personal names indexes.

Bookdealers in North America 1983-85. London: Sheppard Press, 1983. Lists of book trade organizations, overseas antiquarian booksellers' associations, book trade and literary periodicals, current reference books, appraisers, auctioneers, service suppliers, cable addresses. Geographical listing of bookdealers: alphabetical by state or region, and within state or region alphabetical by name of firm, with addresses, location information, notes as to type and size of stock, specialties, catalogs, association affiliation; dealer listing alphabetically by firm name; specialty index; list of advertisers.

Cole's Register of Antiquarian and Second-Hand Bookdealers Active in Britain April 1986. New York: Bowker, 1986. Alphabetical listing by name of firm; specialty index; catalog bookdealers, listed by subject field; geographical listing, alphabetical by area of proprietors.

Collector's Guide to Antiquarian Bookstores. New York: Macmillan, © 1984. Geographical listing for the United States and Canada: alphabetically by state or province, and within state or province alphabetically by name of firm, with location and hours information, notes as to history of firm, size of stock, catalogs, specialties; specialty index.

A Directory of Dealers in Secondhand and Antiquarian Books in the British Isles 1984-86. London: Sheppard Press, 1984. Notes on the British book trade, overseas antiquarian booksellers' associations, current reference books, periodicals, auctioneers, service suppliers. Geographical listing by area, with addresses, location information, notes as to type and size of stock, specialties, catalogs, bank affiliation, association affiliation.

Directory of Specialized American Bookdealers. New York: Moretus Press, © 1984. Geographical listing: alphabetical by state and city, with addresses, hours, catalog information, specialties; index of firms and of proprietors.

In addition, there is a journal literature worth browsing. *AB Bookman's Weekly* (Clifton, N.J.: AB Bookman Publications) provides a weekly view of the trade, usually focusing on some specialty within it. The magazine also contains reviews, notices of events such as books fairs, and long lists of dealer offerings and desiderata; it may be a convenient forum in which to advertise the library's own needs as well. The *Antiquarian Book Monthly Review* (Oxford: ABMR) is a useful and more discursive supplement to *AB Bookman's Weekly* as is the London-based *Book Collector* (London: Pickering & Chatto), both of which contain more scholarly articles and reviews on matters bibliographical and professional. Other relevant journals include:

American Book Collector. New Series. New York: Moretus Press. Bimonthly. Bibliographical articles, bibliographic checklists, news of the trade, list of new dealer catalogs, book reviews, want lists and books for sale.

Rare Books and Manuscripts Librarianship. Chicago: Association of College and Research Libraries. Semiannual. Bibliographical articles, book reviews.

The function of the antiquarian book trade is to mediate between the material and the collector or institution. It positions the material and establishes its commercial value. The various ways in which market value is established are important to appreciate, since they may or may not have anything in common with the values driving the library's special collection programs. Condition of the copy, the nature and status of the author, the size of the edition of the work and its relative rarity in the marketplace, provenance and associations, and authorial corrections and annotations all play a role in fixing the position of an item in the market. The price a dealer charges for a title, a manuscript, a collection, is the ultimate synthesis; it reflects not only the dealer's knowledge and judgments about the nature and quality of the material but also the dealer's place within the trade and the nature and status of the customers. Thus, the selector whose interests are primarily textual and only secondarily artifactual will confront in the modern firsts trade, for example, a system of values focused intensely on the nature of the artifact and oriented principally to the private collector whose concerns and preoccupations may diverge sharply from those of the institutional buyer. Indeed, it is particularly important for the literature bibliographer whose collection development mandate includes selections from major twentieth-century British and American writers to scout the trade carefully for the purpose of finding matches with dealers whose assumptions and values approximate those of the bibliographer and the program. Since there is a range of dealers, so too there is a range of prices which can be expected for given items. The range allows dealers to buy from each other and encourages potential customers to choose carefully.

For manuscripts and correspondence, research value can play a role in determining market value. Research criteria are established with institutional buyers in mind, since that is the reason most academic libraries acquire primary source materials. In the highly competitive market of literary manuscripts, these are especially important criteria since the selector will at every turn need to answer with some surety the question, "What is it worth to us?" Unpublished material, whether fragments, complete manuscripts, correspondence, or journals, will usually fetch higher prices than material already available in some other format. Dealers may have a rather different understanding of "research value" than do librarians and their constituencies. That is one reason why faculty involvement in evaluating potential acquisitions is crucial, since it is presumably their research and that of their students which is to be furthered by the purchase. A special collections development program with a clear sense of purpose and goals will be better able to weigh and evalute potential acquisitions than one with a weakly defined profile.

The antiquarian book trade operates largely through catalogs, lists, and direct quotations. Dealers' catalogs contain information which can vary wildly in accuracy, sophistication, and presentation; their personalities often reflect those of their creators. Some are slick and redolent of overhead; others will not pass the three-fold test. Some have genuine bibliographical value; others betray the haste of the moment and the pressure to get on with it. Orienting oneself to the general organization of the catalog is the first order of business; evaluating the contents follows closely. Entries may often be nothing more that a transcribed title page, an oblique note on condition, and price. At the other extreme, they may be page-long narratives which include a full description of the physical artifact, its place in the bibliographical repertoire, and some sense of its relative rarity.

In evaluating a potential acquisition from a catalog, the selector not only has to focus quickly and precisely his or her knowledge of the collections and the nature of its needs, he or she also has to judge the quality of the effort behind the description. How this is done is a matter of choice. Some selectors prefer to work only with dealers who invest heavily in bibliographical description and content notes—and for that, of course, there is a price to pay, since the dealer's time is folded into the cost of the item. Other selectors find such efforts unnecessary and would prefer to do the work themselves. Either way, costs are involved. Over time, the selector will sift and sort dealers' catalogs into various categories of quality and relevance. Items purchased from catalogs are usually returnable within a certain period of time—a consistent note of good faith throughout the trade. The condition of a work is usually the hardest thing to evaluate, since it generally has to be seen to be believed. Nonetheless, dealers who belong to the ABAA are supposed to adhere to certain conventions when describing condition, and these conventions may be easily consulted in any issue of *AB Bookman*.

Catalogs not only describe what a dealer has and at what price; they also point to what the dealer might have or be expected to have. Thus, for selectors beginning special programs, it is useful to make contact with dealers for the purpose of getting on their mailing lists. The selector needs exposure to the potential as well as to the actual.

Orienting oneself to the marketplace is a gradual process that grows out of experience and hundreds of dealers' catalogs. However, there are ways to get a quick fix on prices and trends. Annual summaries of activity arranged by author may be found in *American Book-Prices Current* a comprehensive and reliable index which may be usefully supplemented by the yearly *Book-Auction Records.* These indexes of prices are published primarily for the trade and have an undisputed working value for those who know how to use them. Librarians need to keep in mind that these price annotations reflect at best the historical *range* an item has commanded in the market. They are primarily orientation tools. Old standbys such as Van Allen Bradley's *Book Collector's Handbook of Values* and *Bookman's Price Index* are more useful for certain collectors than for institutions.

It is a truism that developing collections means developing booksellers: healthy relationships with the trade are essential, particularly when building special collections. Booksellers often like to see themselves as partners in the collection building enterprise, and collaboration with dealers can be beneficial in terms of material. The trade channels material in certain directions and not others. Indeed, there is much material that never makes it into catalogs because it is offered on quotation only. For selectors to get into these loops of the trade is clearly crucial to the success of any collecting effort. But it is just as important that the selector not become encumbered with obligations—real or imagined—to dealers and that he or she retain perspective, judgment, and freedom of action. Relying on a handful of dealers to the exclusion of all others may have obvious benefits; but the tendency to over-rely on certain dealers may also close off other options and insulate the selector from the larger market.

It is always helpful to remember that the bookseller's major problem is not so much selling books as getting good stock. Good stock moves; static stock means ruin. New stock means sales, and sales mean the possibility of acquiring more stock. The increasing scarcity of many kinds of material in combination with growing institutional competition for that material often makes it a seller's market. Developing good relations with the book trade is one way of insuring that the repository gets to see what it needs to see, whether or not it actually buys.

Auctions are a central part of the book trade; indeed, for many dealers, they are a principal source of material. Like dealers, auction houses range from the lavish to the humble. The splashy sales in New

York and London form one end of a continuum that terminates in the local auction gallery where books and papers may be found among procelain dogs, andirons, grandfather's portrait, and other objets d'art. The major houses, Sotheby's and Christies, schedule regular sales in New York and London which the selector can preview through expensively produced catalogs. Unlike booksellers, who usually supply catalogs free of charge to those on their mailing lists, auction firms require paid subscriptions, and for the larger houses these are not necessarily inexpensive. Descriptions of lots up for auction reflect the nature of the house and run from the extraordinary to the oblique. The catalogs provide estimated price ranges for each lot, and these are often pegged low to encourage bidding. While many institutions lack the flexibility to participate effectively in auctions, those who compete usually do so through agents—typically booksellers—who are wise in the ways of the rooms. The other option is simply to mail bids to the house or participate oneself. The advantages of using an agent are many. They can inspect the lots before the sales to answer questions of condition and content; they can provide their clients with a certain flexibility once in the rooms; and, if chosen well, they can usually make sure that their clients are not the underbidders on desired lots. It is important to keep in mind that the auction house will usually tack on 10 percent to the hammer price as its take; agents will add another 10 percent. It adds up.

Why compete at auction? Few libraries routinely do, so the literature selector can relegate the task of tracking auctions to others. However, there are some reasons for at least staying alert. If the selector is building collections in more traditional areas and has an appetite for distinctive items, auctions will turn them up before they enter the trade and acquire the inevitable mark-up. Literary "high spots" dominate the major sales in New York and London, and if the institution has the resources and the programs, it should find an agent and join in the chase. Closer to home, the local auction house may, from time to time, offer surprises which can be grabbed for bargain prices. If the selector, for example, is interested in genre fiction, the local gallery may turn up some interesting examples. Here, too, it repays working with the special collections librarian who may be better tuned into the local scene, its manners and customs.

GOING TO THE SOURCE

Developing donors is as important as developing dealers. Many academic libraries have been developed from major private collections, acquired through gift or purchase. Sometimes these collections are entombed in specially named rooms replete with "atmosphere"; more often, they are dispersed among the stack collections, their identity recorded on a bookplate or in a lone file memo. Whatever their fortune within institutions, these collections play pivotal roles in the intellectual history of libraries, and the literature selector ought to learn this history.

Every college and university has its own donor pool, access to which is usually channelled through one of several bureaucracies. Libraries with development officers may be better placed to survey the possibilities and make contact with bibliophilic friends and alumni. Although the traditions of book collecting among faculty are on the wane, they may also be a good source of material. However, beyond the tried and the true is a large and diffuse world of collectors which encompasses accumulators of every kind. It is likely that somewhere out there someone is doing something relevant. How does one know? One never really knows as much as one would like. Dealers have a view of the population, since they are usually in close contact with it, but how they choose to share their knowledge and contacts is another matter. There are directories of book collectors, such as Judith and Roger Sheppard's *International Directory of Book Collectors,* though these are chiefly comprised of the stratosphere of the collecting world—collectors with substantial monetary and psychological investments in collecting and in their identity as collectors. There are the book clubs, the best known of which will be found in the major metropolitan centers. These clubs usually have regular meetings and offer the librarian an opportunity to meet a cross-section of the local collecting world. Publicity about the institution's special collecting program as well as about its more impressive acquisitions will almost always generate some interest among fellow-travelers.

Turning collectors into patriotic donors is often a matter of assiduous and thoughtful cultivation. It is a long-term process which may involve regular efforts at various levels of the organization. The selector's contribution to the process is critical, since he or she is usually well enough placed to help establish that mutuality of interest necessary for productive donor relations. Most donors need to feel connected in some way not only with the larger institution but with the specific program for which they are being cultivated. Defining and nurturing that connection may fall to the selector, who needs to remain alert to the nuances of a relationship which is invariably complicated. Different donors require different styles and approaches. But a thoughtfully conceived and well-directed program is a product which sells itself.

A donor relationship is rarely a simple matter of give and take. Rather, it is an exchange in which each party gives something in return for something received. What the institution is prepared to give is a matter about which the selector needs to be clear. For many donors, the prestige of the institution and the nature of its mission can provide the necessary long-term satisfactions. For others, the process of exchange will assume more tangible forms: keeping the collection together, a dedicated room, instantaneous processing, curatorial staffing, etc. The extent to which an institution can accommodate a donor depends, of course, on the degree to which it genuinely wants the collection. The selector will thus need to gauge the depth of institutional commitment to the program and the particular collections which would support it as part of the overall donor relations strategy.

Until the Tax Reform Act of 1969, writers themselves were a principal source of gifts to special collections. In disallowing tax deductions for donations by writers of their manuscripts and files, the Tax Reform Act effectively eliminated any financial incentive for writers to be generous to institutions. The effect has been to encourage the expansion of modern literary manuscripts market, making it more costly for institutions to build special literary collections. Established living writers understand well the competition by libraries for their papers and other literary materials and they usually have a sense of how the market works. Many have been "signed up" by a university and regularly sell their papers to it. For a library to begin buying the papers of a living writer is a major step, since it can mean mortgaging other acquisitions, present and planned, to support a particular relationship or single collection. Librarians entering the world of modern literary manuscripts with acquisition in mind should have a treasury equal to their ambitions. Most writers need money and are sensitive to being exploited by institutions; the marketplace puts everything into perspective. The business of building a special collection of literature can be very much a business.

Bringing writers into the fold, even to purchase their papers, is no easy thing. Blanket solicitation efforts do not work well in a vigorously competitive context. Cordial letters that seem to arrive out of the blue will probably go unacknowledged. Besides, writers, like all potential donors (and sellers), need to feel that there is something special in their being approached by a particular institution. No one wants the sense of being but one name on a long and hastily assembled shopping list. Then, too, there is the issue of whose company they will be keeping in the repository once their literary remains are neatly folded and tucked away in archival boxes: an *omnium gatherum* collection with little coherence may not strike all potential donors as the right ambience in which to pass the sleep of future centuries. Solicitations stand a greater chance of being successful if they grow out of some natural relationship between the writer and the institution. That relationship can include everything from alumni status to personal contacts with faculty or bibliographical interests on the part of the selector. Such a relationship will provide a shared context for approaching a writer. The extent to which the selector can put together a solicitation program based on organic ties between the community of the writers and the institution will probably coincide with the program's chances of success. The very best university archives have done this with consistent success for faculty papers.

INTEGRATION

For many selectors, the process of building a special collection includes little beyond getting the material into the building. If it is destined for the special collections department, it is often assumed that the human and physical requirements in those corners of the library are in place and prepared to handle the books, manuscripts, and other items being funneled their way. However, developing special collections is an activity with implications that extend across and beyond the library. The selector whose charge includes curatorial responsibilities should take a broad view of the special collections and make sure that their integration into the working routines of the library and into the intellectual life of the university takes place in appropriate ways.

The identification and acquisition of special materials in any systematic fashion often require special staffing—or at least *more* staffing. Developing relationships with dealers, donors, and writers takes time, energy, and the accumulation of knowledge. Clerical and bibliographical support will surely be necessary at some level. If the acquisitions department is part of the process, its role must be carefully defined and its capacity for handling the type and volume of material critically assessed.

Access to the material once it is in the building is crucial, especially if procedures bypass the acquisitions department. Bibliographic control over special collections is surely worth a chapter in itself, but it is sufficient here to underscore the desirability of carefully planning the cataloging needs of the material. The plan involves evaluating the expertise as well as the levels of staffing. Special collections departments are sometimes departments of special arrearages, and if the latter remain hidden from public view their raison d'etre is compromised. If technical processing support for a particular special collection cannot be secured, that may be a sign of the collection's relative unimportance within the context of larger institutional priorities. Though support for processing special collections can occasionally be provided through timely grants, they can never take the place of long-term institutional commitments. Grants may help, but they do not ultimately sustain programs.

Special collections are assumed to have an artifactual value which gives them importance beyond their textual content. This value may typically imply the need for a special environment as well as for special conservation attention. Special materials usually fall outside the scope of the mass preservation projects which have recently mushroomed into existence—indeed these projects are often inimical to the integrity of the artifact and thus inappropriate for special collections. The conservation of special materials usually requires the attention of a conservator and, at the very least, suggests the need for a regular program of phased care designed to protect whatever meaning is presumed to inhere in the artifact.

The integration of special collections into the daily rhythms of the library ideally takes place in tandem with their interpretation to the university community at large. The process of interpretation can have many goals, but it should always seek to give life and meaning to the material in ways that resonate within the institution or for whatever other constituency the collection is being developed. Interpretive programs are ways of mooring special collections within organizations while also bringing them to wider scholarly attention. The process of interpretation occurs on different levels, from the casual and the social to the formal and the didactic. Indeed, the initial processing of special materials can present opportunities for involving students and faculty in the work of bringing them under bibliographic control; in fact, sometimes that is the rationale for acquiring the materials in the first place. The arsenal of interpretive tools includes a list of familiar possibilities: exhibits, lectures, guides, catalogs, courses, special presentations, etc. The nature of the collection and of institutional needs and resources will shape the overall character of an interpretive program, but its place in the library's larger educational mission should be clear.

While each approach offers a different set of possibilities for putting the material in a new light or perspective, a shared point of departure is the meaning and value of the artifact. These are generally easier to establish with unpublished than with published material, though the problem is equally real for both. The only thing more deadening than an exhibit of densely packed documents is an unimaginative show of an author's corpus, with neat rows of editions presented as if their meaning were self-evident to the viewer. Self-referencing exhibits may be the mode of some galleries and museums but not of libraries. While the interpretation of the artifact is to some extent implicit in its having been chosen for presentation, it also needs to be thoughtfully articulated so that the possibilities for research and discovery are clear. Finally, if the special collection has more than institutional significance, there may be an obligation to the larger scholarly community to issue a guide or catalog to it.

The possibilities for interpretation that a special collection of literature present are legion; they encompass the traditional and bibliographical as well as the new and the critical. The interpretation of special collections offers particular opportunities for imaginative collection mapping; constructing relationships between special and general stack material may represent an important contribution to the intellectual life of the university. The fact that special collections—and in particular special collections of literature—often represent an institution's aspirations as well as its achievements, puts them at the center of libraries' efforts to interpret themselves to their constituencies. An organic view of this effort will not only multiply the possibilities for new views and approaches, it will also provide perspective, balance, and judgment over time.

NOTES

1. The literature on documentation strategies is only just emerging. Some first attempts include Helen Samuels' important article, "Who Controls the Past," *American Archivist*, 49, 2 (1986): 109–24, and Larry J. Hackman's case study, "From Assessment to Action: Toward a Usable Past in the Empire State," *The Public Historian*, 7, 3 (1985): 23–24. The Society of American Archivists has included the development of documentation strategies in its recent statement of goals and priorities, *Planning for the Archival Profession* (Chicago: SAA, 1986), pp. 10–11.

2. See Nancy E. Gwinn and Paul H. Mosher, "Coordinating Collection Development: The RLG Conspectus," *College & Research Libraries* 44 (1983): 128–140, and David Farrell, "The NCIP Option for Coordinated Collection Development," *Library Resources & Technical Services* 30 (1986): 47–56.

WORKS CITED

American Book-Prices Current. New York: Bancroft-Parkman, 1894/95– . (Annual.)

Ash, Lee. *Subject Collections: A Guide to Special Collections and Subject Emphases*. 6th ed. New York: Bowker, 1985.

Book-Auction Records. London: Dawson's, 1903– . (Annual.)

Bookman's Price Index. Edited by Daniel F. McGrath. Detroit: Gale Research Co. 1964– .

Bradley, Van Allen. *The Book Collector's Handbook of Values.* 4th ed. New York: Putnam, 1982.
A Directory of Rare Book and Special Collections in the United Kingdom and the Republic of Ireland. Edited by Moelwyn I. Williams. London: Library Association, 1985.
International Directory of Book Collectors. 4th ed. Beckenham: Trigon Press, 1985. Edited by Roger and Judith Sheppard.
National Historical Publications and Records Commission. *Directory of Archives and Manuscript Repositories in the United States.* Washington: National Archives and Records Service, 1978.
National Union Catalog of Manuscript Collections. Washington: Library of Congress, 1959/61- . (Annual.)
Schreyer, Alice D. *Rare Books 1983-84.* New York: Bowker, 1984.

Editors and Contributors

CHARLES W. BROWNSON is Humanities Co-ordinator in the Collection Development Division of the Arizona State University Libraries. He has published articles and papers on bibliographical control and selection of contemporary literature, two novels, *Ancestors* (1984) and *In Uz* (1985), and numerous short stories.

ERIC J. CARPENTER is Collection Development Librarian at Oberlin College. He served previously as Subject Librarian for English and American Literature, Head of Collection Development, and Acting Curator of the Poetry/Rare Books Collection at SUNY-Buffalo. His publications include a chapter on small presses in *Selection of Library Materials in the Humanities, Social Sciences, and Sciences* (1985), articles in *Literary Research Newsletter* and *New Horizons for Academic Libraries,* and numerous reviews.

PETER V. DEEKLE is Assistant Dean of Academic Affairs at the Harrisburg Area Community College in Harrisburg, Pennsylvania.

ROBERT HAUPTMAN, currently an Assistant Professor at St. Cloud State University, holds a Ph.D. in Comparative Literature in addition to his doctoral work in library science. His 250 publications include *The Pathological Vision: Jean Genet, Louis-Ferdinand Céline, and Tennessee Williams* (1984) and the forthcoming *Ethical Problems in Librarianship.* His essays have appeared in *North Dakota Quarterly, The Review of Contemporary Fiction, Neophilologus, The Reference Librarian, College & Research Libraries,* and other journals.

Editors and Contributors

RICHARD HEINZKILL is the Subject Specialist for English and American Literature, Linguistics, Speech, Film, and Theater at the University of Oregon. In addition to his book, *Film Criticism: An Index to Critics' Anthologies* (1975), he had published articles on both professional and literary topics in such journals as *Library Quarterly*, *Papers of the Bibliographical Society of America*, and *RQ*.

STEPHEN LEHMANN is currently Humanities Librarian at Swarthmore College. Co-translator of Nietzsche's *Human, All-Too Human* (1984) and a reviewer for *Library Quarterly*, *Choice*, and other journals, he is translating the correspondence of Johannes Brahms and Joseph Joachim for publication.

CRAIG LIKNESS is Humanities Librarian and Head Bibliographer at Trinity University's Maddux Library in San Antonio, Texas. He earned B.A. and M.A. degrees in English at St. Olaf College and the University of Illinois. His graduate degree in library science is from the University of Wisconsin–Madison.

WILLIAM McPHERON is Curator for English and American Literature Collections at Stanford University. Most recently author of *Charles Olson: The Critical Reception, 1941–1983* (1986) and *The Bibliography of Contemporary American Poetry, 1945–1985* (1986), he has also published critical and bibliographical articles in *Boundary 2* and *The Review of Contemporary Fiction*.

JOSEPH NATOLI is responsible for the British and American literature collections in the Michigan State University Libraries. In addition to his *Twentieth-Century Blake Criticism: Northrop Frye to the Present* (1982), he has also compiled (with Frederik L. Rusch) *Psychocriticism: An Annotated Bibliography* (1984) and edited the volume, *Psychological Perspectives on Literature: Freudian Dissidents and Non-Freudians, A Casebook* (1984).

MARCIA PANKAKE is Associate Professor and Bibliographer for English and American Literature at Wilson Library of the University of Minnesota. Editor of the humanities section of *Selection of Library Materials in the Humanities, Social Sciences, and Sciences* (1985), she has also published on collection development and selection in *College & Research Libraries*, *Library Acquisitions: Practice & Theory*, *Library Journal*, and *Library Resources & Technical Resources*.

MICHAEL T. RYAN is Curator of Special Collections and Collection Development Officer at Stanford University Libraries.

KATHRYN SOUPISET is Head of the Acquisitions Department at Trinity University's Maddux Library in San Antonio, Texas. She serves as consultant to the ALA/RTSD Library Materials Price Index Committee and annually prepares the "College Book Price Index" published in *Choice* and the *Bowker Annual of Library and Book Trade Information*.

SCOTT STEBELMAN is Coordinator for Bibliographic Instruction and the Subject Specialist for English and American Literature at George Washington University.

Index

Prepared by Pamela Hori

AAP Industry Statistics, 111
AB Bookman's Weekly, 32, 193
ABAA Membership Directory 1986, 192
abstracts, serial, 170
Accessions List, Eastern Africa, 52
Accessions to Repositories, 191
acquisitions, 20-39
acquisitions pre-order, 22
advertising, out-of-print acquisitions, 31
Africa in Modern Literature, 74
African Book Publishing Record (ABPR), 21, 52, 113
African Book World and Press, 113
African Books in Print, 21
African-English Literature, 74
African literature, 74
The Age of Dryden, 63
agents, for auctions, 196-97
alert services, 46, 52
American Book Collector, 32, 193
American Book Prices Current, 195
American Book Publishing Record (ABPR), 21, 46, 108

American Book Review, 109
American Culture Series, 166
American Drama from Its Beginning to the Present, 72
American Drama to 1900, 72
American Fiction, 1900-1950, 71
American Fiction to 1900, 71
American Film, 149
The American Indian Language and Literature, 114
American Literary Magazines, 88
American Literary Manuscripts, 191
American Literary Scholarship, 48, 54, 136, 172
American Literature, 48, 70, 166
American literature, 68-72
The American Novel: Sinclair Lewis to the Present, 71
The American Novel through Henry James, 71
American Periodicals, 1741-1900, 88
American Poetry, 71
American Poetry Review, 109
American Poets from the Puritans to the Present, 71

207

Index

American Reference Books Annual (ARBA), 172
American Writers since 1900, 69
American Writers to 1900, 69
The Americas Review, 114
Amsterdam Review of Books, 54
Anglo-Irish Literature, 68
An Annotated Bibliography of American Literary Periodicals, 1741–1850, 87
Annotated Bibliography of Canada's Major Authors, 73
Annual Bibliography of English Language and Literature, 48, 49, 170
Annual Bibliography of Scottish Literature, 50
Annual Survey of Manufactures, 111
anonymous literature, 160–61
Anthology of Magazine Verse and Yearbook of American Poetry, 110–11
Antioch Review, 149
antiquarian book dealers, (list) 29–30, 31–32
Antiquarian Book Monthly Review, 32, 193
antiquarian book trade, 192–95
Antiquarian Booksellers Association of America (ABAA), 35, 192
appraisal, tools for, (list) 35
approval plans, 23–26; contemporary literature, 117–18; foreign, 26
archival finding aids, 161
Archives and Manuscripts Control (AMC) format, 190
Armchair Detective, 109
Articles on Twentieth Century Literature, 168
Arts & Humanities Citation Index, 55, 86, 170
Asian/Pacific Literatures in English, 115
auctions, of books, 196–97
Australian Book Review, 53
Australian Books in Print, 21, 53
Australian Bookseller and Publisher, 32, 53
Australian Literary Studies, 53, 114
Australian Literature, 73, 115

Australian literature, 73
Australian National Bibliography, 53
author bibliographies, 161
Author Biographies Master Index, 162
author collection, 184–85
Author Newsletters and Journals, 45, 89, 110
Authors and Areas of Australia, 73

Baker & Taylor, and approval plans, 25
Best Reference Books 1970–1980, 172
Bibliographie de la France, 53
bibliographies, 5–6; author, 161; national, (list) 21, 44, 167; retrospective, 60, 168–70; selective, 57; serials, (list) 28, 170; subject, 45; trade, 44
Bibliography of American Literature, 69, 139
A Bibliography of Creative African Writing, 74–75
Bibliography of Indo-English Literature, 115
Bibliography of Modern British Novelists, 168
Bibliography of South African Novels, 1930–1960, 75
A Bibliography of West African Life and Literature, 75–76
Bibliotheca Britannica, 159
The Bibliotheck, 50
A Biobibliography of Native American Writers, 114
biographical encyclopedias, 161–62
biographies, 5
Black African Literature in English, 113, 169
Black American Literature Forum, 113
Black and Blue Guides to Current Literary Journals, 91
The Black Mind, 75
Black Scholar, 113
Blackwell North America, and approval plans, 25
Book-Auction Records, 195
book clubs, 26, 198
Book Collector's Handbook of Values, 195–96

book dealers: *see* dealers
Book Industry Trends, 111
book review journals, 44; Australia, 53; Canada, 51; Europe, continental, 54; Ireland, 49; New Zealand, 53; United Kingdom, 49; United States, 47
book scout, 30
Bookdealers in North America 1983-85, 192-93
Booklist, 109, 149, 173
Bookman's Price Index, 196
Books for College Libraries, 4, 10
Books in Print, 21
The Bookseller, 48-49
Bowker Annual of Library and Book Trade Information, 111
British and Irish Library Resources, 161
British Archives, 191
British Bibliography and Textual Criticism, 137
British Book News, 49, 112
British Books in Print, 21
British Literary Magazines, 88
British National Bibliography (BNB), 48
British Novel: Conrad to the Present, 66
The British Novel: Scott through Hardy, 64
British Union Catalog of Periodicals, 28

Caedmon (publisher), 149
Cambridge Bibliography of English Literature (CBEL), 5-6, 60
Canadian Anthology, 72
Canadian Book Review Annual, 51
Canadian Books in Print, 21
Canadian Literature, 51
Canadian literature, 72-73
"Canadian Literature: An Annotated Bibliography," 51
Canadiana, 50
cataloging, nonprint materials, 154-55
catalogs: antiquarian dealers', 194-96; auction, 196; dealers', 31, 123; out-of-print dealers', 122-23; small press materials, 123
CCLM Catalog of Literary Magazines, 111
CCLM Newsletter, 111
CDS Alert Service, 46
Census of Manufactures, 111
Center for Editions of American Authors (CEAA): *see* Center for Scholarly Editions (CSE)
Center for Scholarly Editions (CSE), 129
chapbooks, 119
Chicago Manual of Style, 163
Chicano Literature, 114
Chicano Perspectives in Literature, 114
Choice, 44, 47, 90, 109, 149, 171
citation analysis, and collection evaluation, 12
Classified List of Periodicals for the College Library, 89
Cole's Register of Antiquarian and Second-Hand Bookdealers Active in Britain April 1986, 193
Collection Building, 110
Collection Development, 90
collection development, 1-19; basic planning methods, 7-17; special collections policy, 187-88; *see also* current selection; retrospective selection; individual topics and formats by name, e.g., Canadian literature; microforms
collection evaluation, steps for, 9-12
collection management, 15
Collector's Guide to Antiquarian Bookstores, 193
College & Research Libraries, 173
College Composition and Communication, 3
College English, 3
Combined Retrospective Index to Book Reviews in Humanities Journals, 1802-1974, 170
Commonwealth Literature Periodicals, 112
compact disk, 146
A Companion to Scottish Culture, 67
Comparative Literature Studies, 45

Comprehensive Dissertation Index (CDI), 164
Computer Programs for Literary Analysis, 153
computer software, 146
Computers and the Humanities, 153
A Concise Bibliography of English-Canadian Literature, 73
Concise Cambridge Bibliography of English Literature, 191
concordances, 162
conservation: and special collections, 200; *see also* preservation
Contemporary Authors, 162
Contemporary Dramatists, 67, 72
The Contemporary English Novel, 66
Contemporary Fiction in America and England, 1950-1970, 66, 71
contemporary literature, 102-26
Contemporary Native American Literature, 114
Contemporary Novelists, 65, 71
Contemporary Poetry in America and England, 1950-1975, 66, 71
Contemporary Poets, 66, 71
Contrast, 115
Critical Survey of Short Fiction, 169
Critical Survey of South African Poetry in English, 75
critical surveys, 44-45; Africa, 52; Australia, 53; Canada, 51; Europe, continental, 54; Ireland, 49; New Zealand, 53; United Kingdom, 49; United States, 48
Critical Writings on Commonwealth Literatures, 74
Cumulative Book Index, 21
current selection, 40-55; administration of, 14-15; nonprint media, 147-53; reference materials, 158-70

databases, computer readable: OCLC, 22; and retrospective selection, 59; RLIN, 22, 190
dealers: antiquarian books, (list) 29-30, 31-32; and approval plans, 24-26; and firm orders, 27; out-of-print, 28-32; and standing orders, 26-27

Decade of Chicano Literature (1970-1979), 114
deselection: *see* weeding
Deutsche Bibliographie, 54
dictionaries, 162-63
Dictionary of American Biography, 161
Dictionary of Anonymous and Pseudonymous Literature, 159, 160
Dictionary of Literary Biography, 162
Dictionary of Modern English Usage, 163
direct orders, and contemporary literature, 118-19
Directory of Archives and Manuscript Repositories, 190
A Directory of Dealers in Secondhand and Antiquarian Books in the British Isles 1984-86, 193
Directory of Rare Book and Special Collections in the United Kingdom and the Republic of Ireland, 190
Directory of Small Magazine/Press Editors and Publishers, 111
Directory of Specialized American Bookdealers, 193
Directory of Spoken-Word Audio Cassettes, 152
Dissertation Abstracts International (DAI), 164
dissertations and theses, acquisition of, 34
Dissertations in American Literature 1891-1966, 164
Dissertations in English and American Literature, 164
distributors, and contemporary literature, 118
documentation program, categories for, 185
documentation strategy, 184-85
donors, and special collections, 197-99
drama, retrospective selection guides, 66-67, 72
Drama Review, 45

Early English Books: Series I, Series II, 6
editions, selection of, 127-43
Educational Film Locator, 152

Eight American Authors, 70
The Eighteenth Century, 63
Eighteenth-Century Studies, 50
England's Helicon, 63
English and American Studies in German, 54
English Drama and Theatre, 1800-1900, 65
English Drama, 1900-1950, 67
English Drama to 1660 (Excluding Shakespeare), 62, 169
English Fiction, 1900-1950, 65
English Fiction, 1660-1800, 63
"English Language and Literature Periodicals," 90
English Language Titles from German Publishers, 54
English Literary Journals, 1900-1950, 87-88
The English Literary Journal to 1900, 87
English Literature in the Sixteenth Century, Excluding Drama, 63
English Poetry, 1900-1950, 66
English Prose and Criticism in the Nineteenth Century, 64
English Prose, Prose Fiction, and Criticism to 1660, 62
English Romantic Poetry, 1800-1835, 64
The English Romantic Poets, 63, 136, 168
The English Romantic Poets & Essayists, 63
equipment: and microforms, 34; for nonprint materials, 146-47, 154-55
Essay & General Literature Index, 55, 164
Etudes irlandaises, 50
"Evaluating Periodicals in English Studies," 89
exchange programs, for acquisitions, 36

Famous Quotations, 167-68
Faulkner's Revision of Sanctuary, 136
Feature Films on 8mm, 16mm, and Videotape, 152

Feminist Studies, 45
Fiction Writer's Market, 111
Fifteen American Authors before 1900, 70
Fifteen Modern American Authors, 70
Film Library Quarterly, 149
Film Literature Index, 151
Filmed Books and Plays 1928-1974, 153
films, 145-46
filmstrips, 146
Fine Print, 109
firm orders, 27
First Printings of American Authors, 69, 136
Focus on English Literature, 1708-1907, 88
footnotes, and literary research, 157
foreign language materials, 2
Fourth Directory of Periodicals Publishing Articles on English and American Literature and Language, 89
From There to Here, 73
funding: nonprint media, 144-45; retrospective selection, 58
Funk & Wagnalls New Standard Dictionary of the English Language, 163

Gale Bibliography of Literature in America, 136
General Catalogue (British Museum), 159
Genreflecting, 110
gifts, 35; and special collections, 197-99
grammar manuals, 163
Granger's Index to Poetry, 164
Grants and Awards Available to American Writers, 109
grants, for retrospective selection, 58
Guide to American Literature, 70, 166
A Guide to American Screenwriters, 153
A Guide to Archives and Manuscripts in the United States, 191
Guide to Current National Bibliographies in the Third World, 113, 115

212   Index

Guide to Doctoral Dissertations in Victorian Literature 1886-1958, 164
A Guide to English and American Literature, 61, 63, 166
Guide to English Literature from Beowulf through Chaucer and Medieval Drama, 61
Guide to Microforms in Print, 88
Guide to Reference Books, 170
Guide to Reference Materials, 171
Guide to Reprints, 33
A Guide to Serial Bibliographies for Modern Literatures, 45
A Guide to Twentieth-Century Literature in English, 75
Guidelines for Collection Development, 9, 10, 11, 13, 14

Harrassowitz Book Digest: Languages, Literature, 54
Harvard Guide to Contemporary American Writing, 72
High Fidelity/Musical America, 149
A History of Scottish Literature, 67
Home Book of Quotations, 167-68
Home Video, 149
The Humanities, 171
Humanities Index (HI), 170

Index of English Literary Manuscripts, 191
Index to Book Reviews in the Humanities, 170
Index to Educational Audio Tapes, 151
Index to Educational Records, 151
Index to Educational Slides, 151
Index to Educational Video Tapes, 151
Index to Literary Biography, 162
Index to Producers and Distributors, 151
Index to Reviews of Bibliographical Publications, 137
Index to 16mm Educational Films, 151
Index to 35mm Educational Films, 151
indexes: anthologies and reprint collections, 163-64; collections, 45-46, (list) 55; dissertations, 164; serial, 170

Indian Literature, 115
Indian Literature in English, 115
Indian Literature in English 1827-1979, 115
interlibrary loan: and collection development, 11-12; and serials, 92-93
The International Association of Independent Publishers' COSMEP Catalogue, 108-9
International Directory of Book Collectors, 198
International Directory of Little Magazines and Small Presses, 91, 111
International Directory of Private Presses, 111
International Index to Film Periodicals, 151
Irish Literary Supplement, 49
Irish literature, 68
Irish Literature, 1800-1875, 68
The Irish Renaissance, 68
Irish University Review, 50

jobbers, 118
Joint Acquisitions List of Africana (JALA), 52
Journal Citation Reports, 86
Journal of American Folklore, 149-50
Journal of Commonwealth Literature, 51, 52, 53, 76, 112
Journal of Modern Literature, 50, 109
Journal of South Asian Literature, 114-15
journals: see serials

Kirkus Review, 109
Kraus Periodical (dealer), 88

Landers Film Reviews, 150
The Landscape of Literatures, 11
LC Alert Service, 52
Les Livres de la semaine, 54
The Library, 137
Library Journal, 47, 90, 173
Library of Congress Main Reading Room Reference Collection, Subjec Catalog, 171

Library of Literary Criticism, 169
literary gazetteers, 164-65
literary handbooks, 165
A Literary History of England, 61
The Literary History of the United States, 68-69, 136, 166, 168
The Literary Journal in America, 1900-1950, 88
The Literary Journal in America to 1900, 88
Literary Magazine Review, 90
Literary Press Group Catalogue, 109
Literary Research Guide, 45, 60, 166
literary research guides, 165
Literary, Rhetorical, and Linguistics Terms Index, 165
Literatura Chicana, 114
Literature and Film, 153
Literature/Film Quarterly, 150
The Literature of Australia, 73
The Little Magazine, 91
Little Press Books in Print, 112
LMP: Literary Market Place, 111
Location Register of Twentieth-Century English Literature Manuscripts and Letters, 190
Locus, 110
London Review of Books, 49, 112

Magazines for Libraries, 89, 90
Magill's Bibliography of Literary Criticism, 168, 169
Magill's Literary Annual, 167
Major Canadian Authors, 73
manuscript finding aids, 161
manuscripts, facsimile, 5
A Map of Modern English Verse, 66
market value, and special collections, 194
Masterplots, 167
Media Review Digest, 150
Medieval Manuscripts in British Libraries, 191
microcomputers, and retrospective selection, 59
microfilms, 6
microform guides, 166
Microform Research Collections, 6, 166

microforms: acquisition of, 33-34; bibliographic guides to, (list) 33, 166
MIMP: Magazine Industry Market Place, 111
MLA Directory of Periodicals, 87, 89
MLA Handbook, 163
MLA International Bibliography of Books and Articles on the Modern Languages and Literatures (MLAIB), 48, 51, 52, 53, 136-137, 159, 164, 170
MLAIB: *see MLA International Bibliography of Books and Articles on the Modern Languages and Literatures*
Modern Australian Prose 1901-1975, 114
Modern British Drama, 67
Modern Drama in America and England, 1950-1970, 72
Modern Irish Literature, 1800-1967, 68
multimedia materials: *see* nonprint media resources

national bibliographies, 44, 167; Africa, 51-52; Australia, 53; Canada, 50; Europe, continental, 53-54; Ireland, 48; New Zealand, 53; United Kingdom, 48; United States, 46
North American Collections Inventory Project (NCIP), 14, 16
National Endowment for the Humanities, 58
National Information Center for Educational Media (NICEM), 151
National Union Catalog, 159
National Union Catalog: Books, 46
The National Union Catalog of Manuscript Collections, 161, 190
The Native American in American Literature, 114
A New Book of South African Verse in English, 75
New Cambridge Bibliography of English Literature (NCBEL), 5, 60, 168
New Pelican Guide to English Literature, 61

A New Reader's Guide to African Literature, 74
The New Schwann, 151
New Serial Titles—Classed Subject Arrangement, 28, 90
New York Review of Books, 47, 110
New York Times Book Review, 47
New Zealand Book World, 32
New Zealand Books in Print, 21
New Zealand Bookseller & Publisher, 53
"New Zealand Literature: A Select List with Some Background Titles," 74
New Zealand literature, 74
New Zealand Literature to 1977, 74
New Zealand National Bibliography, 53
newspapers: *see* serials
nonprint media resources, 144–55; cataloging of, 154–55
North American Film and Video Directory, 152

OCLC, 22
Old and Middle English Literature, 61
Old English Literature, 61
On Cassette, 152
On Editing Shakespeare and the Elizabethan Dramatists, 136
Ottemiller's Index to Plays in Collections, 164
Our English Heritage: South African English Literature, 75
Our Nature, Our Voices, 73
out-of-print materials, acquisition of, 28–32
Oxford History of Australian Literature, 74
Oxford History of English Literature, 61, 63

Pages, 137
paperbacks, acquisition of, 34
The Papers of the Bibliographical Society of America, 137
The Paradise of Dainty Devices, 63
Pelican Guide to English Literature, 61
periodicals: *see* serials

phonodisc recordings, 146
Pilot Bibliography of South African English Literature, 75
Play Index, 55, 164
plot summaries, 167
Plot Summary Index, 167
PMLA, 90
PN Review (Poetry Nation), 112
Poetry Australia, 115
Poetry Explication, 169
Poetry Index Annual, 55
poetry, retrospective selection guides, 66, 71
policy, for collection development, 13–15
precatalog searching: *see* acquisitions preorder
preservation, 2; and collection management, 15; and special collections, 200
previewing, and nonprint media, 148–49
procurement, and contemporary literature, 115–17
Proof, 137
proverb books, 167
pseudonymous literature, 160–61
publicity on retrospective selection, 58–59
Published Screenplays, 152
publishers: audio, 149; directories of, (list) 23
Publishers Weekly, 111
Publishers Weekly Yearbook, 111

Quill and Quire, 51, 112
quotation books, 167

Rare Books and Manuscripts Librarianship, 193
Rare Books, 1983–84, 190
Reader's Guide to English and American Literature, 70
Recent Research on Anglo-Irish Writers, 68
Record and Tape Reviews Index, 151
The Reference Book Review, 172
Reference Books in the Social Sciences and Humanities, 171

reference collections, and literature, 156-80; for graduate students, 4-6
Reference Sources in English and American Literature, 60, 165-66
regional literature, acquisition of, 34-35
Renaissance Quarterly, 50
reprints, 32-33
research, and special collections, 184
Research in African Literatures, 52, 113
Research Libraries and Collections in the United Kingdom, 191
Research Libraries Information Network (RLIN), 22; nonprint materials, 190
research value, and special collections, 194
resource sharing: and collection development, 16-17; and periodical literature, 6
retrospective bibliographies, 168-70
retrospective selection, 56-81; administration of, 15; contemporary literature, 121-23; reference works, 170-71
Review, 137
The Review of English Studies, 50
RLG Task Force on Conspectus Analysis, 187-88
RLIN: *see* Research Libraries Information Network
Romantic Poets and Prose Writers, 64
RQ, 172-73
RSR: Reference Service Review, 172

SANB: Suid-Afrikaanse Nasionale Bibliografie (South African National Bibliography), 52, 115
scholarly book reviews, 45; Africa, 52; Australia, 53; Canada, 51; Ireland, 50; New Zealand, 53; United Kingdom, 50; United States, 48
scholarly journals, and book columns, 45
Scottish literature, 67
Scottish Literature in English and Scots, 67

selection of materials: current *see* current selection; retrospective *see* retrospective selection; *see also* individual topics and formats by name, e.g., Canadian literature; microforms
Selective Bibliography for the Study of English and American Literature, 165
serials, 6, 82-101; acquisition of, 27-28; basic lists of, 94-97; bibliography of, (list) 28; and reference works, 171-74; and textual studies, (list) 137
Serials for Libraries, 87
Serials in Microform, 88
Serials in the British Library, 28
Serials Review, 45, 90, 91, 110
The Seventeenth Century: Bacon through Marvell, 62
Shakespeare: A Study and Research Guide, 62
Shakespeare: Select Bibliographical Guides, 62
Short Stories on Film, 153
Short Story Index, 55, 164
Sight and Sound, 150
Sightlines, 150
Sixteen Modern American Authors, 70-71
The Sixteenth Century: Skelton through Hooker, 62
slides, 146
Small Press, 112
Small Press News, 110
Small Press Record of Books in Print (SPBIP), 21, 108
Small Press Review, 91, 110
small presses, and contemporary literature, 118, 119
The South African Novel in English (1880-1930), 75
The South African Novel in English since 1950, 115
special collections, 181-202; and resource sharing, 16
special materials, and acquisition of, 32-35
special studies, 5

Speculum, 45, 50
Spoken Arts (publisher), 149
Standing Conference of National Universities and Libraries (SCONUL), 190
standing orders, 26–27
statistics, on collection use, 11
Stereo Review, 150
storage, of nonprint materials, 154–55
Strophes, 112
Studies in American Indian Literature, 114
Studies in Bibliography, 137
Studies in English Literature, 49
Studies in Romanticism, 50
style manuals, 163
subject bibliographies, 45; Africa, 52; Australia, 53; Canada, 51; Europe, continental, 54; Ireland 49–50; New Zealand, 53; United Kingdom, 49–50; United States, 48
Subject Collections, 190
Subject Guide to Forthcoming Books, 46–47
subscription agents, 27
Survey of Contemporary Literature, 167
Survey of Modern Fantasy Literature, 169
Survey of Science Fiction Literature, 169

tape recordings, 146
Tax Reform Act of 1969, 198–99
Tech Trends, 150
Televisions, 150
term paper manuals, 163
The Texts of Keats's Poems, 136
textual studies, 127–43
Times Literary Supplement, 49, 112
Tottel's Miscellany, 63
trade bibliographies, 44; Africa, 52; Australia, 53; Canada, 51; Europe, continental, 54; Ireland, 48–49; New Zealand, 53; United Kingdom, 48–49; United States, 46–47
The Transcendentalists, 136
Tudor and Stuart Drama, 62, 169

Twentieth Century British Literature, 65
20th Century Fiction, 65
The Twentieth Century Novel in English, 65, 71

UMI Research Collections, 88
uncataloged collections, 11
Union List of Manuscripts in Canadian Repositories, 191
Union List of Serials in Libraries of the United States and Canada, 28
union lists, serials, 28
Universal Serials and Book Exchange (USBE), 36
University of Toronto Quarterly, 51
The University Publishing New Books Supplement, 47
use studies, 11

vendors, 22; and approval plans, 24–26; and firm orders, 27; and standing orders, 26–27
verification, 20–21
Victorian Fiction: A Guide to Research, 64
Victorian Fiction: A Second Guide to Research, 64, 136
Victorian Poetry, 150
The Victorian Poets, 65
Victorian Poets and Prose Writers, 64
Victorian Prose, 64
Victorian Studies, 50
Video Source Book, 152
videodisc, 146
videorecordings, 146
Virginia Quarterly Review, 150
A Vision of Order, 75

Webster's New Collegiate Dictionary, 163
weeding, 15; serials, 91–93
Weeding Library Collections, 15
Weeding Library Collections—II, 92
Weekly Record, 46, 171
Wellesley Index to Victorian Periodicals, 1824-1900, 88
Westerly, 115

Whitaker's Books of the Month & Books to Come, 48–49
Whitaker's Cumulative Book List, 21, 49
Widener Library Shelflist, 171
World Literature Today, 112
World Literature Written in English, 112
Writers' and Artists' Yearbook, 113

writers, and special collections, 198–99
Writer's Handbook, 109
Writer's Market, 112

Yale Review, 150
Year's Work in English Studies (YWES), 48, 49, 51, 52, 53, 136, 172

Composed by Ampersand, Inc.
in Itek Times Roman and
Helvetica on a Digitek
typesetting system

Printed on 50-pound Glatfelter,
a pH-neutral stock, and
bound in 10-point Carolina
cover stock by
Malloy Lithographing, Inc.